The Flat-Screen iMac For Dummies®

Cheat Sheet

What've You Got There?

To find out how much memory your iMac has and what system-software version, choose About This Mac from the menu (see Chapter 1). Write the answers down here.

Your iMac OS version: _____

Built-in memory: _____

Surviving the First Half Hour

You may need this information only at the very beginning of your iMac career — but you'll really need it.

Turning on the iMac

Press the power button. It's the round button on the white volleyball-shaped dome part of the iMac, about halfway around the back on the left side.

Turning off the iMac

Truth is, you don't need to think about turning off the iMac. After about half an hour, it goes to "sleep" on its own, consuming only a night-light's worth of electricity, ready to wake up when you touch a key or the mouse.

But if you want it all the way off, open the menu and choose Shut Down.

Troubleshooting Keystrokes

One of your programs is frozen: Press ⌘-Option-Esc. In the list of programs, click the balky one and then click the Force Quit button. (Click Force Quit in the confirmation box.) Your other programs are just fine.

The iMac has completely frozen: This hardly ever happens — but if it does, press the Power button on the left side for six seconds to turn the machine off. Then press it again to turn the machine on again.

A CD is stuck in the machine: Restart the computer. As it's turning on, hold down the mouse button continuously until the CD spits out.

You're panicking: Call Apple's hotline: 800-500-7078.

The Dock

This thing is your Dock:

It keeps your favorite programs, documents, folders, and disks handy for quick access. (Point to an icon without clicking to see its name.)

To add an icon to the Dock, drag it there with the mouse (programs go on the left side of the Dock's white divider line, everything else on the right). To remove something from the Dock, drag its icon up and away. To rearrange Dock icons, just drag them sideways with the mouse.

Working with Icons

Finding a file

Each file you create is represented by an icon and is usually stored inside an electronic folder, which looks like a file folder on your screen. Everyone sometimes misplaces a file. Here's what to do.

1. **Open Sherlock (click the detective-hat icon on your Dock).**

2. **Type a few letters of the missing file's name.**

   You don't have to type the whole name — only enough to distinguish it. Capitalization doesn't matter.

3. **Press the Return key or click the magnifying-glass button.**

   The iMac roots through your files. When it shows you a list of all icons that match, click one (to see where it is) or double-click (to open it).

To insert a CD-ROM or DVD

Hold the CD by its edges (or the hole), label side up. Hold down the Eject key on your keyboard (the upper-right key, which looks like this:)

After a moment, the CD tray slides out of the iMac like a big wide tongue. Place the CD or DVD into it, label side up. Tap the Eject key again to close the tray. After another moment, the CD icon now shows up on the screen, or the DVD movie starts to play.

Ejecting a CD or other disk

Tap the Eject key on your keyboard. The tray slides open.

BESTSELLING
BOOK SERIES

The Flat-Screen iMac® For Dummies®

Cheat Sheet

What All These Little Controls Do

They call this box a *dialog box* because the iMac is asking questions it needs answered. Here are the elements of a typical dialog box.

Radio buttons

◉ Entire File   ○ Selection

Named after the pushbuttons on a car radio, where only one can be pushed in at a time. Likewise, only one iMac radio button can be selected at a time.

Check boxes

☑ Ignore Case

Used to indicate whether an option is on or off. Click once to place the checkmark in the box; click again to remove the checkmark (and turn off the option).

Text fields

Replace with: [fish]

You're supposed to type into these blanks. To move from one blank to another, either click with the mouse or press the Tab key.

Pop-up menus

Paper Size: [US Letter ▼]

When you see this, you're seeing a *pop-up menu*. Point to the text, hold down the mouse button, and make a selection from the mini-menu that drops down.

Buttons

(Previous) (Next)

Every dialog box has a clearly marked button or two (usually OK and Cancel) that make the box go away — your escape route.

Click OK (or Print, or Proceed, or whatever the button says) to proceed with the command you originally chose from the menu. Click Cancel if you want to back out of the dialog box, as though you'd never issued the command.

See the Next button above? If you could see the *real* Next button on your screen, you'd see that it's blue and pulsing. Whenever you see a blue, pulsing button, you don't have to use the mouse to click it. Instead, you can press either the Return or Enter key on your keyboard — a few precious seconds saved.

Working with Several Programs

The iMac lets you run more than one program at once. Here are some pointers.

Determining what programs are running

Look for the tiny triangles underneath your Dock icons. These are the programs that are currently open.

Hiding or quitting programs

Many iMac fans *never* quit their programs; instead, they just *hide* the ones they're not using (from the menu next to the menu, choose Hide AppleWorks, or Hide Mail, or Hide whatever). But if you're really, truly finished with a program for the day, you can choose Quit AppleWorks, or Quit Mail, or Quit whatever, from the menu that bears the program's name (next to the menu).

Opening or Closing a Window

Every window was once an *icon* that you double-clicked to see what was inside.

1. Double-click any icon to open its window.

2. To get rid of a window, click the *close button* in the upper-left corner.

For Dummies: Bestselling Book Series for Beginners

iMac
Methodologies
in Theory
and Practice

A technical guide for experienced users

formerly *The Flat-Screen iMac For Dummies*

By D. Welch Pogue

Includes advanced treatment of these topics:

◆ Invoking the commencement of A/C 120V electric power to the CPU unit

◆ Propelling the cursor-control module on a horizontal plane

◆ Insertion and removal of optical data storage media

Look, we use the word *Dummies* on the cover with affection and a twinkle in the eye. Still, we understand if you're not thrilled about leaving a book on your desk called *The Flat-Screen iMac For Dummies*.

We hear you. And we've got the perfect solution: Just rip off the real cover of the book! This phony cover will be all that's left. Leave it on your desk in plain sight, so everybody will know what a computer whiz you are.

The Flat-Screen iMac®

FOR

DUMMIES®

The Flat-Screen iMac FOR DUMMIES®

by David Pogue

Wiley Publishing, Inc.

Best-Selling Books • Digital Downloads • e-Books • Answer Networks • e-Newsletters • Branded Web Sites • e-Learning

The Flat-Screen iMac® For Dummies®

Published by
Wiley Publishing, Inc.
909 Third Avenue
New York, NY 10022

www.wiley.com

Copyright © 2002 by Wiley Publishing, Inc., Indianapolis, Indiana

Published by Wiley Publishing, Inc., Indianapolis, Indiana

Published simultaneously in Canada

For general information on our other products and services or to obtain technical support, please contact our Customer Care Department within the U.S. at 800-762-2974, outside the U.S. at 317-572-3993, or fax 317-572-4002.

Wiley also publishes its books in a variety of electronic formats. Some content that appears in print may not be available in electronic books.

Library of Congress Control Number: 2002107909

ISBN: 0-7645-1663-9

Manufactured in the United States of America

10 9 8 7 6 5 4 3 2

1O/SW/QX/QS/IN

Wiley Publishing, Inc. is a trademark of Wiley Publishing, Inc.

About the Author

Ohio-bred **David Pogue** never touched a computer — nor wanted to — until Apple Computer suckered him into it by selling Macs half-price at Yale, from which he graduated *summa cum laude* in 1985. After a few years as a Broadway theatre conductor, he spent 12 years writing the triple-award-winning "Desktop Critic" column for *Macworld* magazine. He now writes the weekly "State of the Art" personal-technology column for the *New York Times*.

Pogue is one of the world's best-selling how-to authors, having written or co-written seven books in the *For Dummies* series (including *Macs, iMacs, Magic, Opera,* and *Classical Music*), along with *PalmPilot: The Ultimate Guide*, several computer-humor books, and a technothriller, *Hard Drive,* which was a *New York Times* "notable book of the year."

He's also the creator of the Missing Manual series (*www.missingmanuals.com*), whose current and upcoming titles include *Mac OS X, iPhoto, Office X, AppleWorks 6,* and *iMovie 2.*

With his madly adored wife Jennifer, son Kelly, daughter Tia, and Bullwinkle the Wonderdog, he lives in Connecticut, where he does magic tricks and plays the piano. The family photos lurk on the World Wide Web at *www.davidpogue.com.*

Author's Acknowledgments

This book was made possible by the enthusiasm and support of Project Editor Mary Goodwin, Acquisitions Editor Bob Woerner, and everyone else in the sprawling universe of Wiley's voicemail.

Thanks, too, to technical editor Mark Hurlow. And a tip o' the mouse to Apple's cofounder Steve Jobs and his chief designer Jonathan Ive. Their vision and refusal to compromise produced the glorious, smash-hit, flat-panel computer called the iMac.

Above all, my gratitude and love go to the lovely Jennifer, Kelly, and Tia, who stood by me (or crawled by me, as the case may be) during the writing of this book.

The David Pogue Pledge

As in all my Macintosh books, I make the following guarantee:

1. I will reply to every reader e-mail. My address is *david@pogueman.com*. (I'll respond cheerfully to messages that pertain to the material *in this book*. If you ask me for technical help on other topics, I'm afraid I can only refer you to the list of self-help sources in Chapter 16.)

2. I will not use trendoid terms in my writing: *the user* when I mean you, *price point* when I mean price, *performance* when I mean speed, and so on.

3. I will never put an apostrophe in the possessive word *its*.

Publisher's Acknowledgments

We're proud of this book; please send us your comments through our online registration form located at www.dummies.com/register/.

Some of the people who helped bring this book to market include the following:

Acquisitions, Editorial, and Media Development

Project Editor: Mary Goodwin

Acquisitions Editor: Bob Woerner

Technical Editor: Mark Hurlow

Editorial Manager: Constance Carlisle

Editorial Assistant: Amanda Foxworthy

Production

Project Coordinator: Nancee Reeves

Layout and Graphics: Gabriele McCann, Jacque Schneider, Betty Schulte, Jeremey Unger, Erin Zeltner

Proofreader: Betty Kish

Indexer: TECHBOOKS Production Services

General and Administrative

Wiley Technology Publishing Group: Richard Swadley, Vice President and Executive Group Publisher; Bob Ipsen, Vice President and Group Publisher; Joseph Wikert, Vice President and Publisher; Barry Pruett, Vice President and Publisher; Mary Bednarek, Executive Editorial Director; Mary C. Corder, Editorial Director; Andy Cummings, Editorial Director

Wiley Manufacturing: Ivor Parker, Vice President, Manufacturing

Wiley Composition Services for Branded Press: Debbie Stailey, Composition Services Director

Contents at a Glance

Introduction *1*

Part 1: For the Absolute iMac Virgin *5*

Chapter 1: How to Turn On Your iMac (and What to Do Next) 7
Chapter 1½: High-Tech Made Easy 27
Chapter 2: Windows, Icons, and Trashes 35
Chapter 3: Actually Accomplishing Something 53
Chapter 4: Typing, Saving, and Finding Again 83
Chapter 5: A Quiet Talk about Printers, Printing, and Fonts 115

Part 11: The Internet Defanged *129*

Chapter 6: Faking Your Way onto America Online and the Internet 131
Chapter 7: The Weird Wide Web 155
Chapter 8: E-mail for He-males and Females 173

Part 111: Software Competence *187*

Chapter 9: Faking Your Way Through AppleWorks 189
Chapter 10: iPhoto, iTunes — iLove It! 217
Chapter 11: iSpielberg: Digital Movies and DVDs 235

Part 1V: Toward a New, Nerdier You *259*

Chapter 12: Back to Mac OS 9 261
Chapter 13: Mono-Mac, Multi-People 271
Chapter 14: Networks for Nitwits 279
Chapter 15: When Bad Things Happen to Good iMacs 293
Chapter 16: Beyond the iMac: Where to Go from Here 315

Part V: The Part of Tens *319*

Chapter 17: Ten Cool Things You Didn't Know Your iMac Could Do 321
Chapter 18: Ten Features that Didn't Quite Fit the Outline 337
Chapter 19: Ten Back-of-the-Mac Jacks 347

Index *357*

Cartoons at a Glance

By Rich Tennant

page 5

page 187

page 319

page 259

page 129

Cartoon Information:
Fax: 978-546-7747
E-Mail: richtennant@the5thwave.com
World Wide Web: www.the5thwave.com

Table of Contents

Introduction 1

Who Needs an iMac Book? 1
How to Use This Book (Other Than as a Mouse Pad) 2
   Macintosh conventions 2
   Conventions in this book 2
   Apple and obsolescence 3

Part 1: For the Absolute iMac Virgin 5

Chapter 1: How to Turn On Your iMac (and What to Do Next) 7

The Amazing Desk-Lamp Computer 7
   Switching on the iMac 8
   The startup slide show 9
What Happens Next 10
   The Setup Assistant 11
   The Welcome screen 13
   The desktop and menu bar 14
   The big turn-off 15
   Why not to turn off the iMac 15
Desktop, Dock, and Icons 16
   Macintosh syntax 18
   The complete list of window doodads 20
   Double-clicking in theory and practice 21
   One window 22
   Multiple windows 22
Where to Get Help 23
   Pit stop 24
Top Ten Similarities between You and Your iMac 25

Chapter 1½: High-Tech Made Easy 27

How an iMac Works 27
   Storing things with disks 27
   Conceptualizing the hard disk 28
   Understanding memory 28
   Who's Meg? 29
   Understanding RAM 30
   Putting it all together 31
   "I lost all my work!" 32
Top Ten Differences between Memory and a Hard Disk 33

Chapter 2: Windows, Icons, and Trashes 35

Becoming Manipulative 35
Foldermania 35
Your Home folder 36
Folder factory 37
Keyboard shortcuts 38
Icon, List, and Column Views 41
Icon view 42
List view 44
Column view 45
How to Trash Something 47
Top Ten Window and Icon Tips 48

Chapter 3: Actually Accomplishing Something 53

Your Software Collection 54
Getting more software 54
Where to buy it 55
The Dock 56
How the Dock works 56
Adding your own icons 57
Minimizing a window 58
Four fancy Dock tricks 59
The First Tutorial 60
The Calculator 61
Stickies 62
Triangles in the Dock 63
The cornerstone of human endeavor: Copy and Paste 64
Quitting a program 67
System Preferences 67
Desktop 69
General 71
Screen Saver 71
Displays 73
Energy Saver 74
Keyboard 74
Sound 75
Date and Time 75
Software Update 76
Quitting System Preferences 77
The iMac Keyboard 77
Top Ten Freebie Programs 79

Chapter 4: Typing, Saving, and Finding Again 83

Your Very First Bestseller 83
  Top three rules of word processing 83
  The excitement begins 84
  Editing for the linguistically blessed 85
  Puff, the Magic Drag-N-Drop 88
Form and Format 90
  The return of Return 90
  Appealing characters 91
  Formatting paragraphs 93
Working with Documents 94
  Navigating the Save File sheet 95
  Closing a file, with a sigh 99
  How to find out what's going on 99
Getting It All Back Again 100
  Crazy relationships: Parents and kids 100
  File-name suffixes 101
  Fetch: How to retrieve a document 102
Save Me Again! 103
How to Back Up — and Burn CDs 104
  The importance of being backed up 104
  What to back up 104
  Method 1: Burn a CD 105
  Method 2: Back up onto your iDisk 107
  Method 3: Back up onto another Mac 108
  Method 4: Buy a backup drive 108
When What Was Found Is Now Lost 109
  Seeking wisdom in your own words 110
Top Ten Word-Processing Tips 111

Chapter 5: A Quiet Talk about Printers, Printing, and Fonts 115

Inkjet Printers 115
  How to hook up a USB inkjet printer 116
Laser Printers 117
After All That: How You Actually Print 119
  Using the Tab key in dialog boxes 120
  Other options 121
  Micromanaging your printouts 122
  Canceling printing 123
Top Ten Free Fun Font Factoids 123

Part II: The Internet Defanged 129

Chapter 6: Faking Your Way onto America Online and the Internet 131

First, the Modem 132
America Online or Direct to the Internet? 133
America Online (AOL), the Cyber-Grocery 134
  Your first online session 135
  Exploring by icon 136
  Navigating by keyword 137
  How to find your way back to the good stuff 138
  The e-mail connection 139
  The party line 139
  Talking behind their backs 140
  How to find — and get — free software 140
Signing Up for an Internet Account (ISP) 141
  The EarthLink sign-up program 141
  A little ISP housekeeping 142
What's on the Internet 143
  E-mail 143
  Newsgroups 143
  The World Wide Web 145
How to Hang Up 146
When You Can't Open Your Downloaded Goodies 147
  Problem 1: It's encoded 147
  Problem 2: It's a disk image 148
  Problem 3: Wrong format 149
The Internet as Giant Backup Disk 151
Top Ten Best/Worst Aspects of the Net 154

Chapter 7: The Weird Wide Web 155

Getting to the Web via America Online 155
Getting to the Web via an ISP 156
Internet Made Idiotproof: Link-Clicking 156
Where to Go, What to Do on the Web 157
  Ways to search for a particular topic 158
  Searching using Sherlock 160
  Useful Web pages: The tip of the iceberg 163
Internet Explorer Tip-O-Rama 164
  More address shortcuts 164
  Even less typing 165
  Go get the plug-in 165
  Where's home for you? 166
  Faster — please, make it faster! 166

Bookmark it 167
Stop the blinking! 168
Open a new window 168
Extreme browsing 170
Learn to love history — and the Scrapbook 170

Chapter 8: E-mail for He-males and Females **173**

Getting into E-Mail 173
Sending e-mail 174
Five tips for sending mail 179
Checking Your Mail 180
Listening to your mail 182
Processing a message you've read 182
The Anti-Spam Handbook 185

Part III: Software Competence *187*

Chapter 9: Faking Your Way Through AppleWorks **189**

Your Personal Software Store 189
AppleWorks 191
Your first database 192
Data entry time 195
Forming the form letter 198
The graphics zone: Designing a letterhead 200
The return of Copy and Paste 204
The urge to merge 204
AppleWorks: The Other Spreadsheet 206
The AppleWorks Slide Show 211
Other cool stuff AppleWorks does 215

Chapter 10: iPhoto, iTunes — iLove It! **217**

iPhoto: the Digital Shoebox 217
Where to get iPhoto 218
iPhoto meets camera 219
Fun with pictures 220
Organize into "albums" 223
Showing off on the screen 225
Professional bookmaking for the amateur 227
iTunes 2: The CD and MP3 Jukebox 229
Audio CDs 231
Copying CD songs to your hard drive 232
Playlists 233
Burning music CDs 233

Chapter 11: iSpielberg: Digital Movies and DVDs **235**

Got What It Takes? 235
Filming Your Life 237
Step 1: Dump the Footage into iMovie 238
Capturing clips 240
How much footage can your iMac hold? 240
Naming, playing, and trimming clips 241
Step 2: Build the Movie 242
Adding a cross-fade 243
Adding titles 243
Color Effects 244
Grabbing music from a CD 246
Step 3: Find an Audience 247
Sending your movie back to the camcorder 248
Saving your movie as a QuickTime file 248
Burning your movie onto a real DVD 250
The iMac's Built-In DVD Player 255

Part IV: Toward a New, Nerdier You **259**

Chapter 12: Back to Mac OS 9 . . . . **261**

A Tale of Two Systems 261
Two Mac OS 9 Methods 262
Classic: The Mac OS 9 Simulator 263
Understanding the Classic world 265
Getting out of Classic 265
Restarting in Mac OS 9 266
Switching to Mac OS 9 267
Switching to Mac OS X (long way) 268
Switching to Mac OS X (short way) 269

Chapter 13: Mono-Mac, Multi-People **271**

All About Accounts 271
Setting Up Accounts 272
Logging On 275
Shared Folders 276
Logging Off 277
Deleting Accounts 278

Chapter 14: Networks for Nitwits **279**

Two Ways to Build the Network 280
Ethernet made eathy 280
Your ride to the AirPort 281

Sharing Files 285
    Phase 1: Setting up the computers 285
    Phase 2: Connecting from your iMac 287
    Phase 3: What you can do once you're in 290
    Disconnecting yourself 291
Networking with Windows 292

Chapter 15: When Bad Things Happen to Good iMacs 293

Introduction to Computer Hell 293
Frozen Programs 293
    First resort: Force quit 294
    Last resort: Restart the Mac 294
Things Are Too Slow 295
Startup Problems 295
    No chime, no picture 295
    Picture, no ding 295
    Some crazy program launches itself every time you start up 296
    Kernel panic 296
    Freezes during startup 297
    Blue screen during startup 297
    "I don't want to have to log in every day —
        it's my own iMac!" 297
    "I can't log in! I'm in an endless startup loop!" 298
    Forgotten password 298
Software Situations 299
    Minor eccentric behavior 299
    Application won't open 301
    You can't rename a file 301
    System Preferences controls are dimmed 301
    "My hard drive is overrun with alien files!" 302
    Can't empty the Trash 302
Hardware Headaches 303
    Your mouse is jerky or sticky 303
    Double-clicking doesn't work 303
    The CD drawer won't open 304
    The screen is too dim 304
The Wrong Program Opens 304
    File name extensions 304
    Type and creator codes 306
    Reassigning documents to programs 306
Error Messages 308
    "There is no application available" 308
    "You do not have sufficient access privileges" 309
    "DNS Entry not found" or "Error 404" 310
Fixing the Disk 310

Reinstalling Mac OS X 312
 Reinstalling Mac OS X 312
 Wiping out everything 312

Chapter 16: Beyond the iMac: Where to Go from Here **315**

Where to Turn in Times of Trouble 315
 Your 15 minutes of free help 315
 $150 for three years 316
 Free help sources 316
Where to Get the Inside Dirt 317
Upgrading to Mac OS 10.2 — and Beyond 317
Save Changes Before Closing? 318

Part V: The Part of Tens *319*

**Chapter 17: Ten Cool Things You Didn't Know
Your iMac Could Do** **321**

Talk 321
Sing 322
Listen 323
 Turning on speech recognition 323
 What the iMac can understand 323
 Speaking to the Mac 325
Play Movies 325
Send Faxes 326
 Installing FAXstf 326
 Sending a fax 327
Receive Faxes 330
Fit in Your Pocket 331
Take Pictures of the Screen 332
Run Windows Programs 333
Talk to Windows Computers 333

Chapter 18: Ten Features that Didn't Quite Fit the Outline **337**

Closing All Windows at Once 337
Multitasking Methods #1 337
Multitasking Methods #2 338
Make an Alias of a File 338
Self-Launching Programs 339
The Secret Life of a Scroll Bar 340
An Instant "You Are Here" Map 341
Folder Burrowing in the Dock 342

The Secret Programs' Dock Menu 343
Redesigning the Finder Toolbar 343
    Different buttons, smaller buttons 344
    Adding your own stuff 345

Chapter 19: Ten Back-of-the-Mac Jacks **347**
Lock 347
Headphones 348
Speakers 348
FireWire 348
Ethernet 350
Power Cord 350
Phone Line 350
USB 350
    Installing a new USB doodad 354
    Attaching more USB gear 354
External Monitor 355
The Power Button 355

Index *357*

Introduction

· ·

*1*f you bought an iMac, you're unbelievably smart (or lucky). You've neatly
eliminated most of the hassle, frustration, and annoyance that normally
comes with buying a computer. You've saved an incredible amount of money,
while still getting a fast, state-of-the-art machine; and you've significantly
enhanced your office décor. (Especially if you have furniture that looks like
a volleyball sawed in half.)

That's not just PR baloney, either; the iMac truly is a dramatically different
machine. There's that screen, for one thing: it floats before you, at any angle,
as bright and flicker-free as screens get.

The iMac also has everything you need built in: a modem (so you can use the
Internet and e-mail), a CD burner (great for making backups), and a huge
assortment of free programs. Selling a complete computer in one handy
bundle isn't a new idea — but rarely has it all worked together so smoothly.
And, of course, never before has all of this good stuff come in a futuristic-
looking case that you can move from room to room without calling a bunch of
friends over to help.

In short, the iMac is the gadget that comes closest to fulfilling the vision of
Apple founder Steve Jobs: to make a personal computer that's simply another
appliance. You don't have to buy memory upgrades for your TV, do you? You
don't have to hire a consultant to install your toaster oven, right? So why
should computers be any more complicated?

Who Needs an iMac Book?

If the iMac is so simple, then who needs a book about it?

Well, despite all the free goodies you get with the iMac, a *manual* isn't among
them. You need somewhere to turn when things go wrong, when you'd like to
know what the add-on software does, or when you want to stumble onto the
Internet for the first time.

By the way, of *course* you're not a dummy. Two pieces of evidence tell me
so: For one thing, you're learning the iMac, and for another, you're reading
this book! But I've taught hundreds of people how to use their Macs, and an
awful lot of them start out saying they *feel* like dummies when it comes to

computers. Society surrounds us with fast-talking teenagers who grew up learning English from their Nintendo sets; no wonder the rest of us sometimes feel left out.

But you're no more a dummy for not knowing the iMac than you were before you knew how to drive. Learning a Macintosh is like learning to drive: After a lesson or two, you can go anywhere your heart desires.

So when we say *Dummies,* we're saying it with an affectionate wink. Still, if the cover bothers you even a little — I'll admit it, you wouldn't be the first — please rip it right off. The inner cover, we hope, will make you proud to have the book out on your desk.

How to Use This Book (Other Than as a Mouse Pad)

Start with the very basics in Chapter 1; turn to Chapter 15 in times of trouble; and consult the other chapters as the spirit moves you.

Macintosh conventions

Macintosh conventions? Sure. They're called Macworld Expos, and there's one in New York and one in San Francisco each year.

Conventions in this book

Oh, *that* kind of convention.

So that we'll be eligible for some of the more prestigious book-design awards, I've marked some topics with these icons:

Nerdy stuff that's okay to skip but will fascinate the kind of people who read Tom Clancy novels.

The Macintosh is the greatest computer on earth, but it's still a computer. Now and then it does unexplainable stuff, which I'll explain.

A shortcut so you can show off.

Denotes an actual You-Try-It Experience. Hold the book open with a nearby cinder block, put your hands on the computer, and do as I say.

Points out something really cool that your iMac can do that mere mortal computers can only eye jealously.

Apple and obsolescence

One more thing before you delve in: Apple is the gigantic Silicon Valley computer company that started out as a couple of grungy teenagers in a garage. Each time Apple introduces a new iMac model, it's faster, more powerful, and less expensive than the model *you* already bought. People love Apple for coming up with such great products — but they also feel cheated at having paid so much for a suddenly outdated machine.

Feel whatever you want, of course. But if you're going to buy a computer, accept the fact that your investment is going to devalue faster than real estate in Chernobyl.

Here's a promise: No matter how carefully you shop or how good a deal you got on your iMac today, it will be replaced by a less expensive or souped-up version within a year. (It'll still *work* just fine, and be more or less up-to-date, for about five years.)

With that quick and inevitable computer death looming, how can people psych themselves into spending $1,500 for a computer? Simple: They believe that in those few short years, the computer will speed them up enough, and enhance their productivity enough, to cover the costs easily.

That's the theory, anyway.

Part I
For the Absolute iMac Virgin

The 5th Wave   By Rich Tennant

"Because I can't find my regular cake stand."

In this part . . .

There are three ways to learn how to use a new computer: You can consult the manual; unfortunately, your iMac didn't come with one. You can take a course (like you've got time for that?). Or you can read a book.

In these opening chapters, you'll learn, as kindly and gently as possible, how to get up and running on your iMac — and nothing else.

Chapter 1

How to Turn On Your iMac (and What to Do Next)

• •

In This Chapter

▶ How to turn the iMac on (and off)

▶ New meanings for old words like *mouse, menu,* and *system*

▶ Doing windows

▶ Mindlessly opening and closing folders

• •

*O*nce you've paid for your iMac, the hard part is over. Take it home, open the carton, and haul it out of its sculptured Styrofoam blocks. (Believe it or not, you're supposed to use the chrome silver screen arm as a lifting handle.)

The Amazing Desk-Lamp Computer

Once you've put the iMac down somewhere, you should set aside, oh, a good two minutes for getting it all plugged in. One cord goes to a power outlet. The mouse plugs into the end of the keyboard. The keyboard plugs into any of the three USB connectors on the back of the iMac (see Chapter 19). If those transparent globule speakers came with your machine, they plug into the speaker jacks (see Chapter 19 again). That's it.

Now comes one of the most exciting aspects of iMac ownership: goofing around with the screen. With one finger, try pushing this luminous, beautiful flat panel of light to one side or another, as though you want to show it to somebody sitting next to you. Using the same finger with your thumb, try tilting it at an angle, so that it's slanted more or less toward the ceiling.

Note that the screen moves up or down in space, too, to accommodate people with especially short or long necks. The amazing thing is that adjusting the screen height this way never affects its vertical angle, thanks to a fiercely advanced system of pulleys and cables inside that gleaming chrome screen arm.

At this moment, then, you should have a ready-to-roll iMac on your desk, in all its white, spheroid glory, and a look of fevered anticipation on your face.

Switching on the iMac

In this very first lesson, you'll be asked to locate the On button. This particular aspect of the iMac is not, shall we say, its best designed feature. Instead of putting the power switch somewhere logical — oh, say, like *where you can see it* — Apple chose to park it halfway around the back of the base. Stand up and peer at the left side of the machine to find it, or slide your finger around the left curve of the machine until you touch it. It's round, and it bears the universal symbol for iMac On-Turning, like this:

On button

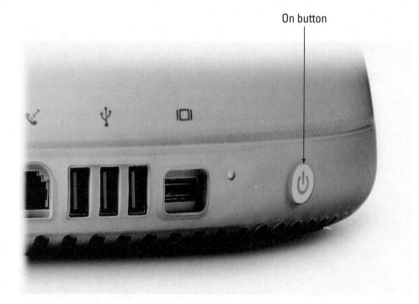

Try pushing this button now. If the iMac responds in some way — a sound plays, the screen lights up, missiles are launched from the Arizona desert — then your machine is working. Skip ahead to the following section, "The startup slide show."

If pressing that button doesn't do anything, then your iMac isn't plugged into a working power outlet. I'll wait here while you get that problem sorted out.

The startup slide show

If your On-button experiment was successful, you hear a chord, and after a few seconds, an image appears on the screen. Now you get to witness the Macintosh Startup Slide Show, revered by millions. First, you see a quick glimpse of the smiling Macintosh. It looks like this:

(In the rare event that your smiling Macintosh looks like this —

— you've rotated that screen just a tad too far.)

Next slide: You see the famous Mac OS logo:

As the startup process proceeds, a progress bar inches its way across the screen as it fills with what looks like shimmering blue water. It telegraphs how much longer you have to wait.

What Happens Next

Life is never easy for computer-book authors (except for the screaming mobs of attractive fans in bookstores, of course). Pity the guy who has to explain what happens once you've turned on the iMac.

The truth is, you may encounter any of three things at this point. If the machine is fresh out of the box, you're guided through an interview in which you set the computer's clock and perform other digital paperwork. If it's already been set up, you might be asked to choose your name from a list before gaining access. And you may go straight to the swirling blue of the iMac *desktop* picture, ready for work. The following pages tell you what to do in each of these three situations.

All three situations, by the way, require your mastery of the *mouse*. If you've never used the mouse before, read the sidebar called "Mouse College."

Mouse College

The *mouse* is the white-and-transparent, domed, capsule-like thing on the desk beside your keyboard. Having trouble visualizing it as a rodent? Think of the cord as its tail and (if it helps you) draw little eyeballs on the domed surface facing you.

To use the mouse, keep it turned so that the cord *always* points away from you.

Now then, scrape the mouse across the desk (or mouse pad). See how the arrow pointer moves across the screen? For the rest of your life, you'll hear that pointer called the *cursor*. And for the rest of your life, you'll hear moving the mouse called *moving the mouse*.

Try lifting the mouse off the desk and waving it around in midair like a remote control. Nothing happens, right? The mouse controls the cursor only when it's on a flat, opaque surface. (An electronic eye on the bottom of the mouse is

constantly scanning the table surface. That's how it knows when you're moving it. That's also why dragging it across a glass or mirrored surface is a mean prank to play on this helpless little gadget.)

You can pick up the mouse when you run out of desk space, but the cursor will stay in place on the screen. Only when you set the mouse down and begin to roll it again will the cursor continue moving.

Now put your index finger on the far end of the mouse and briefly press down (and then release). If all goes well, you should feel the mouse *click*.

Congratulations — you've learned how to *click the mouse*. You'll encounter that instruction over and over again in your budding computing life.

The Setup Assistant

If you are the first person ever to turn on the iMac, the entire screen fills with a movie. Lights! Music! Simulated water! Sea sickness! (If you don't hear music right away, somebody must have set up the machine already. Skip to the next section.)

During this show, you'll be interviewed, one question per screen. It's kind of unfortunate that your computing experience has to begin with paperwork instead of, say, blasting aliens, but that's life in the fast lane.

In any case, this setup program asks you what country you're in (twice), what your name and address are, and whether or not you want to get junk mail. Fill in the answers by clicking the multiple-choice buttons with the mouse and typing into the empty boxes with the keyboard. When you're finished with each screen, click the Continue button with your mouse.

Registration Information

Please fill out the requested information. Press the Tab key to move between boxes.

First Name
Mary

Last Name
Jones

Address
212 West 95 St

City
New York

State   Zip Code
NY   10024

Email Address (if you have one)

Area Code   Phone Number
262   512 6655

Company/School

Apple takes your privacy very seriously. Click
the button to see Apple's Privacy Policy.

Privacy

Go Back   Continue

Eventually, you arrive at a Create Your Account screen. It's somewhat technical looking, but as computer screens go, this one is pretty important.

This is where you identify yourself to the iMac. Fill in the boxes called Name (example: *Huckleberry Finn*), Short Name (example: *Huck*), Password (no longer than eight characters — *don't forget it!*), and Password Hint (which the iMac will show you if you ever *do* forget your password). You can change your password or its hint later, but not your name.

If this is your own personal iMac that nobody else uses, count your blessings: you'll only rarely need to type in this password. If you share the computer with other people in your family, school, or office, you'll be grateful that that little password keeps your own stuff safe from the inquiring minds of your comrades. (Details on this *user accounts* feature in Chapter 13.)

When you click Continue again, you're asked how you want to get onto the Internet:

✔ If you don't have an Internet account, click "I'd like a free trial account with Earthlink." (When you click an option like this, you can click *either* the little round button *or* the sentence itself.) When you click Continue, you'll be guided through the process of getting an account with Earthlink, one of the biggest Internet service companies. It won't let you into its hallowed halls, however, without your credit-card number, even though the first month is free. (Your iMac will actually dial into the Internet during this process, so make sure that you've connected the included beautiful white telephone cable to a phone jack.)

✔ If you already have an Internet account, choose "I'll use my existing Internet service." This option is not for the technically timid, however. When you click Continue, you'll be asked what kind of connection you have (telephone modem, cable modem, and so on), and then asked for a lot of technical parameters like IP addresses and DNS addresses. Unless you're some kind of competent Internet guru, skip this option and set up your account later, as described in Chapter 6.

✔ If all of this red tape is giving you a tension headache, you can always confront the Internet later. In that case, choose "I'm not ready to connect to the Internet" and click Continue. You can set up an Internet account when you're reading Chapter 6.

The interview continues. You'll be asked to register (click Register Later, unless you're a real fan of junk mail). You'll be shown a map of the world, which you can click to specify your time zone. You'll be asked to set the iMac's clock, like this:

1. Click the arrow buttons to change the month and year.

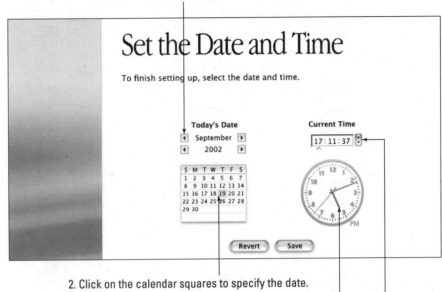

2. Click on the calendar squares to specify the date.

3. Drag the clock hands to set the time (or click in the Current Time box and type new numbers, or click the up and down arrow buttons to choose higher or lower numbers).

Finally, the iMac thanks you for your bureaucratic efforts. Click the Done button.

At last, the colored full-screen pattern, called the *desktop,* appears. Congratulations! You've arrived.

(If you saw anything else during the startup process — a blinking question-mark icon, a strange error message, or thick black smoke — you've just met your first computer problem. Proceed directly to Chapter 15, which is all about troubleshooting.)

The Welcome screen

If turning on the iMac produces a list of people's names, like this —

— then you're not the first person to use this machine. Somebody has beat you to the setup process. Click your name, if you see it; type your password, if you've been given one; and then read on.

In any case, you'll find an explanation of this name-and-password signing-in process at the end of Chapter 13.

The desktop and menu bar

For some people, turning on the iMac takes you directly to the *desktop,* as shown in the upcoming illustration.

You also wind up here *after* encountering the Setup Assistant or list of names described in the previous pages. In any case, the machine is officially on now, and ready to do work for you.

Let's try some real computing here. Move the cursor up to the lightly striped strip at the top of the screen. It's called the *menu bar,* named after a delightful little pub in Silicon Valley. Touch the arrow on the logo at the upper-left corner of the screen. (The *tip* of the iMac's arrow is the part you need to worry about. Same thing with real-life arrows, come to think of it.)

Pointing to something on the screen in this way has a technical term: *pointing*. (Think you're going to be able to handle this?)

The big turn-off

Before we get into 3-D color graphs, space-vehicle trajectories, and DNA analysis, I guess I should tell you how to turn the iMac *off*.

In a pinch, sure, you can just yank the power cord out of the wall. But regularly turning off the iMac by chopping off its power can eventually confuse the poor thing and lead to technical problems.

Instead, you're supposed to turn off your iMac using one of the commands listed in the menu that you opened just a moment ago. Click the logo; when the list of commands appears, roll the mouse downward so that each successive command turns dark. When each menu command turns dark, it's said to be *highlighted*.

(The only commands that don't get highlighted are the ones that are dimmed, or *grayed out*. They're dimmed because they don't make any sense at the moment. For example, if no disc is in the CD-ROM drive, choosing Eject wouldn't make any sense. So the Mac makes that command gray, which means it's unavailable to you.)

If you've had enough of a computer lesson for now, let the cursor come to rest on the *Shut Down* command — and then click the mouse again. The computer promptly shuts itself off. See? This thing's no harder than a toaster.

If you're ready to read on, though, confident that you now know how to turn this thing off, move the mouse cursor away from the menu and click anywhere else on the screen. The iMac, amazingly, does nothing at all but continue looking extremely cool.

Why not to turn off the iMac

Believe it or not, many iMac owners *never* turn the machine off. Instead, whenever they're not using it, they let the iMac drift off to *sleep*.

When the iMac is asleep, the screen is dark, the components inside stop whirring, all activity stops, and electricity consumption slows to a trickle. When you press a key later, the computer brightens right up. Whatever was on the screen is still there, ready for you to begin working again.

When you first buy an iMac, it's set to sleep automatically several minutes after you've stopped using it. But you can also make the machine sleep instantly, on your command, which is useful when you're browsing the "Survivor" Web site at work just as the boss walks by.

To do so, open the menu again and then click the Sleep command. The iMac blinks right off to sleep.

While it's dozing, the little white light at the lower-right corner of your screen stays on, your cue that the machine isn't entirely off. It makes a handy night light for the office (well, if your office is about one inch wide).

Desktop, Dock, and Icons

Take a look around the screen. At the bottom is a row of icons called the *Dock*. Most of these icons represent the various programs that came with your iMac. (To find out their names, try pointing to them without clicking.) The Dock is described in Chapter 3.

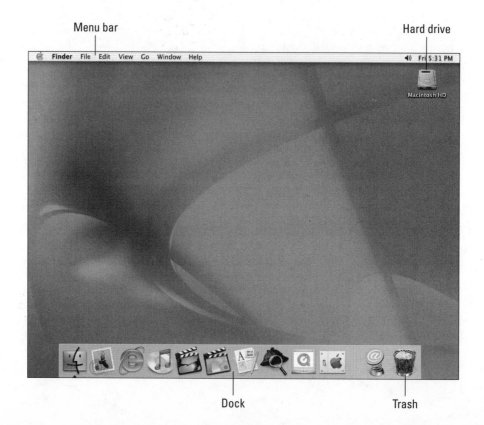

Menu bar   Hard drive

Dock   Trash

All systems are go

An *operating system* is the behind-the-scenes software that runs your computer. But because everyone's in such a hurry these days, people now just call it the *OS.* (Say it "O. S.," not "oss.") Your computer, in fact, runs one of the most advanced and beautiful operating systems on earth: Mac OS X.

(That X is supposed to be a roman numeral 10. Say "Mac Oh Ess Ten." Don't say "Mack Ossex," unless you want people to look at you funny.)

Just like car companies, Apple Computer piles on a few new features to Mac OS X every year. It distinguishes one version from the previous by tacking on additional decimal points. Your iMac may run Mac OS X version 10.1.4, or 10.1.5, or even 10.2-point-something.

Want to find out what you've got? Get a pencil.

Remember the logo in the upper-left corner of the screen? Point your arrow cursor tip on the apple and click the button to open the menu. Click the first command here, About This Mac.

A window appears, like the one shown here, revealing what version of Mac OS X you have.

The version is a number you'll need to know later in this book and later in your life. Therefore, take this opportunity to write it onto your Cheat Sheet (the yellow cardboard page inside the front cover of this book). You'll find a little blank for this information in the upper-left corner of your card, where it says, "Your System version."

But write it in pencil, because as Apple improves its software, fixes bugs, and dreams up speed enhancements, it will send them to your iMac automatically the next time you connect to the Internet. One day, you'll wake up to discover that your 10.1.4 machine now runs 10.1.5, or whatever. Strange, useful — and freaky.

When you're finished with this little piece of homework, close the About This Computer window by clicking the little, round, red button in the upper-left corner — the Close button.

About This Mac

X
Mac OS X
Version 10.1.4

Memory: 256 MB
Processor: PowerPC G4

™ & © Apple Computer. Inc. 1983–2001

Near the upper-right corner of the screen, you see an *icon,* a little, inch-tall, symbolic picture. Unless you've changed it, that icon is called *Macintosh HD.*

Icons represent everything in the Mac world. They all look different: One represents a letter you wrote, another represents the Trash can, another represents a CD you've inserted. Here are some examples of icons you'll probably be seeing before long:

A CD   A hard drive   A folder   A picture   A program

You can move an icon by dragging it. Try this:

1. Point to the Macintosh HD icon.

2. Press and then hold down the mouse button continuously — and, while it's down, move the mouse to a new position.

This sophisticated technique is called, by the way, *dragging.* You're dragging the hard drive icon now.

3. Let go of the mouse button.

Hey, this thing isn't so technical after all, right?

Other than the fact that there's a Trash can at the lower-right corner, nobody's really sure why they call this main screen the *desktop.* It has another name, too: the *Finder.* It's where you file all your work into little electronic on-screen file folders so that you can *find* them again later. The word *Finder* even appears at the top of the screen, next to the menu.

Used in a sentence, you might hear it like this: "Well, no wonder you don't see the Trash can. You're not in the Finder!"

Macintosh syntax

Point once again to the hard-disk icon in the upper-right corner of the screen, like this:

This particular icon represents the giant disk inside your iMac, known as the *hard drive* or *hard disk*, which serves as your filing cabinet. It's where the computer stores all your work, all your files, and all your software.

So how do you see what's in your hard drive? Where do you get to see its table of contents?

It turns out that you can *open* any icon into a window, where you'll see every item inside listed individually. The window has the same name as the icon you opened.

Before we proceed, though, it's time for a lesson in Macintosh syntax. Fear not; it's nothing like English syntax. In fact, everything that you do on the Macintosh has this format: *noun-verb*. Shakespeare it ain't, but it's sure easy to remember.

Let's try a noun-verb command, shall we?

1. **Click the hard-disk icon in the upper-right corner of the screen.**

   The icon turns black, indicating that it's *selected*. Good job — you've just identified the *noun*.

2. **Move to the File menu and choose Open.**

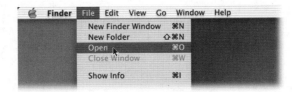

You guessed it — Open is the *verb*. And, sure enough, your hard disk opens into a window, where you can see its contents. (If another window was already on your screen, it immediately disappears to make way for the Macintosh HD window.)

In the world of Macintosh, you always specify *what* you want to change (using the mouse) and then you use a menu command to specify *how* you want it changed. You'll see this pattern over and over again: *Select* something on the screen and then *apply* a menu command to it.

The complete list of window doodads

Look over the contents of your hard-drive window, as shown in the following figure. (Everybody's got different stuff, so what you see on your screen may not exactly match the illustration.)

Better yet, look over the various controls and gadgets around the *edges* of this window. Using these controls and buttons, you can do all kinds of neat things to a window: stretch it, move it, or make it go away. These various gadgets are worth learning about — you're going to run into windows *everywhere* after you start working.

CLOSE BUTTON — Click here to close the window.

MINIMIZE BUTTON — Click the yellow globe to hide the window.

ZOOM BUTTON — Click to make the window just big enough to show all its contents.

TITLE BAR ICON — Click and hold, and then drag, to move the entire window to Trash, to another disk, or to another window.

TITLE BAR — Drag anywhere in this striped area to move the whole window.

TOOLBAR BUTTON — Click to hide (or bring back) the toolbar.

TOOLBAR — Filled with buttons that take you to important folders.

VERTICAL SCROLL BAR — It has a blue handle, indicating that you're not seeing everything in the window. Drag the blue, shimmery handle to bring the rest into view.

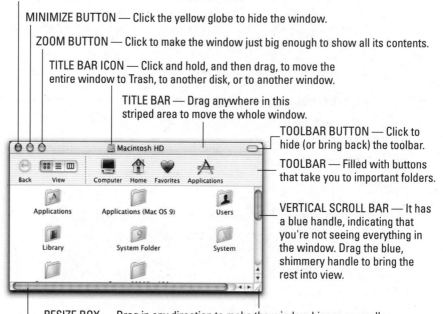

RESIZE BOX — Drag in any direction to make the window bigger or smaller.

HORIZONTAL SCROLL BAR — There's no blue handle, so you're seeing everything in the window (left to right, anyway).

Go ahead and try out some of the little boxes and scroll bars. Click them. Tug on them. Open the window and close it again. No matter what you do, *you can never hurt the machine by doing "the wrong thing."* That's the wonderful thing about the iMac: It's the Nerf appliance.

Double-clicking in theory and practice

So far, all of your work in the Finder (the desktop) has involved moving the mouse around. But your keyboard is useful, too. For example, do you see the System folder, the one with a big X on it? Even if you don't, here's a quick way to find it: Quickly type **SY** on your keyboard.

Presto, the iMac finds the System folder (which happens to be the first thing that begins with those letters) and highlights it, in effect dropping it in front of you, wagging its tail.

Now try pressing the arrow keys on your keyboard — right, left, up, down. The iMac highlights neighboring icons as you do so.

Suppose you want to see what's in the System folder. Of course, using your newfound noun-verb method, you could (1) click the System folder to select it and then (2) choose Open from the File menu.

But that's the sissy way. Try this power shortcut: Point to the System folder icon so that the tip of the arrow cursor is squarely inside the picture of the folder. Keeping the mouse still, click twice in rapid succession. With stunning originality, the Committee for the Invention of Computer Terminology calls this advanced computing technique *double-clicking.*

If all went well, your double-click opened a new window, showing you the contents of the System folder. (If it didn't work, you probably need to keep the mouse still or double-click faster.)

Remember this juicy golden rule: *Double-click means "open."*

In your iMac life, you'll be asked (or tempted) to click many an item on-screen: buttons that say "OK"; tools that look like paint brushes; all manner of multiple-choice buttons. In every one of these cases, you're supposed to click *once.*

The only time you ever *double*-click something is when you want to *open* it. Got it?

One window

Now you have the System window open. Well, that's just great, but what happened to the hard drive window?

The iMac tries to keep your life simple by showing you only one window at a time. When you open one folder, its window *replaces* whatever window you were just looking at. It works like a TV: you can change channels, but the frame around your screen always looks the same.

That's all great, but what if you want to backtrack? What if, now that you've savored the System folder for a moment, you want to return to the Macintosh HD window that you opened first?

That's what the Back button is for. Just click the button to go back to whatever window you had open before. In fact, if you'd opened several folders in succession, you can click the Back button *repeatedly* for a little reverse slide show of the windows you've recently opened.

Multiple windows

This business of keeping only one window before you at all times is fine for timid beginners, and it certainly keeps your screen tidy. But sooner or later, you're going to wish you could open two windows simultaneously — when you want to move a picture or a chapter from one window into another.

Try this: From the File menu, choose New Finder Window. Presto: a second window appears. (It probably says "[Your Name]'s Computer.")

You can tell that this window is in back, because it looks sort of faded. Click anywhere in the window to bring it to the front.

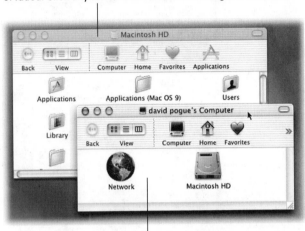

You can tell that this window is in front, because its title bar is bright and bold.

Windows on a computer are like pieces of paper on a desk: there may be a whole pile of them, but only one can be on top. And on a Mac, you bring a window to the top just by clicking it.

Take a stress-free moment to prove the point, using the two windows now before you: Click the back one to bring it forward; then click the one that was in front to bring it to the front again. To move a window, drag it with the mouse, using the pinstriped strip at the top (the title bar, which Apple evidently made of recycled pajamas).

When you're finished goofing around, close each window by clicking its Close button (the little red glob of Colgate Very Berry Gel in the upper-left corner).

Where to Get Help

It's true that your iMac didn't come with a printed manual. If you're cynical, you might guess that Apple was hoping to save a few bucks. If you're idealistic, you might assume that Apple is simply concerned about the rampant logging and paper industries.

In any case, your computer does come with a manual, of sorts — an electronic one. It's very terse, somewhat incomplete, and contains no jokes whatsoever, but it's there. To find it, open the Help menu, and choose Mac Help. You get a window that looks something like this:

You can use this Help Center in two ways. First, you can type a Help topic into the blank at the top of the window (such as *naming files* or *dialing the Internet*) — and then click the Ask button. If you're having a good night, the window will then show you a list of Help pages that might contain the answer you're looking for; click the name of the topic that seems to hold some promise.

Second, you can click your way through this little Help program. In the previous illustration, see all the topics written in blue underlined type?

Of course not. This is a black-and-white book. How silly of me.

But on *your* screen, all those underlined phrases show up in blue lettering. That blueness, and that underlining, means *click me to jump to a different page*. By clicking on successive blue underlined phrases, you can often hone in on the precise Help article you're interested in.

Pit stop

Shut the iMac down now, if you want (flip back a few pages to the section "The big turn-off" for complete instructions). Or just walk away, confident that it will put itself into an energy-saving Sleep mode after half an hour.

Chapter 1½ is something of a chalk-talk to help you understand what's really happening inside the computer's puny brain.

Top Ten Similarities between You and Your iMac

Before you move boldly forward to the next chapter, ponder the following frightening similarities between an iMac and its owner:

1. Each is pulled out of a very special container on Day One.

2. Each has a neck that permits the head to look around or nod.

3. Each has slots to provide adequate ventilation.

4. Each reacts to sudden movements of mice.

5. Each may crash when asked to do too much at once.

6. Each has a button on its abdomen.

7. Each lights up when turned on.

8. Each occasionally enjoys a good CD.

9. Each may be connected to a phone line for days at a time.

10. Sooner or later, each goes to sleep automatically.

Chapter 1½

High-Tech Made Easy

In This Chapter

▶ Why memory and disks aren't the same thing
▶ Why you'll never lose work to a computer glitch
▶ What to remember about memory

How an iMac Works

I'm a little worried about sticking this chapter so close to the front of the book. Plenty of people firmly believe that the iMac has a personality — that when something goes wrong, the iMac is being cranky; and when a funny message appears on the screen, the iMac is being friendly. Don't let the following discussion of cold, metal, impersonal circuitry ruin that image for you; the iMac *does* have a personality, no matter what the wireheads say.

For the first time, you're going to have to roll up your brain's sleeves and chew on some actual computer jargon. Don't worry — you'll feel coolly in control by the time it's over. Besides, it's a short chapter.

Storing things with disks

Human beings, for the most part, store information in one of two places. Either we retain something in our memory, or we write it down on the back of an envelope.

Computers work pretty much the same way. They can either store what they know in their relatively pea-brained *memory,* which I'll cover in a moment, or they can write it down. A computer writes stuff down on a computer disk.

Conceptualizing the hard disk

Every iMac has a gigantic disk built inside it — a *hard disk*. The concept of a hard disk confuses people because it's hidden inside the iMac's case. Since you can't see it or touch it, it's sort of conceptual — like beta-carotene or God, I guess. But it's there, spinning quietly away, and a hefty chunk of your iMac's purchase price paid for it.

Why all this talk of disks? Because a hard disk is where your life's work is going to live when the computer is shut off. You will, like it or not, become intensely interested in the overall health of your computer's hard disk.

The hard disk isn't the only one you'll encounter in your lifetime, by the way. For example, your iMac can also play, and even record, CDs. You may also one day decide to buy an *external disk drive* that plugs into the back of the iMac; it might be a second hard drive, or it might be a Zip drive or floppy drive into which you can insert *removable* disks. (The iMac doesn't have a built-in floppy-disk slot.) Copying your important work onto a pocketable disk is a handy way to *back up*, or make a safety copy of, whatever you've been working on.

Understanding memory

Now we get to the good stuff: how a computer really works. I know you'd just as soon not know what's going on in there, but consider this information mental broccoli: It's good for you, and later in life, you'll be glad you were forced to digest it. If, at this point, your brain is beginning to hemorrhage, skip this section and find serenity in Chapter 2.

There's actually a significant difference between an *iMac*'s memory and *your* memory (besides the fact that yours is probably much more interesting). When you shut down the iMac (not just put it to sleep), it forgets *everything*. It becomes a dumb, metal-and-plastic doorstop. That's because a computer's memory, just like yours, is kept alive by electrical impulses. When you turn off an iMac, the electricity stops.

Therefore, each time you turn *on* an iMac, it has to relearn everything it ever knew, including the fact that it's a computer, what kind of computer it is, how to display text, how many days until your warranty expires, and so on.

Now we arrive at the purpose of those disks we've been droning on about — it's where the computer's knowledge lives when the juice is off. Without a disk, the iMac is like someone with a completely hollow skull (and we've all met *that* type). If you're ever unlucky enough to experience a broken hard drive, you'll see how exciting an iMac can be without a disk: It shows a completely gray screen with a small blinking question mark in the middle. (I've met a few people like *that,* too.)

When you turn on a completely shut-down iMac, there's whirring and blinking. The hard disk inside begins to spin. When it hits about 5,400 rpm, the iMac starts reading the hard disk — it "plays" the disk like a CD player. It finds out: "Hey, I'm an iMac! And this is how I display text!" and so on. The iMac is reading the disk and copying everything it reads into *memory.* (That's why the computer takes a minute or so to start up.)

Memory is really neat. After something's in memory, it's instantaneously available to the computer. The iMac no longer has to read the disk to learn something. Memory is also expensive (at least compared to disks), probably because it's a bunch of complicated circuits that people in dust-proof spacesuits etch onto a piece of silicon the size of a piece of Trident.

Because memory is more expensive, computers have far less of it than disk space. For example, even if your hard disk holds every issue of *National Geographic* ever published, you're probably only going to *read* one article at a time. The iMac reads "The Nocturnal Nubian Gnat: Nature's Tiniest Vampire" from your hard disk, loads it into memory, and displays it on the screen.

So it doesn't matter that your iMac's memory doesn't hold as much as your entire hard disk. The iMac uses the hard disk for *long-term, permanent* storage of *lots* of things, and it uses memory for *temporary* storage while you work on *one thing at a time.*

Who's Meg?

You often hear computer jocks talk about *megs.* Only rarely are they referring to Meg Ryan and Meg Tilly. Meg is short for *megabyte.* So is the abbreviation *MB.* (*Mega* = 1,000,000, and *byte* = an iota of information so small it can only specify a single letter of the alphabet.)

What's highly confusing to most beginners is that you measure memory (fast, expensive, temporary) and hard-disk space (permanent, slower) in the *same units*: megabytes. A typical iMac might have 128 or 256 megs of memory (silicon chips) but 40,000 or 60,000 megs of hard-disk space (spinning platters).

(*Free bonus fact:* If a hard drive's size reaches 1,000 megs, it gets a new measurement name — its size is said to be one *gigabyte.* The abbreviation for one gigabyte is 1GB. Your iMac's hard drive may hold, for example, 60 GB. Computer nerds sometimes use shorthand for this measurement — "My iMac's hard drive has 60 gigs," much to the confusion of jazz-club musicians.)

Why they call it RAM

You know what an *acronym* is, right? It's a bunch of initials that, together, spell out an actual word, such as M.A.D.D. or SALT Treaty . . . or RAM.

When the Committee for Arbitrary Acronyms (the CAA) ratified the abbreviation RAM, it probably

stood for *Random Abbreviation for Memory.* Today, it supposedly stands for *Random Access Memory.*

Whatever *that* means.

With these vital facts in mind, see if you can answer the following paradoxical dinner party question:

"*How many megs* does your iMac have?"

The novice's answer: "Um . . . say, have you tried those little cocktail weenies?"

The partly initiated's reply: "I . . . I think 256?"

The truly enlightened response: "What do you mean, how many megs? Are you referring to *memory* or to *hard-disk space?* Here, have a cocktail weenie."

Understanding RAM

Let's add another term to your quickly growing nerd vocabulary list. It pains me to teach you this word, because it's one of those really meaningless terms that was invented purely to intimidate people. Trouble is, you're going to hear it a lot. You may as well be prepared.

It's *RAM.* You pronounce it like the sheep. RAM is memory. A typical iMac has 128 megs, 256 megs, or even more megs of RAM — in other words, of memory. (Don't say, "I have 256 RAMs." People will think you're a livestock farmer.)

Incidentally, this might be a good time to find out how much RAM *you* have. Here's how to find out.

Wake up, or turn on, your iMac.

See the logo in the upper-left corner of the screen? It's no ordinary logo. It's actually a menu, just like the ones you've already experienced. Click it with your mouse cursor, and watch what happens.

As with any menu, a list drops down. This one, however, includes an extremely useful command. This command is so important that it's listed first in the menu: *About This Mac.*

Slide the pointer down until About This Mac turns black, and then click the mouse button. A window appears:

The number labeled Memory (which I've circled in the picture) is how much actual RAM your iMac has. It's some multiple of eight.

In any case, your iMac's RAM endowment is a statistic you'll enjoy reviewing again and again. Therefore, take this opportunity to write this number onto your yellow cardboard Cheat Sheet at the front of the book. There's a little blank for this information.

When you're finished with this little piece of homework, close the About This Computer window by clicking the little red button in the upper-left corner — the Close button.

Putting it all together

Now that you know where a computer's information lives, let me take you on a tour of the computer's guts. Let's get into our little imaginary Disney World tram. Keep hands and feet inside the car at all times.

When you turn on the iMac, the hard disk spins, and the iMac copies certain critical information into its memory. So far, the iMac knows only that it's a computer. It doesn't know anything else that's stored on your hard disk. It doesn't yet know about Nocturnal Nubian Gnats, your new screenplay, or how much you owe on your credit card.

To get any practical work done, you now have to transfer the article (or screenplay or spreadsheet) into memory. In Macintosh terminology, you have to *open a file*. In Chapter 2, you'll find out how easy and idiot-proof this process is. Anyway, after you open a file, it appears on-screen. It's *in memory* now.

While your document is on the screen, you can make changes to it. This, of course, is why you bought a computer in the first place. You can delete a sentence from your novel or move a steamy scene to a different chapter. (The term for this process is *word processing*.) If you're working on your finances, you can add a couple zeros to your checking-account balance. (The term for this process is *wishful thinking*.)

Readers who haven't already gotten bored and gone off to watch TV will recognize that you're making all these changes to what's in *memory*. The more you change the screenplay that's up on the screen, the more it's different from that *permanent* copy that's still on your disk, safe and sound.

At this point, you're actually in a pretty precarious position. Remember that memory is sustained by electricity. In other words, if your four-year-old mistakes the iMac's power cord for a handy suckable plaything and jerks it out of the wall, then the electricity stops. The screen goes blank, and all the changes you've made disappear forever. You're left with the original copy on the disk, but any work you've done on it vanishes, along with anything else in the iMac's memory.

However, every software program has a simple command, called Save, that saves your work back onto the hard drive. That is, the computer *updates* the original copy that's still on the hard drive. Now you're safe. Even if a sun storm wipes out all power plants in the Northern Hemisphere and your iMac goes dark, your novel or letter or spreadsheet is safe on the disk. Most people use the Save command every five or ten minutes so that their work is always up-to-date and preserved on the disk. (You'll learn how to use the Save command in Chapter 4.)

"I lost all my work!"

So that you'll quit worrying about it, the precariousness of memory accounts for the horror stories you sometimes hear from people who claim that they lost their work to a computer. "I was on volume Y of the encyclopedia I've been writing," they'll say, "and I lost all of it because of a computer glitch!"

Now you can cry crocodile tears and then skip back to your office with a smirk. *You* know what happened. They probably worked for hours with some document on the screen but forgot to use the Save command. Then the unthinkable happened — someone tripped on the power cord — and, sure enough, all the changes they'd made got wiped out. A simple Save command would have stored everything neatly on the hard disk.

Top Ten Differences between Memory and a Hard Disk

May you never confuse memory with a hard disk again.

1. You usually buy memory 128 or 256 megs at a time. Hard disks come in sizes like 40 gigs, 60 gigs, and on up. (A *gigabyte* is 1,000 *megabytes*.)

2. Memory comes on a little minicircuit board. A hard disk is a metal-cased box with cables hanging out of it.

3. You can install memory only inside the computer. A hard disk may be either inside the iMac (an *internal* drive) or in a separate box you plug into the side (an *external* drive).

4. Memory delivers information to the iMac's brain almost instantly. The hard disk sometimes seems to take forever.

5. Some disks are removable. When one fills up, you can insert a different one. (Some examples: floppy disks, Zip disks, and recordable CDs.) Removing RAM is a more serious proposition, generally involving the assistance of a knowledgeable geek.

6. Not every computer on earth has a hard disk. (The earliest Macs used nothing but floppy disks, and pocket organizers like the PalmPilot have no disks at all.) But every computer ever made has memory.

7. If you listen carefully, you can hear when the iMac is reading information off a hard disk; it makes tiny frantic scraping noises. You can't tell when the iMac is getting information from RAM.

8. As a very general rule, RAM costs about 50 cents per meg. Hard drives average about *1/3 of one cent* per meg.

9. Memory's contents disappear when you shut down the computer. A disk's contents stay there until you deliberately throw them away.

10. To find out how much *hard-disk* space you have left, open any window on your desktop. The strip at the top shows you how much space is available, as shown here.

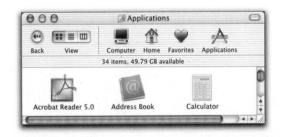

(If you don't see this information strip, click the View menu at the top of your screen, and choose Show Status Bar to make it appear.)

But there's no similar way to see how much *RAM* you have left. The beauty of Mac OS X, the operating software of your iMac, is that it smoothly and masterfully dishes out memory to as many programs as you care to run, taking excess memory from here, tucking it there, constantly redistributing your iMac's memory so that no program ever goes hungry.

Chapter 2

Windows, Icons, and Trashes

- -

In This Chapter

▶ All about windows, folders, and icons

▶ Three window views for three moods

▶ Learning keyboard shortcuts

▶ Tips on using windows and disks to raise your social status

- -

Becoming Manipulative

All the clicking and dragging and window-shoving you learned in Chapter 1 is, in fact, leading up to something useful.

Foldermania

I've said that your hard disk is like the world's biggest filing cabinet. It's where you store all your stuff. But a filing cabinet without filing *folders* would be about as convenient to handle as an egg without a shell.

The folders on the iMac screen don't occupy any space on your hard drive. They're electronic fictions whose sole purpose is to help you organize your stuff.

Mr. Folder

Your Home folder

As far as you're concerned, the most important folder on the iMac is your *Home folder*. It's the one that will soon contain all of your work, the one that will remember all of your favorite Web pages, the one that will keep track of your preference settings in every program you use, and so on.

But the Home folder isn't just a convenient folder that offers one-stop shopping for all your stuff. It's also a security feature. Nobody else who uses this iMac is allowed to see, mess with, or delete anything in your folder (assuming all of you sign in using the accounts feature described at the end of Chapter 13).

In short, the Home folder, gentle reader, is your new digital home.

Because this folder is so important, Apple has equipped your machine with a long list of ways to get there. For example:

✔ Open the Go menu. Choose Home.

✔ Press Option-⌘-H. (Instructions on deciphering this instruction in a moment.)

✔ Click the Home icon on the toolbar at the top of any open window, like this:

✔ Double-click the Macintosh HD icon near the top right of your screen. In the hard drive window, double-click the Users folder, and then double-click the folder inside it that bears your name and looks like a house.

In any case, your Home folder now appears, filled with folders that you'll grow to know and love:

Leave it open for the following exercise. As a matter of fact, you might even want to make it a little bigger by tugging its lower-right corner handle.

Folder factory

The iMac provides an infinite supply of folders. Want a folder? Do this:

From the File menu, choose New Folder.

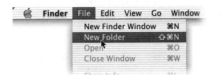

Ooh, tricky, this machine! A new folder appears. Notice that the iMac gracefully proposes "untitled folder" as its name.

Notice something else, though: The name is *highlighted* (black). Remember our earlier lesson? Highlighted = selected = ready for you to *do* something. When *text* is highlighted, the iMac is ready for you to *replace* it with anything you type. In other words, you don't even have to backspace over the text. Just type away:

1. **Type *USA Folder* and press the Return key.**

   The Return key tells the iMac that your naming spurt is over.

   Now, to see how folders work, create another one.

2. **From the File menu, once again choose New Folder.**

   Another new folder appears, once more waiting for a title.

3. **Type *Ohio* and press Return.**

You're going to create one more empty folder. But by this time, your wrist is probably weary from the forlorn trek back and forth to the File menu. Don't you wish you could make a folder faster?

You can.

Keyboard shortcuts

Open the File menu, but don't select any of the commands in it yet. See those weird notations to the right of some commands?

Get used to 'em. They're *keyboard shortcuts,* and they appear in almost every menu you'll ever see. Keyboard shortcuts let you select certain menu items without using the mouse.

Some people love keyboard shortcuts, claiming that if you're in a hurry, pressing keys is faster than using the mouse. Other people loathe keyboard shortcuts, pointing out that using the mouse doesn't require any memorization. In either case, here's how keyboard shortcuts work.

When you type on a typewriter, you press the Shift key to make a capital letter, right? Computer nerds call the Shift key a *modifier key* because it turns ordinary, well-behaved citizen keys like 3 and 4 into madcap symbols like # and $.

Welcome to the world of computers, where everything is four times more complicated. Instead of having only *one* modifier key, the iMac has *four* of them! Look down next to your space bar. There they are: In addition to the Shift key, one says Option, one says Ctrl, and another has a little ⌘ symbol on it.

Menu symbols unlimited

Besides the little keyboard-shortcut symbols at the right side of a menu, you'll occasionally run into a little downward-pointing arrow, like this:

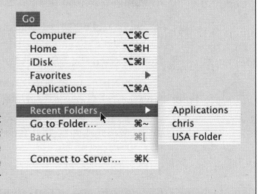

That arrow tells you that the menu is so long, it doesn't even fit on the screen. The arrow is implying that still more commands are in the menu that you're not seeing. To get to those additional commands, carefully roll the pointer

down the menu all the way to that down-pointing triangle. Don't let the sudden jumping scare you: The menu commands will jump upward, bringing the hidden ones into view.

And then there are the little black triangles pointing to the *right* (left side of the illustration). These triangles indicate that, when selected, the menu command won't do anything except offer you several *other* commands, which pop out to the side:

It's that little cloverleaf — the *command key* — whose symbol appears in the File menu. Next to the New Folder command, you see ⌘-N. That means:

1. **While pressing the Shift and ⌘ keys, press the N key and then release everything.**

   Bam! You've got yourself another folder. (Sometimes you might see *two* symbols next to a menu command, like the ones next to Computer in the Go menu. That means press *both* the Option and ⌘ keys before typing the specified letter.)

2. **Type *Michigan* and press Return.**

   You've just named your third folder. So why have you been wasting a perfectly good afternoon (or whatever it is in your time zone) making empty folders? So you can pretend you're getting organized.

3. **Drag the Ohio folder on top of the USA Folder.**

Make sure that the tip of the arrow actually hits the center of the USA Folder so that the folder becomes highlighted. The instant it turns black, let go of the Ohio folder — and watch it disappear into the USA Folder. (If your aim wasn't good, you'll now see the Ohio folder sitting next to the USA Folder; try the last step again.)

4. Put the Michigan folder into the USA Folder in the same way — by dragging it on top of the USA Folder.

As far as you know, though, those state folders have *disappeared*. How can you trust me that they're now neatly filed away?

5. Double-click the USA Folder.

Yep. Opens right up into a window, and there are your two darling states, nestled sweetly where they belong.

Okay, so how do you get these inner folders *out* again? Do you have to drag them individually? That would certainly be a bummer if you had all 50 folders in the USA Folder.

Turns out there are several ways to select more than one icon at a time.

6. Click above and to the left of the Michigan folder (Step 1 in the upcoming picture) and, without releasing the mouse, drag down and to the right so that you enclose both folders with a light gray rectangle (Steps 2 and 3).

Release the mouse button when you've got both icons enclosed.

Now that you have several folders selected, you can move them en masse to another location.

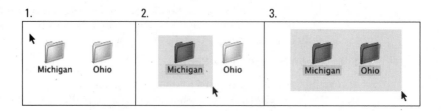

7. **Drag the Ohio folder outside of the USA Folder window — onto the blue desktop, for example.**

   The Michigan folder goes along for the ride.

This was a somewhat unproductive exercise, of course, because you were only working with empty folders. It gets much more exciting when you start working with your own documents, as you will in the following chapters. All of these techniques work equally well with folders and with documents.

Icon, List, and Column Views

Whenever you visit your Home folder, you see attractive little pictures that represent the files and folders inside. In other words, you're viewing this window in *icon view* — a fact that you can confirm by opening the View menu. See the check mark next to "as List" in the View menu?

But lovely though icon view may be, it's not ideal for every folder. What if you had a folder containing 250 pictures from a digital camera? You'd go nuts trying to swim through 250 little icons in random order.

Fortunately, Mac OS X lets you call up any of three different views for any window you're perusing: icon, list, or column. You switch among them either by choosing "as Icons," "as List," or "as Columns" from the View menu — or just by clicking the corresponding buttons in your toolbar, shown here:

Each view is appropriate for different kinds of windows, as you're about to find out.

Icon view

Icon view is ideal for windows that contain only a few icons — your Home folder when you're just starting out, for example.

Icon view is also by far the most fun view. Play your cards right, and just fiddling with icon-view options can provide hours of hilarity for the whole family.

For example, all those attractive little folders don't have to be attractive *little* folders. You can make them as large or small as you like. For proof, open the View menu and choose View Options. As you can see here, the resulting dialog box contains a slider that lets you make your icons minuscule, gigantic, or anything in between:

Bonus technique for extra credit

The method of selecting several icons by dragging a rectangle around them is fine if all the icons are next to each other. But how would you select only the icons that begin with the letter A in this picture? You can't very well enclose each A by dragging the mouse — you'd also get all the *other* icons within the same rectangle.

The power-user's secret: Click each icon *while pressing the Shift key*. As long as you're pressing Shift, you continually add additional, non-adjacent icons to the selection. (And if you Shift-click one by accident, you can deselect it by Shift-clicking *again*. Try it!)

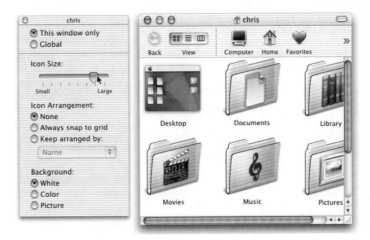

See the controls at the bottom of this dialog box? If you click Color and then the small rectangular button that appears beside it, you're offered a color wheel. Use it to choose a solid color for the background of an icon-view window — just the ticket when you feel the urge to interior-decorate your Home folder in a soothing sea green.

In fact, the wallpaper for an icon-view folder can even be a photo. If you click Picture, and then Select, the iMac offers you its Open File dialog box, which lets you navigate your hard drive in search of the perfect photo background. (More on the Open File dialog box in Chapter 4.)

List view

The second standard view for folder windows will make Type A personalities wriggle with delight: a list, sorted alphabetically, chronologically, or any way you like. This is the perfect view for windows that hold more than a handful of icons.

Click a column heading to sort the list that way.
(Click again to sort the opposite way.)

Drag a column heading sideways to rearrange the columns.

Once a window's contents are in a list, each folder *within* the window is marked by a tiny triangle. You can open one of these folders-within-a-folder in the usual way, if you wish — by double-clicking. But it's much more satisfying for neat freaks to click the *triangle* instead. In the following figure, the before-and-after view of the Library folder (inside your Home folder) shows how much more organized you can be.

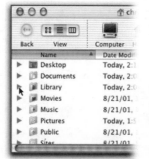 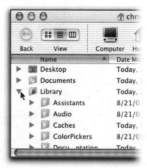

When you click the triangle, in other words, your window contents look like an outline. The contents of that subfolder are indented. To "collapse," or close, the folder, click the downward-pointing triangle.

Column view

As noted in Chapter 1, you usually see only one window at a time. When you open folder B, folder A's window closes automatically. Apple's trying to keep your life tidy.

In column view, however, you see exactly where you're going, and where you've come from, as you burrow through folders-within-folders on your hard drive.

That's because column view divides your window into several vertical panes. The pane at the far left (you may have to use the scroll bar to see it) shows all the icons of your disks, including your main hard drive.

How column view works

When you click that hard drive icon, the second pane shows a list of all the folders on it. When you click one of those folders, the third pane shows all the folders inside *it*. And so on. Each time you click a folder in one pane, the pane to its right shows what's inside; the other panes slide off to the left. (Use the horizontal scroll bar to bring them back, if you like.)

You can keep clicking until you're actually looking at the file icons inside the most deeply nested folder. If the file is a picture or movie, you can even take a look at it right there in the window:

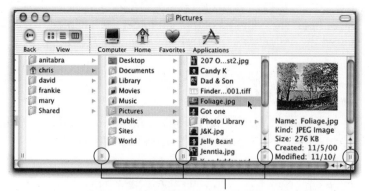

Drag one of the circled handles to adjust all columns' widths.
Option-drag to make only one column wider or narrower.

If you discover that your hunt for a particular file has taken you down a blind alley, you can easily backtrack, thanks to the trail of folders that's still visible on the screen. Just click a different folder in one of the earlier panes to start burrowing down a different rabbit hole.

In short, column view not only keeps your screen tidy (by showing several windows' worth of information in a single window), but you're less likely to get lost, wondering what folder you're in and how you got there. Your trail of digital breadcrumbs is visible at all times.

Manipulating the columns

Every now and then, the column widths in column view aren't ideal. You may have a list of files with very short names, wallowing in space in very wide columns. Or maybe your files have very *long* names, and the columns are far too narrow to show the full names.

You have considerable control in these situations. For example:

- ✔ You can make all the columns wider or narrower simultaneously by dragging any of the small handles at the bottom of the columns (see the previous illustration).

- ✔ To make a *single* column wider or narrower, drag the column handle (the one at its right edge) while pressing the Option key.

- ✔ To read a file name that's too long to fit in its column, just point to it without clicking. After a moment, you'll see a yellow, rectangular balloon pop up at your arrow tip, revealing the full name.

- ✔ If you'd like to see more columns at once, make the window wider (drag the resizing handle at its lower-right corner).

How to Trash Something

Of all the computers on earth, the iMac is probably the most conducive to helping you be productive and creative. But even Mozart crumpled up the occasional half-finished overture and threw it into the fireplace.

You, too, can throw away files or folders you no longer need. You might decide to throw away that USA Folder you made in your Home folder, for example. (If the Home folder isn't on the screen right now, choose its name from the Go menu. Put the window back into icon view, if you like.)

To do so, just point to the USA Folder (or whatever you're trying to delete). Then, carefully keeping the far end of the mouse "clicked down," drag the folder down and to the right, until it's right on top of the Trash can at the right end of the Dock.

Don't let go until the Trash icon actually turns black (when the tip of the arrow cursor is on it). When you do let go, notice how the Trash icon changes from a wastebasket to a wastebasket-filled-with-crumpled-up-papers, to let you know there's something in there.

That's how you throw things out on the iMac: Just drag them onto the Trash. (There's even a keystroke for this: Highlight an icon and then press ⌘-Delete. The chosen icon goes flying into the Trash as though it's just been drop-kicked.)

What's really hilarious is how hard Apple made it for you to get rid of something. Just putting something into the Trash doesn't actually get rid of it; technically, you've only put it into the Oblivion Waiting Room. It'll sit there forever, in an overflowing trash basket. To rescue something, you just double-click the Trash basket to open its window, and then drag whatever-it-was right back onto the screen.

So if putting something into the Trash doesn't really delete it, how *do* you really delete it? You choose Empty Trash from the Finder menu.

But even *then* your stuff isn't really gone. You get a final warning like this:

Only when you click OK is your file finally gone.

Now you can understand why you never hear iMac owners complain of having thrown away some important document by accident — an iMac won't *let* you get rid of anything without fighting your way through four layers of warnings and red tape.

Pretty cool computer, huh?

Top Ten Window and Icon Tips

Staggering through the basics of using your iMac unattended is one thing. Shoving around those on-screen windows and icons with grace is quite another. Master the following, and then invite your friends over to watch some evening.

1. To rename an icon, click carefully on its name. Wait for a second or so, until a rectangle appears around the name. That's your cue to type away, giving it a new name. (You can type really long names, too, like *The chapter I started on Saturday night after "When Harry Met Sally" on TV but stopped when I got to the part about the vampire's wedding, because Chris came over with pizza and who could possibly work under those circumstances?*) Press Return when you're done.

1.   2.   3.

Layoffs   Layoffs   Downsizing

2. To make a copy of a file the traditional way, click the icon and then choose Duplicate from the File menu. Or, while pressing the Option key, drag the icon into a new window or folder.

3. To move some files from one window into another the modern way, start by selecting them (click them — or Shift-click them, if there's more than one). Then, from the Edit menu, choose Copy.

You've just socked them away onto the Mac's invisible Clipboard storage area.

Now click the folder, or click inside the window, where you want the copies to appear. From the Edit menu, choose Paste. As though by magic, the icons you copied reappear in their new home.

4. Every time you choose Empty Trash from the Finder menu, the iMac asks you if you're absolutely sure. If you're *always* sure, you can make it stop asking you that. To do so, open the Finder menu and choose Preferences. In the dialog box, turn off "Show warning before emptying the Trash." Close the window and savor the resulting time savings.

5. If you have a very important document, you can prevent it from getting thrown away by accident. Click its icon. From the File menu, choose Show Info. Turn on the Locked check box. Now, the iMac won't even let you put it into the Trash, let alone empty it.

6. Isn't it frustrating to open a window that's too small to show you all its contents (shown on the next page at left)?

Of course, you could spend a weekend fussing with the scroll bars, trying to crank the other icons into view. Or, by using trial-and-error, you could drag the lower-right handle (the resize box) to make the window bigger.

There's a much quicker solution. Click the green *zoom button* in the upper-left corner of the window (shown in the following figure at right by the cursor). The iMac automatically makes the window exactly large enough to show all of the icons.

7. In column view, you can press the arrow keys to navigate the different panes. Press the left and right arrow keys to jump from pane to pane, or the up and down arrow keys to "walk" up or down the list of files and folders in it.

8. Try this sneaky shortcut: While pressing the Control (Ctrl) key, point the cursor tip on an icon, disk, or the inside of a window. Keep the Control key pressed; if you now hold down the mouse button, a pop-up menu appears at your cursor tip, listing commands that pertain only to that icon, disk, or window.

For example, if you Control-click a disk or CD, you'll be offered commands like Eject, Help, and Open. If you Control-click an icon, you get commands like Show Info, Duplicate, and Move To Trash. And if you Control-click anywhere inside a window — but *not* directly on an icon — you're offered New Folder, Help, and Show Info. (The geek term for this phenomenon is *contextual menus,* because the menu is different depending on the context of your click.)

9. When your life overwhelms you with chaos and random events, at least your iMac can give you a sense of control and order.

Want proof? Open a crowded window, such as the Library folder in your Home folder. From the View menu, choose "as Icons." Just for the sake of this hypothetical example, drag the icons around until they look disorganized, messy, and random.

Now, from the View menu, choose View Options. In the window that appears, click "Keep arranged by," like this:

Then, from the pop-up menu, specify what order you want your icons to snap into (sorted by name, size, or whatever). Close the View Options window. Now, no matter how many icons you add to this window, and no matter what size you make the window, your icons will always remain in neat alignment.

Before

After

You can even perform this cosmetic surgery on the icons lying loose on your *desktop.* Just click the desktop before using the View Options command. In fact, you can even change the icon size for desktop icons, just by adjusting the slider in the View Options dialog box.

10. You don't have to clean up your windows before you shut down the computer. The windows will be right where you left them the next time you turn on the iMac.

Chapter 3

Actually Accomplishing Something

In This Chapter

▶ The Dock made awesome

▶ What software is, for those who care

▶ Copying and pasting

▶ Desk accessories and the fruit-shaped menu they're listed in

▶ The pure, unalloyed joy of System Preferences

The iMac, if you think about it while squinting, is like a VCR. The software programs you install on the iMac are like the tapes you slip into your VCR. Without tapes (software), the VCR (iMac) is worthless. But with tapes (software), your VCR (iMac) can take on any personality.

A VCR might let you watch a Western one night and a *60 Minutes* exposé about corruption in the contact-lens industry the next. In the same way, your iMac can be a typing instructor, a checkbook balancer, or a movie-editing machine, depending on the software you use. Each piece of software — called a *program* or an *application* — is like a different GameBoy cartridge: It makes the iMac look, feel, and behave differently. The average iMac user winds up using about six or seven different programs regularly.

In the next chapter, you're going to do some word processing. This chapter is the warm-up. It tells you where to find the programs that came with your iMac, explains how to use the Dock that dishes them up, and illustrates some of the basic principles of using programs on the iMac.

Obsolescence therapy

Your relationship with a software company doesn't end when you buy the program. First, the company provides a technical help staff for you to call when things get rocky. Some firms are great about this relationship — they give you a toll-free number that's answered immediately by a smart, helpful, customer-oriented technician. More often, though, sending out an SOS is a long-distance call . . . and a long-distance ten-minute wait before somebody can help you.

Like the computers themselves, software programs are continually being improved and enhanced by their manufacturers. Just as in owning a computer, owning a software program isn't a one-time cash outlay. Each time the software company comes out with a new version of the program, you'll be offered the chance to get it for a small "upgrade fee" of $25 or $99, for example.

You'd think people would get fed up with this endless treadmill of expenses and just stick with the version they've got, refusing to upgrade to successive versions. Some manage it. Most people, however, succumb to the fear that somehow they'll be left behind by the march of technology and wind up forking over the upgrade fees once a year or so. Let your budget and sense of independence be your guide.

Your Software Collection

The iMac comes with a handsome bonus gift of software preinstalled on the hard disk. That's fortunate, because software, for the most part, is expensive.

The crown jewel of the collection is called AppleWorks — a single program containing several *other* programs mashed into one: word processor, data-base, spreadsheet, drawing program, and so on. Chapter 9, "Faking Your Way through AppleWorks," covers this program in detail.

Your iMac also came with a suite of amazing programs that turn the computer into what Apple calls a "digital hub" — a headquarters for music players, digital cameras, and camcorders. That's what the programs called iTunes, iPhoto, and iMovie are all about (Chapters 10 and 11). You also have an e-mail program (Chapter 8), a Web browser (Chapter 7), a couple of games, and a whole raft of cute little accessory programs (see the end of this chapter).

Getting more software

Some people are set for life with the programs that came on the iMac.

But if you deal with anyone in the business world, you'll probably wind up buying something called Microsoft Office X for Macintosh — a single CD that contains Microsoft Word (the most popular word-processing program), Excel (a spreadsheet, for number crunching), PowerPoint (a slide-show program for making pitches around a board-room table), and Entourage (a calendar/e-mail program). (You can also buy these programs individually.)

Want a database for handling order forms, tracking phone calls, and creating form letters? Check out the fantastic FileMaker Pro (around $200). Try, *try* not to focus on the fact that what you *get* for that money is a 50-cent CD and a $2 manual.

Where to buy it

There are two places to buy software: via mail order and at a store. Unfortunately, as you'll quickly discover, today's computer stores generally offer a pathetically small selection of Macintosh software. (The exception: Apple Stores, which are cropping up in affluent cities all over America.)

On the other hand, mail-order companies like *www.buy.com, www.macmall. com,* and *www.macwarehouse.com* offer thousands of choices, give much bigger discounts, take returns after you've opened the box, and generally don't charge sales tax. And, of course, you don't have to fire up the old Toyota. You get your stuff delivered to your door by the next day.

Overnight mail-order companies like these are bright spots in the computer world. You can call some of them until midnight, in fact, and get your new programs by midmorning, only hours later. After ordering from these companies, you'll start to wish there were overnight mail-order grocery stores, gas stations, and dentists.

All right, maybe not dentists.

El cheapo software

Once you've read Chapter 6, and you've decided it might be fun to plug your iMac into the telephone line to dial up faraway computers, you may stumble onto another kind of software: *shareware.* These are programs written by individuals, not software companies, who make their programs freely available on the Internet. You can grab them, via telephone, and bring them to your own iMac. And get this: Only the

honor system, for heaven's sake, compels you to pay the authors the $15 or $20 they're asking for.

Sure, shareware often has a homemade feel to it. On the other hand, some of it's really terrific. You can search for the kind of shareware program you want (and also for acres of sounds, pictures, clip art, and games) on America Online and on the Internet (such as at *www.macdownload. com* or *www.versiontracker.com*).

The Dock

Every program you'll ever use on your iMac is conveniently parked in a single place: the Applications folder. Want to see this impressive list of software tools? You can get to it by choosing Applications from the Go menu, or by pressing Option-⌘-A, or just by double-clicking the Macintosh HD icon on your desktop (and then the Applications icon inside it).

In general, though, that's a lot of hassle, especially for the programs you wind up using often. Fortunately, Apple has provided you with a much more convenient shelf that puts your favorite programs only a click away: the Dock.

How the Dock works

See the fine white line running down the Dock in this picture?

Point to an icon to see its name

←—— Programs on this side   Files, folders, disks on this side ——→

That line separates all your favorite *programs,* on the left side, from your favorite everything-else (files, documents, folders, and disks), on the right.

As you've probably noticed, none of these icons are identified by name, at least not until you point to a Dock icon without clicking. Then the name appears just above the icon.

To open an icon that's on the Dock, just click it. If you click a program, its icon hops up and down excitedly during the time it takes that program to start up — you can't help share its enthusiasm — and then finally settles down with a little triangle underneath it, as shown in the previous picture.

Adding your own icons

Apple starts off the Dock with the icons of some built-in iMac programs — but that's just a tease. The Dock won't truly win your heart until your *own* favorite icons are on it.

Doing so couldn't be easier: Just *drag* any icon onto the appropriate half of the Dock. (Remember: Programs go on the left.) For example, you might open your Applications folder and drag, say, the Calculator from there onto the Dock, like this:

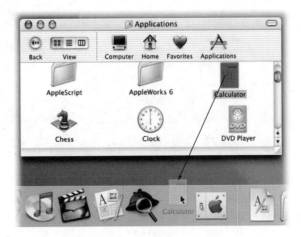

The other Dock icons politely scoot aside to make room.

It won't take you long to guess how you *remove* an icon from the Dock, either: you just drag it up and away. Once your cursor has cleared the Dock, let go of the mouse. A cheerful little puff of cartoon smoke appears, as your icon vanishes to the Great Mac in the Sky. The other Dock icons slide together to close the gap. (You can't ever ditch the Finder, the Trash, or a program or document that's currently open.)

Minimizing a window

The Dock isn't only a parking place for favorite iMac goodies. It can also be a handy shelf for windows you'd like to get out of your way temporarily.

Try this: Open up some window — your Home folder, let's say. (From the Go menu, choose Home.) Now suppose that you'd like to see what's behind it.

You could just close the window, of course. But if you want to return to it momentarily, there's a better way: you can *minimize* it. To do that, click the button that looks like a round, yellow glob of gel in the window's upper-left corner — the *minimize* button, as it's called. (Alternative-lifestyle fans may prefer to choose Minimize Window from the Window menu, or just press ⌘-M, to achieve the same effect.)

As you can see here, the entire window collapses, shrinking like a genie through a transparent funnel, to the right end of the Dock:

The window isn't gone; it hasn't actually closed. It's just out of your way for the moment, as though you've set it down on a shelf. When you want to bring it back, click the newly created Dock icon. The window genies its way right back to its original position on the screen.

Minimizing a window in this way is a great window-management tool. In the Finder, doing so lets you see whatever icons are covered by a window. In a word processor, this technique helps you type up a memo that requires frequent consultation of a spreadsheet behind it.

Four fancy Dock tricks

If your iMac were a Thanksgiving dinner, the Dock would be the turkey. All right, maybe that's not the best analogy, but the Dock *is* the centerpiece of the iMac, and a very big deal. You'll spend a lot of time with it.

In fact, you may as well start spending time with it right now. Put it through the paces with these stunts:

✔ The Dock doesn't have to sit at the bottom of the screen like some kind of muck-eater. It's just as happy on either *side* of your screen. Considering the fact that your screen is wider than it is tall, in fact, the side of the screen might be a less space-hogging position for it.

To put it there, open the menu, mouse down to the Dock command, and choose "Position on Left" or "Position on Right" from the submenu. (You can see these commands in the next illustration.)

When you position your Dock vertically, the "right" side of the Dock becomes the bottom. In other words, the Trash now appears at the bottom of the vertical Dock.

✔ You can also hide the Dock completely, which can come in very handy when it's overlapping some window that you're trying to read. From the Dock command in the menu, choose Turn Hiding On. (Or just press Option-⌘-D. Are you beginning to notice how all of the important keystrokes work alike? You always hold down the Option and ⌘ keys, plus the D for Dock, H for Home, A for Applications folder, and so on.) The Dock disappears promptly, sliding off the screen into oblivion.

That doesn't mean you have to do without it altogether. You can bring it back, either by pressing the same keys you used to make it disappear (Option-⌘-D) or by moving your cursor to the Dock's edge of the screen. Presto: It slides back into view. Click whatever it is you were intending to click on the Dock — and then move the cursor back to the middle of the screen. The Dock slithers out of view once again.

✔ As you may eventually notice for yourself, the icons on the Dock get smaller as the Dock gets more crowded. (If they didn't, the icons would have to extend beyond the edges of your screen, a condition definitely not covered by your warranty.)

Once they reach that point, you may run into a small problem: How are you supposed to make out the pictures on the icons when they're the size of atoms?

Easy: Just tell the iMac to enlarge them as your cursor passes across them. To turn on this strange and wonderful feature, open the menu, slide down to the Dock command, and choose Turn Magnification On from the submenu.

Now your Dock icons puff up bigger as your cursor passes over them, as shown here — an effect whose novelty takes minutes on end to wear off.

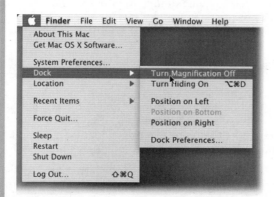

✔ If your Dock isn't yet crammed full, you can also make *all* of the icons bigger or smaller, just by tugging upward or downward on the little white divider line shown here. (When you're in the right spot, your cursor shape changes to look like it does here.)

The First Tutorial

This handy lesson involves two of the iMac's freebie programs: the Calculator, whose function you can probably guess, and Stickies, whose function you probably can't. The trouble is, they're not on your Dock yet, so the only way to find them is to open your Applications window.

Remember how to do that? From the Go menu, choose Applications. (Or press — what else? — Option-⌘-A.)

Once the Applications window opens, finding the Calculator shouldn't be very hard. (If it's not staring you in the face, type *CA* quickly to highlight its icon.) If you occasionally perform little calculations at your desk, install the Calculator onto the left side of your Dock by dragging it there from your Applications window.

Let's start simple. If you have indeed put the Calculator icon onto your Dock, click it. Otherwise, find the Calculator icon in your Applications window and double-click it. Either way, the Calculator pops up in a window of its own.

The Calculator

Using the mouse, you can click the little Calculator buttons. The iMac gives you the correct mathematical answer, making you the owner of the world's most expensive pocket calculator.

What's neat is that you can also type the number keys on your keyboard. As you press these real keys, you can watch the on-screen keys in the Calculator window get punched accordingly. Try it out!

Take a moment to reinforce your love of windows: By dragging the *title bar* (above the "readout" that shows your calculations), move the Calculator window into a new position. If you were tired of looking at it, you could also make the Calculator go away by clicking its close box (the little red dot in the upper-left corner, like on all windows).

But don't close the Calculator just yet. Leave it open on the screen.

Stickies

For your next trick, you'll need another freebie iMac program called Stickies. Once again, you'll find it in your Applications window. (Click in the Applications window to bring it to the front, and then type *ST* to jump to Stickies.)

Once again, you can install it onto your Dock to make it easier to get to in the future. Try opening Stickies right now (click its icon on the Dock, or double-click its icon in the Applications window).

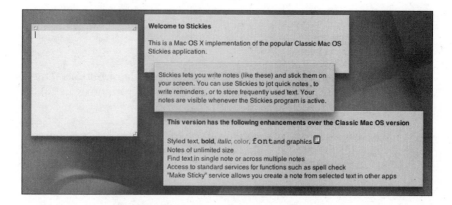

Stickies is the electronic version of those little yellow sticky notes that people stick all around their computer screens. Frankly, the iMac is much too beautiful a machine to junk up with little scraps of gluey paper, so Apple has created an electronic version of the same thing.

You can use Stickies to type quick notes and to-do items, paste in phone numbers you need to remember, and so on. All of your stickies appear on the screen simultaneously whenever you open the Stickies program.

The first time you launch Stickies, a few sample notes show up automatically, describing some of the program's features. You can dispose of each sample by clicking inside it, and then clicking the tiny close box in the upper-left corner of each note. Each time you do so, the iMac asks if you want to save the note. If you click Don't Save, the note disappears permanently.

To create a new note, choose New Note from the File menu and just start typing. (You can also paste stuff into a note, or even *drag* some highlighted text out of a word processor or an e-mail message.) Don't forget that you can make a note bigger just as you would any window: by dragging the small resize handle on the lower-right corner of each note.

For now, with Stickies open on your screen, click inside an empty note and then type this: *Dear Son, I've been a bit concerned with your spending habits lately. By my calculation, you currently owe me $*

And stop right there. (If you make a mistake as you type, press the big Delete key at the upper-right corner of your keyboard. This key means "Backspace.")

Now, by dragging your sticky note's title bar, move it so that you can see the Calculator window, too.

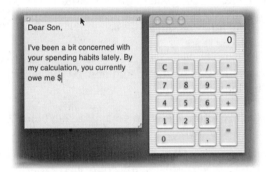

 You're going to use two programs at once, making them cooperate with each other — one of the most remarkable features of the iMac.

Triangles in the Dock

Check your Dock. See how there are *two* tiny triangles under the icons there? The Stickies icon has a triangle, and so does the Calculator. That's the sign that both of these programs are *open* at the moment. You multitasking maniac, you.

Now see the menu name next to the menu? It says Stickies. That's the program you're in *right now*.

So how would you switch back to the Calculator? Right — you'd click the Calculator icon on the Dock.

The Calculator window moves to the front, and the name next to the menu changes to say Calculator.

Those of you still awake will, of course, object to using the Dock to bring the Calculator forward. You remember all too plainly from Chapter 1 that simply *clicking* in a window brings it to the front, which would have required less muscular effort.

Absolutely right! You may now advance to the semifinals. However, learning to use the Dock to switch programs was a good exercise. Many times in your upcoming life, the program in front will be covering up the *entire* screen. So *then* how will you bring another program forward, big shot? That's right. You can't *see* any other windows, so you can't click one to make it active. You'll have to use the Dock.

In any case, the Calculator should now be the active application. (*Active* just means it's in front.)

1. **Press the letter C key on your iMac keyboard, or click the C button on the Calculator.**

    You just cleared the display. We wouldn't want your previous diddlings to interfere with this tightly controlled experiment.

2. **Using the numbers in the block of keys at the far right side of your keyboard, type in an equation like this:** *52+981*17+85-223=*

    In the computer world, the asterisk (*) means "times," or multiply.

With characteristic modesty, the iMac displays the answer to your math problem. (If you typed the numbers shown above, the answer is 17423. That's $17,423 your kid owes you.)

The cornerstone of human endeavor: Copy and Paste

Here's where the fun begins. Choose Copy from the Edit menu.

Thunder rolls, lightning flashes, the audience holds its breath . . . and absolutely nothing happens.

Behind the scenes, though, something awesomely useful occurred. The iMac looked at the number in the Calculator's little display window and memorized it, socking it away into an invisible storage window called the *Clipboard*. The Clipboard is how you transfer stuff from one window into another and from one program into another.

Now then. You can't *see* the Clipboard at this point, but in a powerful act of faith, you put your trust in me and you believe that it contains the high-lighted material (the equation).

Now switch back to Stickies. (Click any visible sticky note, or click the Stickies icon on the Dock.) Now, believe it or not, you can paste the copied number into the word processor, right after the dollar sign: just click there and then choose Paste from the Edit menu.

Dear Son,

I've been a bit concerned with your spending habits lately. By my calculation, you currently owe me $17423

Memo to NASA scientists

Don't rely on the little Calculator program for calculating launch times or impact statistics, at least not without understanding how its math differs from yours.

The Calculator processes equations from left to right. It does *not* solve the multiplication and division components before the addition and subtraction, as is standard in math classes worldwide.

For example, consider this equation: 3+2*4=. (The * means "times" in computerland.) The scientific answer is 11, because you multiply before you add when solving such puzzles. But the Mac's answer is 20, because it processes the numbers from left to right.

Incidentally, the Clipboard holds one thing at a time — whatever you copied *most recently*. If you copy something new right now, you'd wipe out the 17423 that's already on the Clipboard.

On the other hand, whatever's on the Clipboard stays there until you copy something new, or until you turn off the machine. In other words, you can paste it over and over again. Try it now — from the Edit menu, choose Paste again. Another 17423 pops into the window.

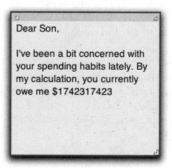

But you don't have to use the menu to issue a command. If you wish, you can use a keyboard shortcut to do the same thing. You may remember having used the ⌘ key in Chapter 2 to issue commands without using the mouse.

And how are you supposed to remember which letter key corresponds to which command? Well, usually it's mnemonic: ⌘-P means Print, ⌘-O means Open, and so on. But you can cheat; try it right now. Click the Edit menu to open it.

There's your crib sheet, carefully listed down the right side of the menu. Notice that the keyboard shortcuts for all four of these important commands (Undo, Cut, Copy, Paste) are adjacent on the keyboard: Z, X, C, V.

C is Copy. And V, right next to it, is Paste. (I know, I know: Why doesn't *P* stand for Paste? Answer: Because *P* stands for Print! And anyway, V is right next to C-for-Copy on your keyboard, so it *kind* of makes sense.)

Try it right now:

1. **While holding down the ⌘ key, type a V.**

   Bingo! Another copy of the Clipboard stuff (17423) appears in your Stickies note. (In the future, I'll just refer to a keyboard shortcut like this as "⌘-V.")

2. **Press ⌘-V again.**

   Yep, that kid's debt is really piling up. He now owes you $17423174231742317423!

But after all, he's your son. Why not just let him make a down payment? In other words, why not *undo* that last pasting?

3. From the Edit menu, choose Undo Paste.

The most recent thing you did — in this case, pasting the fourth 17423 — gets undone.

Rewriting history is addicting, ain't it?

Remember, though, that Undo only reverses your *most recent* action. Suppose you (1) copy something, (2) paste it somewhere else, and then (3) type some more. If you choose Undo, only the typing will be undone (Step 3), *not* the pasting (Step 2).

Did you get what just happened? You typed out a math problem in a word processor (well, in Stickies), copied it to the Clipboard, and pasted it into a number-cruncher (the Calculator). Much of the miracle of the Macintosh stems from its capability to mix and match information among multiple programs in this way.

Quitting a program

If you're finished fiddling with these program-ettes, quit each one. See the menu next to the , the one named after the program you're using? From the Stickies menu, choose Quit Stickies. Then switch to the Calculator, and choose Quit Calculator from the Calculator menu. That's how you get out of a program (and dismiss all its windows).

If you expect to use a certain program again later in your work session, though, don't bother quitting it. Instead, open the menu next to the menu and choose Hide Calculator (or whatever the program's name is). The program's windows disappear, but its icon remains on the Dock. Technically, the program is still open, ready for action when you click its Dock icon.

By hiding programs instead of quitting them, you save yourself the time it takes to quit and reopen them.

System Preferences

Now that you're familiar with the Dock, you should meet another very important Mac program: System Preferences, whose icon on the Dock looks like a light switch. Try clicking that icon — or if you're not in the mood for Dock-clicking, open the menu and choose System Preferences.

System Preferences contains a bunch of icons, each of which controls some aspect of your iMac. It's a veritable playground for the control freak:

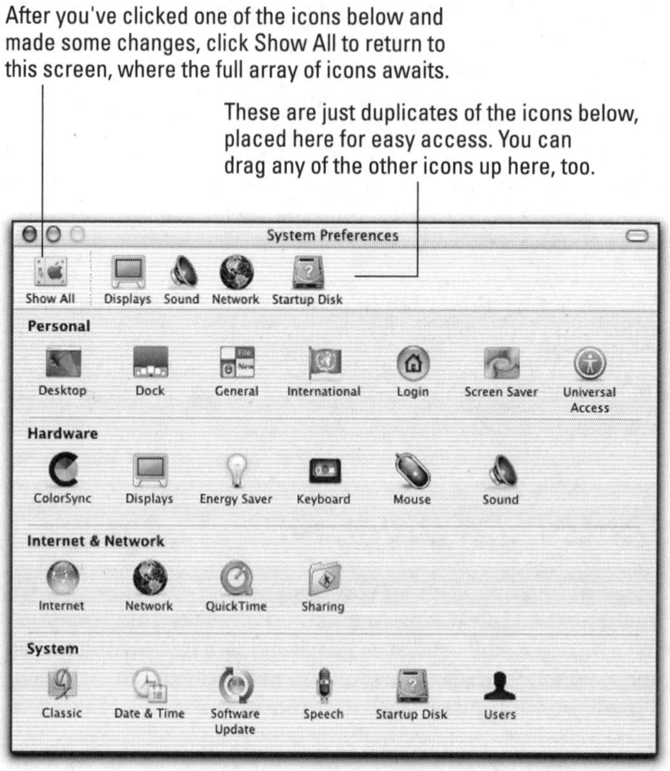

After you've clicked one of the icons below and made some changes, click Show All to return to this screen, where the full array of icons awaits.

These are just duplicates of the icons below, placed here for easy access. You can drag any of the other icons up here, too.

When you click one of the icons, the window fills with the corresponding controls. For example, if you click Date & Time, the window fills with the knobs and buttons you need to set your iMac's clock.

Then, once you're done adjusting the time (for example), you return to the menu of controls shown in the previous picture just by clicking the Show All button in the upper-left corner.

Your iMac would work perfectly well even if you never touched any of these controls. But taking ten minutes for a tour of these controls is easy, free, and better exercise than, say, lying on the couch. And besides, poking around in System Preferences will teach you about sliders, checkboxes, and other screen elements that you'll encounter over and over again in your upcoming computing career.

Here's a glance at a few of the most useful doodads in System Preferences.

Desktop

I've saved the best for first.

By clicking the Desktop icon, you open up this panel:

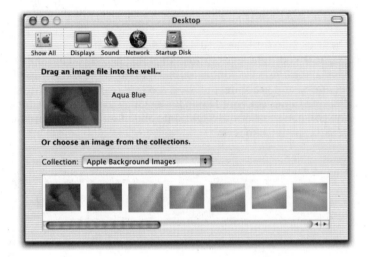

Here's where you choose a different background picture for your desktop — one that can replace the swooshy blue background that's probably been greeting you every morning since the day you first turned on the computer.

Interior decoration

To try a different piece of computer wallpaper, click one of the design swatches in the bottom row. With each click, the iMac's background changes.

Those alternatives are fine for the timid or the lazy. But you, bold and motivated reader that you are, no doubt thirst for more. See the word Collection? The rounded rectangle next to it is what scientists call a *pop-up menu*. A pop-up menu works just like the menus at the top of the screen, except that — well, it's not at the top of the screen.

Click the Collection pop-up menu to see the choices it's hiding. They include Apple Background Images (muted, soft-focused swishes and swirls), Nature (plants, ponds, insects), Abstract (swooshy swirls with vibrant colors), or Solid Colors (your basic grays, blues, and greens). After you choose a collection's name, the row of color swatches changes at the bottom of the window. Just click one to try it on for size.

Using your own pictures

Apple's canned wallpaper options may be professional and shimmering, but they're not *yours.* It's much, much more fun to dress up your desktop with one of your *own* pictures. (This means you, scanner or digital camera owners.)

The trick is to find the actual graphics file that represents the photo you want to use. If your relationship with the iMac is only 30 minutes old, you may not have any photos yet. But eventually, thanks to the miracle of digital cameras, scanners, and grabbing pictures you find on the World Wide Web, your Pictures folder (in your Home folder) may eventually contain a few pictures. You can just drag one straight onto the mini-desktop displayed in the Desktop panel, like this:

After a moment, the iMac plasters that picture across your monitor. (If you use the program called iPhoto to organize your photos — as you should — you can also use any of its pictures as your desktop background. Chapter 10 has details.)

You'll quickly discover that some pictures work better as screen backgrounds than others. For example, if it's too small to fill the whole screen, the iMac either repeats it over and over again like bathroom tiles — or just weirdly stretches it until it fills the screen. Photos of family, pets, or Britney Spears do just fine if you generally keep all of your files and folders in your Home folder, as Steve Jobs hopes you do. But if you like to leave files and folders out on the desktop for quick access, complex photos may make it tough for you to find them. There's nothing worse than having to dig the latest draft of your speech out of Britney Spears's armpit.

General

There's nothing general whatsoever about the controls on this panel of System Preferences — if anything, they're specific and tweaky beyond description. For example, the Appearance pop-up menu lets you choose the color that Mac OS X uses for the menu, scroll bars, progress bars, and so on: either blue or gray. (The gray option — or Graphite, as it's called here — is for graphic designers who claim to be shocked by the standard bright blue.)

Screen Saver

You're probably too young to remember *screen burn-in,* an upsetting phenomenon in which certain more or less permanent elements of the screen display — the menu bar, for example — would, over time, burn a ghostly, permanent image into the screen. But even you have probably seen the solution that programmers came up with: *screen savers.* These programs bounce around moving images on the screen when it's not in use, so that no image remains fixed long enough to do any damage.

Nobody's seen burn-in for years, thanks to advances in computer monitors. In fact, a flat screen like your iMac's *cannot* burn in, screen saver or no.

But screen savers are still with us, not as screen protection but as showoffware. To use the official terminology, they look really cool.

In the Screen Saver panel, you can choose from six different screen saver modules. Most of them look like nature shows in a planetarium, featuring jaw-dropping photographs (Beach, Cosmos, Forest) that grow, shrink, fade, and otherwise glide across the screen. These photo shows are so brilliant and captivating that otherwise level-headed iMac fans have been known to bring the computer downstairs for dinner parties, just for dramatic effect.

When you click a name in the Screen Savers list (Cosmos or Forest, for example), a mini-version of it plays back in the Preview screen. Click Test to give the module a dry run on your full screen. (Moving the mouse or pressing any key kicks you out of test mode.)

A screen saver to call your own

The iMac is perfectly willing to use your *own* collection of photos as fodder for one of these amazing slide shows. Just click Slide Show in the Screen Savers module list, click Configure, and then navigate to the folder of pictures you want to use. Click its name, and then click Choose. Now, whenever the screen saver kicks in, you'll see your own pictures, complete with spectacular zooming and dissolving effects. (Once again, the iPhoto program offers a more direct way of doing this; see Chapter 10.)

Activating the screen saver

Unless you tell it otherwise, the screen saver kicks in automatically about five minutes after the last time you actually used the iMac.

If you'd like to tell it otherwise, you need to visit a different section of this control panel. See the three "file folder tabs" called Screen Savers, Activation, and Hot Corners? You'll spot these fairly often in dialog boxes. For obvious reasons, these divider buttons are called *tabs*.

Click the Activation tab, for example, to specify how long you want the screen saver to wait after the last time you used the mouse or keyboard. The duration can be as short as five minutes or as long as an hour, or you can drag the slider to Never to turn the screen saver off completely.

You can also summon the screen saver instantly, on command, without having to wait a certain number of minutes. (This option is cherished by people who would otherwise be caught bidding in eBay.com auctions just as their bosses walk by.)

To set this up, click the Hot Corners tab. Here you see a map of your screen. Click the boxes in the corners that you'd like to turn into *hot spots* — places that, when visited by your cursor for a few seconds, call up the screen saver. (Click a second time to turn the check mark into a – sign. If you push your cursor into a corner designated by that symbol, the screen saver will *never* come on. That's how you'd want it when you're reading something on the screen or watching a DVD.)

Displays

These System Preferences controls have various effects on your screen — your heartbreakingly beautiful, 15-inch, flat-panel screen.

Most people, most of the time, won't find much here worth fiddling with. You could conceivably be curious about the Brightness slider — maybe you'd turn down the screen brightness when you're working in dim light — but there's a much easier way to adjust the screen brightness. Just press the F14 and F15 keys on the top row of your keyboard to make the screen dimmer or brighter, respectively. (You may want to put tiny stickers on these keys to help you remember them. Don't worry — it won't void your warranty.)

Tech note: All about resolution

The Resolution choices at the left side of the Displays panel are intriguing, especially for the technically inclined.

On a traditional, bulky computer screen, you can use these controls to magnify or shrink the screen image. The numbers here indicate how many tiny picture dots *(pixels)* fit onto the screen. When you click higher numbers, such as 1024 by 768, you're choosing higher *resolution*. At high resolutions, more fits onto your screen — two full side-by-side pages, for example — because those pixels are pretty tiny.

When you click lower numbers, like 800 by 600, you're switching to a *lower* resolution. Now fewer pixels — but bigger ones — fill the screen, in effect magnifying the image.

But on a flat-panel screen like your iMac's, low resolutions don't just mean a bigger screen image — they also mean a *blurry* one. In fact, on your iMac, only one resolution setting looks really great: the maximum one (1024 by 768). That's because your screen is actually made up of 1024 by 768 tiny square shutters. At lower resolutions, the iMac does what it can to blur them together, but the effect is fuzzy and unsatisfying. (On a traditional, not-flat screen, by contrast, the electron gun can actually make the pixels larger or smaller, so there's no fuzziness at different resolutions.)

Energy Saver

As noted in Chapter 1, your iMac nods off to sleep — its screen goes black and its appetite for electricity drops down to almost nothing — about 30 minutes after you stop using the machine.

Of course, if the whole point of your putting your iMac in a public area of the house or office is to show off its stunning screen saver, you certainly don't want its screen to go black in the name of saving a little power. Using the slider at the top of this dialog box, you can tell the iMac how long you want it to wait before nodding off — or *never* to do so.

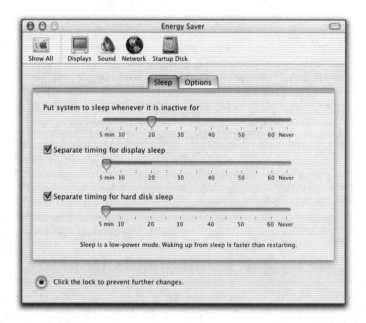

Keyboard

On the obsolete invention known as *electric typewriters,* you could hold down the X key to cross out something you'd typed — XXXXXXX. On the very modern invention known as a Macintosh, *every* key behaves this way, making it a snap to type things like "Woo-HOOOOOOO!" or "GRRRRRRRRRRRR!"

The two sliders on this panel govern this behavior. The right-side slider determines how long you must hold down the key before it starts repeating (to prevent triggering repetitions accidentally). The left-side slider controls how fast each key spits out letters once the spitting has begun.

Sound

Whenever you do something that the iMac doesn't like — clicking somewhere it considers unseemly, for example — it beeps at you. But it doesn't have to *beep* at you; if you like, it can honk, bray, boop, or boing at you. Click each sound name in this list to find the one that seems the least intrusive (or the most intrusive, depending on your personality).

Date and Time

The iMac's résumé features a long list under the Special Talents heading: DVD player, pocket calculator, Post-It Note simulator, and so on. But way, way down the list is another one: desk clock. As you may have noticed, the current time always appears in the upper-right corner of your screen. (And if you *click* the current time, a menu drops down showing the current *date.* The menu also lets you switch between digital and analog clock types, as befits your mood.)

Setting the date and time manually

Here, on the Date and Time screen of System Preferences, is where you *set* this computer calendar and clock. Of course, you probably set the clock already, during the setup process described in Chapter 1. But if your iMac has accidentally drifted through a gap in the time-space continuum when you weren't looking, you can adjust the date by clicking the little arrow buttons next to the month and year labels. Then specify the *day* of the month by clicking a date on the mini-calendar. Click Save.

Never set your clock again

"They can send a man to the moon," many a computer fan mutters, "but they can't come up with a computer that sets its own clock!"

Actually, they can. If you set things up properly, your iMac can adjust its own clock by checking in, every now and then, with a highly accurate scientific clock — via the Internet. If you go online by dialing, this feature isn't very practical, since you probably won't be online at the particular moment when the iMac wants to check the time. But if you have a cable modem or DSL, you'd be crazy to miss this chance.

Click the Network Time tab. Turn on the "Use a network time server" checkbox, select one of the *time servers* (Web-site clocks) listed in the pop-up menu, and then click Set Time Now.

From now on, your iMac will adjust its own clock each time it goes online. It will even adjust itself for daylight saving time — something the clocks on your microwave and car dashboard can only dream about.

To set your clock, you can drag the actual hands on the clock face. (If you prefer, you can do it numerically: Click one of the numbers in the time boxes under the Current Time label, and then adjust the corresponding number by typing or by clicking the tiny up or down arrow buttons. To jump to the next number for setting, press the Tab key.) Finally, click Save.

Indicating your time zone

You probably told your iMac what time zone it's in during the startup process described at the beginning of Chapter 1, too.

But if you (a) discover your geography was a bit off or (b) move to another country, click the Time Zone tab. Then click a section of the map to select a general region of the world. Finally, use the pop-up menu to specify your country within that region.

Software Update

It's almost impossible to write completely bug-free software. Just ask any programmer. (Better yet, ask anyone who's ever used a computer.)

Fortunately, Mac OS X isn't frozen in time. Each time you go online to the Internet, the Software Update feature sends an invisible query to Apple: "Got anything for me?"

If Apple has indeed fixed a few bugs or added a few new features, the company's Web site automatically sends a software update — an *updater* or a *patch* — straight to your machine.

One day you'll be merrily working away, and you'll see a dialog box like this:

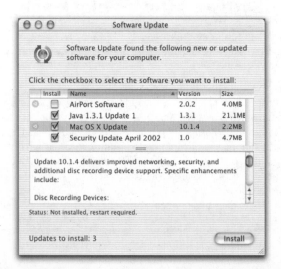

That's your notice that the blessed event has occurred: Apple has sent you a morsel of software it believes will make your iMac better. You don't have to install it, of course, but these updates are *usually* worth accepting.

The purpose of this System Preferences pane is to specify *how often* the iMac checks for updates. Turn on the Automatically option and use the "Check for updates" pop-up menu to specify daily, weekly, or monthly.

Quitting System Preferences

You quit System Preferences just as you would any other program: Choose the Quit command (Quit System Preferences, in this case) from the bottom of its application menu, the one next to the menu.

The iMac Keyboard

One look at the iMac's gleaming, clear-and-white keyboard, and you'll realize that this is not your father's typewriter. If you've never used a computer before, you might be bewildered by the number of keyboard keys. After all, a typewriter has about 50 keys; your iMac has about 100.

The "Just say no" keystroke

There's a wonderful keyboard shortcut that means no in iMac language. It could mean *No, I changed my mind about printing* (or copying or launching a program); stop right now. It could mean *No, I didn't mean to bring up this dialog box; make it go away.* Or: *No, I don't want to broadcast my personal diary over worldwide e-mail!* Best of all, it can mean *Stop asking for that CD! I've already taken it out! Be gone!*

And that magic keystroke is ⌘-period (.).

When you begin to print your Transcripts of Congress, 1952 to 2002, and you discover — after only two pages have printed — that you accidentally spelled it "Transcripts of Congrotesque" on every page, ⌘-period will prevent the remaining 14 million pages from printing. Because the iMac has probably already sent the next couple of pages to the printer, the response won't be immediate — but it will be light-years quicker than waiting for Congress.

Or let's say you double-click an icon by mistake. If you press ⌘-period right away, you can halt the launching and return to the Finder. And if the iMac keeps saying, "Please insert the disk: Purple Puppychow" (or whatever your CD, floppy, or Zip disk was called), you can tell it to shut up by doing that ⌘-period thing over and over again until the iMac settles down with a whimper. Show it who's boss.

Only some of the bizarro extra keys are particularly useful. Here's a list of the oddball extra keys and what they do.

✔ **F1, F2, F3...** In most programs, including the Finder, only the first four keys do anything at all: F1, F2, F3, and F4 correspond to Undo, Cut, Copy, and Paste. On your iMac, the F14 and F15 keys also make your screen dimmer and brighter.

In Microsoft programs, a few of these F-keys (sometimes called function keys) act as menu-command shortcuts. You can also buy programs like QuicKeys X that let you attach these keys to your favorite programs, so that pressing F5 opens up AppleWorks, F6 launches your Web browser, and so on. Otherwise, though, these keys generally don't do anything. They're spares, sitting around for the benefit of add-on software.

✔ ◄ ◄)) ◄: These three buttons control your speaker volume. Tap the first one repeatedly to make the sound level ever lower, the middle one to make it louder. The rightmost button is the Mute button; tap it once to cut off the sound completely, and again to bring it back to its previous level. In any of these cases, you'll see a big white version of these same speaker logos on your screen as you tap, your iMac's little wink to let you know that it appreciates your efforts.

✔ ▲: This is the Eject key. When there's no CD or DVD in your iMac, hold it down for about a second to make the CD/DVD tray slide open, as though the iMac is sticking its big black tongue out. When there *is* a disc in there, just tap the key once to make the computer spit it out.

✔ **Home, End:** "Home" and "End" are ways of saying "jump to the top or bottom of the window." If you're word processing, the Home and End keys jump to the first word or last word of the file, respectively. If you're looking at a list of files, they jump you to the top or bottom of the list.

✔ **Pg Up, Pg Down:** These keys mean "Scroll up or down by one screenful." Once again, the idea is to let you scroll through word-processing documents, Web pages, and lists without having to use the mouse.

✔ **NumLock, Clear:** Clear means "get rid of this text I've highlighted, but don't put a copy on the invisible Clipboard, as the Cut command would do." In Microsoft Excel, the NumLock key actually does something obscure, but I'll let you nuzzle up to the manual for that.

✔ **Esc:** *Esc* stands for *Escape*, and it actually means "Click the Cancel button," such as the one found in most dialog boxes.

Wanna try? Open a program like TextEdit. From the File menu, choose Page Setup. Then press Esc, and marvel as the box goes away.

✔ **Delete:** This is the backspace key.

✔ **Del:** Many a Mac fan goes for years without discovering the handiness of this delightful little key. First of all, force yourself to acknowledge that *Delete* and *Del* are two different keys.

The difference is that Delete, like Backspace, erases whatever letter is just *before* the insertion point. This key, the Del (also called Forward Delete) key, deletes whatever is just to the *right* of the insertion point, like this:

press Delete

a sudden f|light → a sudden light

press Del

a sudden f|light → a sudden fight

Anyway, the Del key really comes in handy when, for example, you've clicked into some text to make an edit — but wound up planting your cursor in just the wrong place.

✔ **Return and Enter:** In general, these keys do the same thing: wrap your typing to the next line. Be careful, though: Some programs distinguish between the two. In AppleWorks, for example, Return begins a new paragraph, but Enter makes a *page break*, forcing the next typing to begin on a fresh page.

✔ **Command (⌘):** This key triggers keyboard shortcuts for menu items, as described in Chapter 2.

✔ **Control, Option:** The Control key *triggers contextual menus,* as described in Chapter 2; the Option key lets you type special symbols (see Chapter 9) and access secret features (discussed earlier in this chapter).

✔ **Help:** Oddly enough, this key doesn't do anything in most programs. Typical, huh?

Top Ten Freebie Programs

Your iMac came with at least 30 programs designed to charm and amaze you. Take a few minutes to savor your riches.

As you read, you might consider double-clicking each one in your Applications folder to get a feel for the process. When you're finished examining each one, close it up by choosing Quit, or hide it by choosing Hide, from the program's first menu, like this:

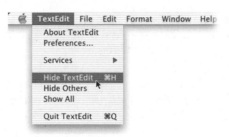

And, of course, if you fall in love with a program or two, by all means drag their icons onto the left side of your Dock so you'll be able to call them up again later when you need a software fix.

1. **Address Book.** It's the digital version of the little black book. To add some-body's information, click the New button, type the name and address into the appropriate boxes (you can press the Tab key to jump from box to box), and then click Save. You'll get much more mileage out of the Address Book when you start doing e-mail (Chapter 8) and faxes (Chapter 17).

2. **Chess.** This little game is a lot like regular chess, with one big difference: It's on your screen. Your opponent, facing imminent devastation, can't knock over the chessboard in a hissy fit.

3. **Clock.** Yes, you already have a clock on your menu bar, but what fun is that? If you open *this* clock program, you have a much bigger, more attractive way to tell the time: an actual clock face in your Dock, where its icon continues to tell the time.

4. **DVD Player.** Yes, your iMac can play DVDs from Blockbuster. See Chapter 11.

5. **iTunes.** Welcome to the digital jukebox. If you feed some music CDs into your iMac, iTunes can copy the songs to your hard drive, where they'll play any time you want them to — no hunting for the CD. Details in Chapter 10.

6. **Preview.** You'll rarely open this program yourself. Most of the time, it opens automatically when you double-click a graphics file — because Preview is nothing more than a picture viewer. (Check out its display menu, whose commands let you rotate or flip the picture.)

7. **Quicken.** Your iMac may have come with Quicken, the famous checkbook-balancing and home-finance program. It's a terrific piece of work, and it's described in Chapter 9.

8. **TextEdit.** The iMac comes with AppleWorks, of course, a program that includes a full-fledged word processor. But for people who prefer a half-fledged word processor, TextEdit is here. It's a handy stripped-down bucket for typing short documents.

9. **Apple System Profiler.** This program — which sits in the Utilities folder that's *in* the Applications folder — is like the printout that's taped to the inside of the window on a new car: it lists the features and options you've paid for. By clicking the various tabs and triangles, you can find out exactly what iMac version you have, how much memory and speed it offers, what kind of disk drives it has, and so on.

10. **Key Caps.** This program, too, is in the Utilities folder. It displays a picture of your keyboard, so that by pressing Option, ⌘, and other modifier keys, you can figure out which keys to press when you need special symbols like ¢ and ¶ and ø. (Details in Chapter 9.)

Chapter 4

Typing, Saving, and Finding Again

In This Chapter

▶ Unlearning years of typewriter lessons

▶ Dragging and dropping

▶ How to save your files so they're not lost forever

▶ You — yes, you — the desktop publisher

*L*et's not kid ourselves. Yeah, I know, you're gonna use your iMac to do photo retouching, to create 3-D animations, or to compose symphonies. But with the possible exception of e-mail and Web exploits, what you'll probably do the *most* of is good old *word processing*.

But just because everybody does it doesn't mean word processing isn't the single most magical, amazing, time-saving invention since microwaveable pasta. Master word processing, and you've essentially mastered your computer.

Your Very First Bestseller

Lucky for you, your iMac comes with a superb word-processing program. It's called AppleWorks, and you can read about it in Chapter 9.

For this quick and dirty typing lesson, though, you may as well use a quick and dirty program: the super-budget word processor known as TextEdit. As usual, it's in your Applications folder. (From the Go menu, choose Applications — or press Option-⌘-A.) Once the Applications folder is open, type *TE* to jump to TextEdit. Drag TextEdit onto your Dock, if you like.

Top three rules of word processing

The first rules of typing on a computer are going to be tough to learn, especially if you've been typing for years. But they're crucial:

✔ **Don't press the Return key at the end of each line.** I'm dead serious here. When you type your way to the end of a line, the next word will automatically jump down to the next line. If you press Return in the middle of a sentence, you'll mess everything up.

✔ **Put only one space after a period.** From now on, everything you write will come out looking like it was professionally published instead of being cranked out on some noisy Selectric with a bad ribbon. A quick glance at any published book, magazine, or newspaper will make you realize that the two-spaces-after-a-period thing is strictly for typewriters.

✔ **Don't use the L key to make the number 1.** Your iMac, unlike the typewriter you may have grown up with, actually has a key dedicated to making the number 1. If you use a lowercase L instead, the 1 will look funny, and your spelling checker will think you've gone nuts.

If those statements give you uncontrollable muscular facial spasms, I don't blame you. After all, I'm telling you to do things that you were explicitly taught *not* to do by that high-school typing teacher with the horn-rimmed glasses.

There are a few other rules, too, but breaking them isn't serious enough to get you fired. So let's dig in. Make sure you have a blank piece of electronic typing paper open in front of you — a clean, fresh TextEdit screen.

The excitement begins

Double-click the TextEdit icon to open a new, blank sheet of "typing paper." You should see a short, blinking, vertical line at the beginning of the typing area. They call this the *insertion point*. It shows you where the letters will appear when you start to type.

 Type the upcoming passage. If you make a typo, press the Delete key, just as you would Backspace on a typewriter. (For a rundown of the iMac's other unusual keys, see Chapter 3.) *Don't* press Return when you get to the edge of the window. Just keep typing, and the iMac will create a second line for you. Believe. *Believe.*

> The screams of the lions burst Rod's eardrums as the motorboat, out of control, exploded through the froth.

See how the words automatically wrapped around to the second line? They call this feature, with astonishing originality, *word wrap.*

But suppose, as your novel is going to press, you decide that this sleepy passage really needs some spicing up. You decide to insert the word *speeding* before the word *motorboat.*

Remember the blinking cursor — the insertion point? It's on the screen even now, blinking calmly away at the end of the sentence. If you want to insert text, you have to move the insertion point.

You can move the insertion point in two ways. First, try pressing the arrow keys in the lower-right cluster of your keyboard. You can see that the up- and down-arrow keys move the insertion point from line to line, and the right- and left-arrow keys move the insertion point across the line. Practice moving the insertion point by pressing the arrow keys.

If the passage you want to edit is far away, though (on another page, for example), using the arrow keys to move the cursor is inefficient. Your fingers would be bloody stumps by the time you finished. Instead, use this finger-saving technique:

1. **Using the mouse, move the cursor (which, when it's near text, looks like this: I) just before the word *motorboat,* and then click the mouse.**

   The I-beam changes to the insertion point.

   This is as confusing as word processing ever gets — there are *two* little cursors, right? There's the blinking insertion point, and there's this one I, which is called an *I-beam* cursor.

   In fact, the two little cursors are quite different. The blinking insertion point is only a *marker,* not a pointer. It always shows you where the next typing will appear. The I-beam, on the other hand, is how you *move* the insertion point; when you click with the I-beam, you set down the insertion point.

   In other words, editing stuff you've already typed, on the Macintosh, is a matter of *click and then type.*

2. **Type the word *speeding.***

   The insertion point does its deed, and the iMac makes room on the line for the new word. A word or two probably got pushed onto the next line. Isn't word wrap wondrous?

Editing for the linguistically blessed

So much for *inserting* text: You click the mouse (to show the iMac *where*) and then type away. But what if you need to delete a bunch of text? What if you decide to *cut out* the first half of our sample text?

Well, unless you typed the challenging excerpt with no errors, you already know one way to erase text — by pressing the Delete key. Delete takes out one letter at a time, just to the left of the insertion point.

Deleting one letter at a time isn't much help in this situation, though. Suppose you decide to take out the *first part* of the sentence. It wouldn't be horribly efficient to backspace over the entire passage just so you could work on the beginning.

No, instead you need a way to edit any part of your work, at any time, without disturbing the stuff you want to leave. Once again, the Macintosh method, noun-then-verb, saves the day. Try this:

1. **Using the mouse, position the I-beam cursor at the beginning of the sentence.**

   This takes a steady hand; stay calm.

2. **Click *just* to the left of the first word and, keeping the mouse button pressed down, drag the I-beam cursor — *perfectly horizontally*, if possible — to the end of the word as.**

   As you drag, the text gets highlighted, or *selected*.

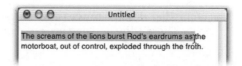

If you accidentally drag up or down into the next line of text, the highlighting jumps to include a big chunk of that additional line. Don't panic; without releasing the mouse button, simply move the cursor back onto the original line you were selecting. This time, try to drag more horizontally.

If you're especially clever and forward-thinking, you'll also have selected the blank space *after* the word *as*. Take a look at the previous illustration.

All right, in typical Mac syntax, you've just specified *what* you want to edit by selecting it (and making it turn black to show it's selected). Now for the verb:

1. **Press the Delete key.**

   Bam! The selected text is gone. The sentence looks pretty odd, though, since it doesn't begin with a capital letter.

2. **Using the mouse, position the cursor just before (or after) the letter *t* that begins the sentence. Drag the cursor sideways across the letter so that it's highlighted.**

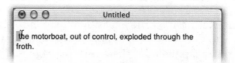

Here comes another ground rule of word processing. See how you've just selected, or highlighted, the letter *t?* The idea here is to capitalize it. Of course, using the methods for wiping out (and inserting) text that you learned earlier, you could simply remove the *t* and type a *T*. But since you've selected the *t* by dragging through it, replacing it is much easier.

3. Type a capital *T.*

The selected text gets replaced by the new stuff you type. That, in fact, is the fourth ground rule: *Selected text gets replaced by the new stuff you type.* As your iMac life proceeds, keep that handy fact in mind; it can save you a lot of backspacing. In fact, you can select 40 pages of text so that it's all highlighted and then type *one single letter* to replace all of it. Or you could *select* only one letter but replace it with 40 pages of typing.

Take a moment now for some unsupervised free play. Try clicking anywhere in the text (to plant the insertion point). Try dragging through some text: If you drag perfectly horizontally, you select text just on one line (shown below at top). If you drag diagonally, you get everything between your cursor and the original click (bottom).

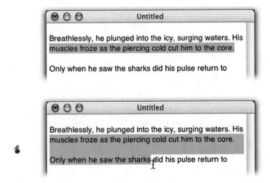

You *deselect* (or, equally poetically, unhighlight) text by clicking the mouse. Anywhere at all (within the typing area).

Here's about the most fabulous word-processing shortcut ever devised: Try pointing to a word and then double-clicking the mouse! You've easily selected *exactly* that word without having to do any dragging.

As you experiment, do anything you want with any combination of drags, clicks, double-clicks, and menu selections. It's nice to know — and you might want to prepare a fine mahogany wall plaque to this effect — that *nothing you do using the mouse or keyboard can physically harm the computer.*

Puff, the Magic Drag-N-Drop

You kids today, with your long music and loud hair! You don't know how lucky you are! Why, when I was your age, if I wanted to rearrange a couple of words, I'd have to *copy and paste them!*

But not anymore. Nowadays, you can move text around on the screen just by *pointing* to it! This profoundly handy feature is known as *drag-and-drop*.

1. **In TextEdit, open the File menu and choose New.**

   If you've been following along with the chapter already in progress, TextEdit is still on the screen. Press the Return key a couple of times to move into an empty part of the page.

2. **Type up two phrases, as shown here:**

3. **Highlight *Eyes of blue*.**

   You've done this before: Position the insertion-point cursor just to the left of the word *Eyes* and *carefully* slide directly to the right, highlighting the phrase (below, left).

4. **Now position the arrow cursor right smack in the middle of the black-ened phrase. Hold down the mouse button for about one full second, motionless — and then *drag* the arrow to the end of the line (above, right).**

   When your arrow is correctly positioned at the end of the line, you'll see the new insertion point appear there. (Troubleshooting note: If you don't see the actual words move along with your cursor, then you didn't wait long enough with your mouse button down before dragging.)

5. **Release the mouse!**

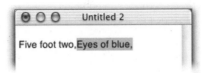

As you can see, you've just *dragged* the first phrase into position after the second phrase! Sam Lewis and Joe Young would be very grateful for your correcting their lyrics.

Now how much would you pay? But wait — there's more! Once you've mastered the art of dragging text around your screen, the sky's the limit! To wit:

✔ If you press the *Option* key while you drag some highlighted text, instead of *moving* that phrase, you actually make a *copy* of it, as shown here:

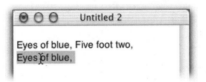

✔ You can actually drag text *clear out of the window* and into another program — for example, from AppleWorks into the waiting TextEdit.

✔ You can also drag text clear out of the window and *onto the desktop*. When you release the mouse button, you'll see that your little drag-and-dropped blurb has turned into a *text clipping*, as shown here:

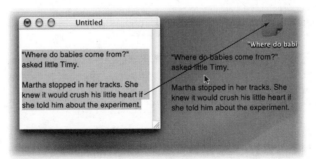

Next time you need that blob of text, you can point to the text clipping and drag it back into your word-processing program, and — presto! — the text appears there, exactly as though you'd typed it again.

Now if they'd only work it out so we could edit our *printouts* using drag-and-drop. . . .

Form and Format

One of the most important differences between a typewriter and its replacement — the computer — is the sequence of events. When you use a typewriter, you set up all the formatting characteristics *before* you type: the margins, the tab stops, and (for typewriters with interchangeable type heads) the type style.

But the whole point of a word processor is that you can change anything at any time. Many people type the text of an entire letter (or proposal, or memo) into the iMac and *then* format it. When you use a typewriter, you might discover, after typing the entire first page, that it's slightly too long to fit, and your signature will have to sit awkwardly on a page by itself. With an iMac, you'd see the problem and nudge the text a little bit higher on the page to compensate.

Word processing has other great advantages: no crossouts; easy corrections that involve no whiteout and no retyping; a permanent record of your correspondence that's electronic, not paper, so it's always easy to find; a selection of striking typefaces — at any size; paste-in graphics; and so on. It's safe to say that once you try processing words, you'll never look back.

For your next trick, you'll dress up your typing the way professional typesetters have for decades before you, although at much higher hourly rates. Open TextEdit, if you're not already in it. Choose New from the File menu, so you're looking at a clean, untitled page.

The return of Return

With all the subtlety of a Mack truck, I've taught you that you're forbidden to use the Return key *at the end of a line*. Still, that rectangular Return key on your keyboard *is* important. You press Return at the end of a *paragraph*, and only there.

To the computer, the Return key works just like a letter key — it inserts a *Return character* into the text. It's just like rolling the paper in a typewriter forward by one notch. Hit Return twice, and you leave a blank line.

The point of Return, then, is to move text higher or lower on the page. Check out this example, for instance:

Dearest·Todd,¶
¶
I·have·never·loved·so·much·as·I·did·last·
night.·Imagine·my·joy·as·I·watched·you·
plunch·your·shining·scimitar·into·the·
greasy·flesh·of·that—that—hideous·thing·
from·the·deep.¶
¶
Unfortunately,·the·IRS·has·determined·
that·you·failed·to·file·returns·for·the·years·
1982–1986.·They·have·asked·that·I·notify·
you·of·¶

¶
Dearest·Todd,¶
¶
I·have·never·loved·so·much·as·I·did·last·
night.·Imagine·my·joy·as·I·watched·you·
plunch·your·shining·scimitar·into·the·
greasy·flesh·of·that—that—hideous·thing·
from·the·deep.¶
¶
Unfortunately,·the·IRS·has·determined·
that·you·failed·to·file·returns·for·the·years·
1982–1986.·They·have·asked·that·I·notify·
you·of·¶

Return characters move text down on the page. So, if you want to move text up on the page, drag through the blank space so that it's highlighted (above, left); of course, what you've really done is select the usually invisible Return characters. If you delete them, the text slides up the page (right).

Combine this knowledge with your advanced degree in Inserting Text (remember? you *click and then type*), and you can see how you'd make more space between paragraphs or push all the text of a letter down on the page.

Appealing characters

Another big-time difference between word processing and typing is all the great *character formatting* you can do. You can make any piece of text **bold**, *italic,* <u>underlined</u>, all of these, and more. You also get a selection of great-looking typefaces — only a few of which look like a typewriter. By combining all these styles and fonts randomly, you can make any document look absolutely hideous.

Here's the scheme for changing some text to one of those character formats: noun-verb. Sound familiar? Go for it:

1. **Select some text by dragging through it.**

   Remember you can select a single word by double-clicking it; to select a bunch of text, drag the cursor through it so that it turns black. You've just identified *what* you want to change.

   Each word processor keeps its Bold, Italic, and Underline commands in its own specially named menu; in TextEdit, they're in the Format menu, in the pop-out submenu of the Font command.

2. **From the Font submenu of the Format menu, choose Bold.**

   You've just specified *how* you want to affect the selected text.

You can apply several of these formats to the same text, too, although you won't win any awards for typographical excellence. Try changing the typeface also; the various fonts are called things like American Typewriter, Arial, Big Caslon, Times, and so on. Changing fonts works the same way: Select text and then choose the font.

You can make type bigger or smaller, too. Most word processors offer a Format menu or a Text menu that contains a Size submenu — AppleWorks works that way, for example (Chapter 9).

In TextEdit and a few other programs, the list of sizes hides on something called the Font Panel. Call it up by opening the Format menu, and then choosing Font Panel from the Font submenu, as shown here at top. The font panel window opens, as shown at bottom:

Now select some text and then choose a type size from the list of sizes in the font panel. The font sizes are measured in points, of which there are 72 per inch. Works out nicely, too — a typical iMac monitor has 72 *screen* dots per inch, meaning that 12-point type on the screen really is 12-point.

Before you know it, you'll have whipped your document into handsome shape.

The efficiency zealot's guide to power typing

Because you *can* format text after you've typed it doesn't mean you *have* to. Most power-users get used to the keyboard shortcuts for the common style changes, like bold and italic. They're pretty easy to remember: In nearly every word-processing program, you get bold by pressing ⌘-B and italic with ⌘-I.

What's handy is that you can hit this key combo just *before* you type the word. For example, without ever taking your hands off the keyboard, you could type the following:

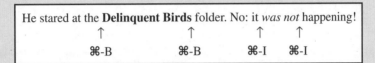

In other words, you hit ⌘-B once to turn bold *on* for the next burst of typing, and ⌘-B again to turn it off — all without ever having to use a menu. (You do the same with ⌘-I.)

Formatting paragraphs

Whereas type styles and sizes can be applied to any amount of text, even a single letter, *paragraph formatting* affects a whole paragraph at once. Usually these styles are easy to apply. To select a paragraph, you don't have to highlight all the text in it. Instead, you can just click *once,* anywhere within a paragraph, to plant the insertion point. Then, as before, choose the menu command that you want to apply to that entire paragraph.

This figure shows some of the different options every word processor provides for paragraph formatting — left-justified, right-justified, fully justified, and centered:

Her heart pounding, she looked toward the door. It swung open with a creak. The stench hit her first—an acrid, rotting swamp smell. She covered her mouth with the blood-soaked handkerchief and stepped backward, her naked back pressed hard against the fourposter.

Left-justified

Her heart pounding, she looked toward the door. It swung open with a creak. The stench hit her first—an acrid, rotting swamp smell. She covered her mouth with the blood-soaked handkerchief and stepped backward, her naked back pressed hard against the fourposter.

Right-justified

Her heart pounding, she looked toward the door. It swung open with a creak. The stench hit her first—an acrid, rotting swamp smell. She covered her mouth with the blood-soaked handkerchief and stepped backward, her naked back pressed hard against the fourposter.

Fully justified

Her heart pounding, she looked toward the door. It swung open with a creak. The stench hit her first—an acrid, rotting swamp smell. She covered her mouth with the blood-soaked handkerchief and stepped backward, her naked back pressed hard against the fourposter.

Centered

(In TextEdit, you get these effects by clicking a paragraph, and then choosing Align Left, Center, Justify, or Align Right from the Text submenu of the Format menu.)

You can control paragraphs in other ways, too. Remember in high school when you were supposed to turn in a 20-page paper, and you'd try to pad your much-too-short assignment by making it two-and-a-half spaced? Well, if you'd had an iMac, you could have been much more sneaky about it. You can make your word-processed document single-spaced, double-spaced, quadruple-spaced, or any itty-bitty fraction thereof. You can even control how tightly together the letters are placed, making it easy to stretch or compress your writing into more or fewer pages.

Take this opportunity to toy with your word processor. Go ahead, really muck things up. Make it look like a ransom note with a million different type styles and sizes. Then, when you've got a real masterpiece on the screen, read on.

Working with Documents

It might terrify you — and it should — to find out that you've been working on an imaginary document. Only a thin thread of streaming electrical current preserves it. Your typing doesn't exist yet, to be perfectly accurate, except in your iMac's *memory*.

You may recall from the notes you took on Chapter 1½ that memory is fleeting. (Specifically, I mean *computer* memory, but if you find a more universal truth in my words, interpret away.) In fact, the memory is wiped away when you shut the iMac down — or when a system crash, a rare but inevitable event for any computer, turns it off *for* you. At that moment, anything that exists on the screen is gone forever.

Therefore, almost every program has a Save command. It's always in the File menu, and its keyboard shortcut is always ⌘-S.

When you save your work, the iMac transfers it from transient, fleeting, electronic memory onto the good, solid, permanent disk. There your work will remain, safely saved. It will still be there tomorrow. It will still be there next week. It will still be there ten years from now, when your computer is so obsolete that it's valuable again.

Therefore, let's try an experiment with your ransom note document on the screen. From the File menu, choose Save.

Uh-oh. Something weird just happened: A slithery, semi-transparent rectangle that Apple calls a *sheet* just dripped out from the top of your document window, like this:

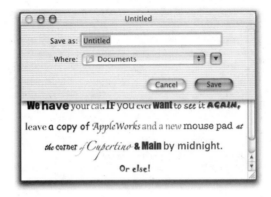

The iMac makes it pretty clear that it wants to know: "Under what name would you like me to file this precious document, Masssssster?"

And how do you know this? Because in the box where it says "Save as," a proposed title is highlighted (selected already). And what do you know about highlighted text? *Anything you start typing will instantly replace it.*

The iMac, in its cute, limited way, is trying to tell you that it needs you to type a title. Go ahead, do it: Type *Ransom Note*.

At this point, you could just click the Save button. The iMac would take everything in perilous, fleeting memory and transfer it to the staid, safe hard disk — in your Documents folder (which is in your Home folder), to be precise. There it would remain until you were ready to work on it some more.

However, a bunch of other stuff lurks in this sheet. A quick tour may be in order.

Navigating the Save File sheet

Before Mac OS X came along, some people *lost* files every day. They'd click Save, and wind up with some document filed somewhere in some folder of the hard drive where they never saw it again.

But on your iMac, it's almost impossible to lose a file you've created. If you just click Save whenever you see the Save sheet, the iMac will always keep your stuff in the Documents folder. When you want to work on something again, you can always find it like this:

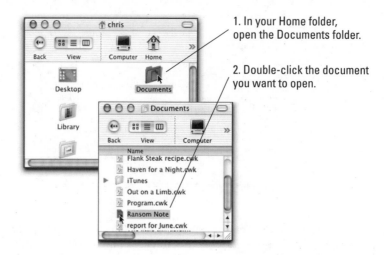

1. In your Home folder, open the Documents folder.

2. Double-click the document you want to open.

When you're feeling good about your mastery of the machine, though, you may one day want to explore the possibility of filing your documents into *other* folders.

For advanced thinkers like you, Apple has provided a small, black triangle button, shown in the picture below. When you click it, the sheet expands to reveal additional controls, like this:

The idea here is simple. You've already learned about the way your computer organizes files: with folders and with folders *in* folders. Remember the little exercise from Chapter 2, where you put state-named folders inside the USA Folder?

Well, all the stuff in the Save File box is a miniature version of that same folder-filing system. In fact, it looks just like column view, which was described in Chapter 2.

Here are some of the ways you might choose a filing folder for a document you're saving:

✔ Click the "Where:" pop-up menu at the top of the box, like this:

Here you see a list of the places you're most likely to want to stash a file you've just written: on the desktop, in your Home folder, on your iDisk (see Chapter 6), and so on. (Some people like to save everything onto the desktop, where they'll find it sitting out on the colored backdrop of the screen when they're done working. At that point, they file it manually, by dragging it into a folder.)

This menu also lists any folders you've designated as Favorites (see the box called "Favorite Places"), plus any folders or disks you've opened recently ("Recent Places"). The idea is the same: to let you choose a filing location for your new document just by picking its name from a menu.

✔ Using the column-view arrangement, navigate to the folder you want. When you've finally highlighted the name of the folder, click the Save button at the bottom of the box.

✔ Create a *new* folder in your Home folder or on the desktop. This is a great option when you've just finished writing Chapter 1 of something; after all, at this moment, you haven't yet created a folder to hold your new masterpiece.

So you'd choose Home or Desktop from the "Where:" pop-up menu at the top of the box (to tell the iMac *where* you want the new folder to appear). Then you'd click the New Folder button, type a name for the new folder, and click Create. Then you'd click Save to file Chapter 1 into that newly created folder.

For the purposes of following along with this exercise, open the "Where:" pop-up menu and choose Documents from the pop-up menu. Then click the Save button at the lower-right corner of the box. The Save sheet slurps away upward, and behind the scenes, your file has been snugly tucked away into the Documents folder, which will be an increasingly important folder in your life.

Want proof, O Cynic? Try this cool trick: From the TextEdit menu, choose Hide TextEdit. Suddenly all open word-processing windows disappear. You haven't lost your work — you've just temporarily hidden it, so that you can see the desktop that they were covering up.

Now you're back at the Finder, where your friends the folders, windows, and Dock pop up. If you wanted to make sure your file really exists, and it really got put where you wanted it, you could now go to your Home folder (choose Home from the Go menu). Inside, you'd find a Documents folder, which you could double-click to open. There, sure enough, is your ransom note, represented as an icon.

Why are we kicking this absolutely deceased horse? Because that same Sheet business (including the "Where:" pop-up menu) is used for *retrieving* files you've already created. You need to know how to work that sheet if you ever want to see your files again. More on this in a moment.

Worrywarts' corner

From the way I've described the terrifyingly delicate condition of a document that's on the screen (that you haven't saved to disk yet) — that is, precariously close to oblivion, kept alive only by electric current — you might think that closing a window is a dangerous act. After all, what if you forgot to save some work? Wouldn't closing the window mean losing that critical memo?

Not really — if you try to close a document, the iMac won't *let* you proceed until it asks you whether you're *sure* you want to lose all the work you've done. It will say something like:

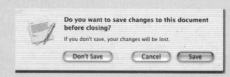

Click Save if you do want to save your work. Click Don't Save if you were only goofing around and don't want to preserve your labors.

Click Cancel if you change your mind completely about closing the document and want to keep working on it.

Closing a file, with a sigh

Return to TextEdit by clicking its icon on the Dock. All of your word-processing windows should pop back onto the screen, including your ransom note.

Close all of your windows by clicking the close button (the little red, leftmost dot in the upper-left corner). Once. If the iMac invites you to save the changes you've made to one of these windows, well, that's up to you. Clicking Don't Save is perfectly OK, especially because the work you've done in this chapter consists primarily of worthless noodlings.

In the iMac's universal language of love, clicking the small square up there means *close the window,* as you'll recall. If all went well, the window disappears.

How to find out what's going on

This gets sort of metaphysical. Hold onto your brain.

Just because you closed your *document* doesn't mean you've left the *program*. In fact, if you inspect the menu just to the right of the menu, you'll see that the TextEdit program is, in fact, still running. Its name still appears on your menu bar.

You could return to the desktop by clicking its Dock icon, or just by clicking anywhere on the desktop — without exiting the word processor. The Finder and TextEdit can both can be running at the same time, but only one can be in front.

In fact, that's the amazing thing about a Macintosh. You can have a bunch of programs all open and running at once.

What gets confusing is that one program (say, TextEdit) may be active, but you'll *think* you're in the Finder. After all, you'll see your familiar icons, Trash, folders, and so on. But you'll be confused, because the menu commands you might be looking for, like Empty Trash or New Folder, won't be in the menus at all!

You need to understand that all this is simply *shining through* the emptiness left by TextEdit, which has no windows open at the moment. If a window *were* open, it would cover up the desktop behind it. The menus you're seeing now, in other words, are the menus of *TextEdit* (which, of course, has no Empty Trash or New Folder commands).

If that momentary disorientation strikes you — you're looking for a menu that doesn't seem to be there any more — your first thought should be to figure out what program you're actually in. Its name always appears next to the menu.

For the moment, stay in TextEdit.

Getting It All Back Again

Okay. You've typed a ransom note. Using the Save command, you turned that typing on your screen into an icon on your hard disk. Now it's time for a concept break.

Crazy relationships: Parents and kids

Two kinds of files are lying on your hard disk right now: *programs* (sometimes called *applications*) and *documents*. A program never changes; it's like a Cuisinart on your kitchen counter, sitting there day after day. Documents are what you *create* with a program — they're the coleslaw, crushed nuts, and guacamole dip that come out of the Cuisinart. You pay money to buy a program. After you own it, you can create as many documents as you want for free.

For example, you could use the Word Proc-S-R program (above, top) to create all the different word-processing documents below it and thousands more like them. If you love analogies as much as I do, you can think of the application as the mommy and the documents as the kiddies.

Here's what their family relationships are like:

✔ Double-click the *program* icon when you want to open a brand-new, untitled, clean-slate document.

✔ Double-click a *document* icon to open that document. Unbeknownst to you, double-clicking a document simultaneously opens the program you used to create the document.

When you double-click to open a document...

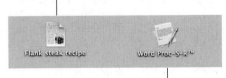

...the Mac automatically opens the program that gave it birth, even if it's buried in a folder somewhere.

File-name suffixes

How does a document know who its mommy is? That's an excellent question with a somewhat technical answer. It turns out that behind the scenes, almost every document you create has a secret three-letter suffix at the end of its name. Your AppleWorks document may look to you like it's called "Robin's Last Will and Testament," but its real name is "Robin's Last Will and Testament.cwk." The Mac has an internal table that indicates which three-letter suffix "belongs" to which program.

So how come you've never seen these suffixes? Because the Mac normally *hides* them, in an effort to make the Mac look less intimidating and geeky.

If you'd like a peek at the secret suffix (also called a *file name extension*), highlight a document icon and, from the File menu, choose Show Info. From the pop-up menu at the top of the resulting dialog box, choose Name & Extension. You'll see something like this:

If this sort of thing gets your pulse racing, you'll find more about it in the troubleshooting chapter (Chapter 15) because you can generally ignore this entire topic until things go wrong.

Fetch: How to retrieve a document

Let's pretend it's tomorrow. Yawn, stretch, fluff your hair (if any). You find out that the person you've kidnapped actually comes from a wealthy Rhode Island family, and so you can demand much more ransom money. Fortunately, you created your ransom note on the iMac, so you don't have to retype anything; you can just change the amount you're demanding and print it out again.

But if you've been following the steps in this chapter, then there's *no* document on the screen. You're still *in* TextEdit, though (or should be; check the name of the program next to the menu). So how do you get your ransom note file back?

Like this:

1. **From the File menu, choose Open.**

   A *dialog box* appears, so called because the iMac wants to have a little chat with you.

This one looks just like the Save dialog box, where you were asked to give your document a title. This one, navigationally speaking, works exactly the same way.

Unfortunately for my efforts to make this as instructional as possible, if you've been following these steps, your ransom note is staring you in the face right now. It's in whichever folder you saved it into. The iMac is nice that way — it remembers the most recent folder you stashed something in and shows you that location the next time you try to save or open something.

If you want to emerge from this experience a better person, pretend that you can't find your ransom note. Pull down the Where: pop-up menu and choose, for example, Desktop. Now the display changes to show whatever's sitting on your desktop.

And from here, you know how to get back into your own stuff, don't you? Correct — from the Where: pop-up menu, choose Home. From here, you can double-click your way into the Documents folder, or whatever folder you keep your criminal records in. Sooner or later, you'll spot the icon for your Ransom Note file.

2. **Double-click the ransom note.**

This is what you've been working up to all this time. The ransom note appears on your screen in its entirety. Now, at last, you can edit it to your heart's content.

Save Me Again!

To continue this experiment, make some changes to your document. Once again, you have to worry about the fact that your precious work only exists in a fragile world of bouncing electrons. Once again, turning the iMac off right now means you'll lose the *new* work you've done. (The original ransom note, without changes, is still safe on your disk.)

Therefore, you have to use that trusty Save command each time you make changes that are worth keeping. (For you desk potatoes out there, remember that ⌘-S is the keyboard shortcut, which saves you an exhausting trip to the menu.) The Save dialog box will *not* appear on the screen each time you use the Save command (as it did the first time). Only the very first time you save a document does the iMac ask for a title (and a folder location).

As mentioned in Chapter 1½, you've probably heard horror stories about people who've lost hours of work when some glitch made their computers crash. Well, usually it's their own darned fault for ignoring the two most important rules of computing:

> **Rule 1. Save your work often.**

> **Rule 2. See Rule 1.**

"Often" may mean every five minutes. It may mean after every paragraph. The point is to do it a lot. Get to know that ⌘-S shortcut, and type it reflexively after every tiny burst of inspiration.

Now you know how to start a new document, edit it, save it onto the disk, reopen it later, and save your additional changes. You know how to launch (open or run) a program — by double-clicking its icon. But now you have to learn to get out of a program when you're finished for the day. It's not terribly difficult:

Choose Quit TextEdit (or whatever the program's name is) from the File menu.

If TextEdit was the only program you were running, then you return to the Finder. If you were running some other programs, then you just drop down into the next program. It's as though the programs are stacked on top of each other; take away the top one, and you drop into the next one down.

How to Back Up — and Burn CDs

Duty compels me to keep this chapter going just long enough to preach one other famous word of advice to you: Back up.

To *back up,* or to *make a backup,* means to make a safety copy of your work.

The importance of being backed up

When you're in the Finder, the documents you've worked on appear as icons on the hard disk. Like any of us, these disks occasionally have bad hair days, go through moody spells, or die. On days like those, you'll wish you had made a *copy* of the stuff on the hard disk so your life won't grind to a halt while the hard disk is being repaired.

You know the cruel gods that make it rain when you forget your umbrella? Those same deities have equal powers over your hard disk and an equal taste for irony. That is, if you don't back up, your hard disk will *certainly* croak. On the other hand, if you back up your work at the end of every day or every week, nothing will ever go wrong with your hard disk, and you'll mumble to yourself that you're wasting your time.

Life's just like that.

What to back up

The beauty of the Mac OS X system is that your whole world of files and settings lives in a single folder: your Home folder. That's the only folder you care about.

Even if a bolt of lightning, or a midnight thief, takes out your iMac, you're almost completely covered. You already have a backup of the operating system itself, and all programs that came with it, in the form of the backup CDs that came with your machine (more on this in Chapter 15). If you've bought more programs, you can back them up from the CDs they came on. The only thing you need to keep backed up, then, is your Home folder.

Method 1: Burn a CD

Among your iMac's many other skills, it can actually *record CDs,* a feat that once required a $25 million fabrication plant in Korea.

A couple of blank, all-silver CDs came in the box with your iMac. (They're stashed into the envelope of software CDs.) If the faint etched writing on them says *CD-R,* then they're just *recordable* blanks — you can fill them up only once. Which isn't so bad, really, since blanks cost less than 30 cents each.

But you can also buy slightly more expensive *CD-RW* blanks, which stands for *rewritable.* You can *re*-record these discs, using one CD as a backup disk that you erase and re-use over and over again. At discount-computer Web sites like *www.buy.com* (search for "CD-R spindle" or "CD-RW spindle"), you can buy a pack of 50 blank CD-R discs, or 25 blank CD-RW discs, for $17 or less. Prices have probably dropped even more since this book was published — in fact, they've probably dropped since you began reading this sentence.

Either way, the process couldn't be simpler:

1. **Open the CD tray by holding down the Eject button on your keyboard.**

   It's the up-arrow key at the upper-right corner of the whole keyboard. Press for about two seconds, until the white, capsule-shaped door, right smack on the front of your iMac's base, snaps down and opens like the entrance to the Bat Cave, and the black CD tray shoots open with considerable power. (Oh, I almost forgot: First remove any Styrofoam cups of coffee that you may have placed directly in front of the computer.)

2. **Put a blank CD (or a CD-RW disc) into the tray.**

   Handle the CD by its hole and its edges; never touch the underside. The disc goes label side up.

3. **Close the tray.**

   You can either push its front edge until it closes automatically, or just tap the Eject key on your keyboard again.

   If you've inserted a new, blank disc, you see this message:

Type a name for your backup disk and then click Prepare. (Or press the Return key. Remember that any blue, pulsing button on your screen can also be "clicked" by pressing Return.)

In any case, a shiny CD icon appears on your desktop.

(Red-tape alert: If it's a CD-RW disc that you've used before, you have to erase it before you can re-use it. To do that, open the Disk Utility program, which is in the Applications folder, inside the Utilities folder. When the Disk Utility screen appears, click the Erase tab, click the listing in the left-side list that represents the disc [it probably says just, "641.04 MB" or something], click Erase, and then click Erase again. Wait a few minutes, and then quit Disk Utility. From now on, the disc will behave exactly as though it's a blank, which it is.)

4. **Open your Home folder window. Drag it, using the little "home" icon in the title bar as a handle (circled in the following picture), onto the CD icon.**

(Don't start dragging until the little house icon turns dark.)

That's it. The Mac begins copying your Home folder onto the blank CD.

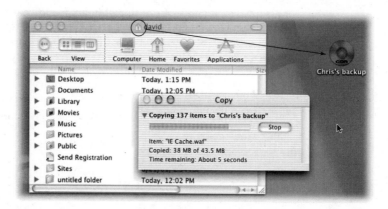

On a Macintosh, making a copy of something is as easy as dragging it to the disk you want it copied onto. You can also drag something into the disk's *window* (instead of onto its *icon*).

Nor should you feel limited to backing up your Home folder; you can drag folder icons from anywhere on your hard drive onto the CD icon.

5. **From the File menu, choose Burn Disc. In the confirmation dialog box, click Burn.**

   (Alternatively, eject the CD by choosing Eject from the File menu, or by dragging its icon onto the Trash icon on the Dock; the iMac will ask you if you want to burn it before ejecting it.)

   Burning the CD takes a few minutes. When the progress bar indicates that the job is complete, you've got yourself a backup. You can open the CD to confirm that your files and folders are really there, or just take it out of the iMac (press the Eject key on your keyboard again). Remove the CD carefully, avoiding touching the bottom, and label the top with a magic marker. Your data is safe — for now.

Burning CDs is also great for taking files and folders from one place to another, or for distributing files to other people. In fact, the CDs you make this way even work on Windows PCs.

You can make as many copies of a file as you want without ever experiencing a loss of quality. You're digital now, kids.

Method 2: Back up onto your iDisk

Your iMac came with a free, though *very* slow, backup disk out there on the Internet: something called the iDisk.

Floppy? What floppy?

Many computer users back up their work by copying their important icons onto floppy disks. Unless your computer-store salesman was a fast-talking slimeball, however, it should be no surprise to you by now that your iMac *doesn't have* a built-in floppy-disk drive.

The truth is, floppy disks don't hold nearly enough to make good backup disks. If you have your heart set on one, though, you can buy an external floppy drive for about $80.

Getting it operational is described in Chapter 6. To bring it onto the screen so you can back up your work, though, connect to the Internet, open the Go menu, and choose iDisk. Once the iDisk icon appears on your screen, open it.

Then drag your Home folder onto one of the folders on the iDisk (not onto the iDisk itself), exactly as shown in Step 4 of the preceding instructions. You have to drag your stuff into one of the folders *on* the iDisk — you can't drag files into the main iDisk window.

Note, though, that the iDisk holds only 20 megabytes of files. That's plenty if you intend to back up AppleWorks, Microsoft Word, and Microsoft Excel files. But if you work with disk-hungry files like digital photos and movies, you'll quickly run out of space. In that case, use one of the other backup systems described here.

Method 3: Back up onto another Mac

If you have more than one Mac, here's a brilliant idea: Connect them with a network wire, a scheme described in Chapter 14. Then use your two Macs as backup disks for *each other.* Chapter 14 tells all.

Method 4: Buy a backup drive

All of the backup methods described so far are especially likeable because they're free, free, free!

But if your cheapskate gene isn't quite as dominant as mine, you may find comfort in *buying* a solution to the backup problem. You can, for example, buy a backup disk drive that plugs into the back of your iMac: a second hard drive, for example, or a doodad that accepts removable disks like Zip disks. (Details in Chapter 19.) The advantage here is that you don't have to use up a CD, or completely erase a CD-RW, each time you want to back up; you can copy and erase files and folders to these disks selectively, as the mood suits you.

Once it's hooked up, turned on, and running, insert a disk; if it's a floppy or Zip disk, it goes metal side first, label side up. Put the disk into the disk drive *slot.* Keep pushing the disk in until the disk drive gulps it in with a satisfying *kachunk.*

Eventually, its icon shows up on the right side, just beneath your hard-disk icon. Drag your Home folder onto it, just as shown in Step 4 of the previous step-by-steps.

When What Was Found Is Now Lost

Okay. You've practiced saving and retrieving files. Yet still it happens: You can't find some file you were working on.

This is nothing to be ashamed of! Thousands of people lose files every day. But through the intervention of caring self-help groups, they often go on to lead productive, "normal" lives.

Here's what to do: Sit up straight, think positive thoughts, and press ⌘-F. Or do it the mousy way: Click the Sherlock icon (the detective hat, of course) on your Dock.

On the screen, you see the Sherlock box: your personal electronic butler who's prepared to spend the next few seconds rummaging through the attics, garages, and basement of your iMac.

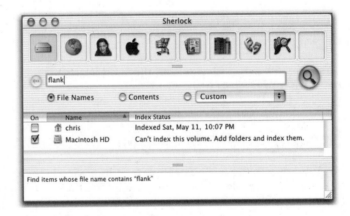

Type a few letters of the missing file's name. (Capitals don't matter, but spaces do!) Then click the green magnifying-glass button (or press Return).

A new window appears, listing everything on your hard drive whose name contains what you looked for. At this point, you can perform any of the following stunts.

1. Double-click an icon to open it. Or drag it someplace — onto the desktop, perhaps, or even directly to the Trash. To open the window a file is in, click it and then press ⌘-E.

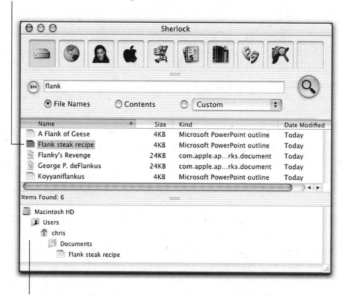

2. This area shows you where the highlighted file is, no matter how many folders deep it's buried. You can double-click any file or folder in this list, too, to open it.

When you're finished playing with the Sherlock thing, choose Quit from its File menu (or press ⌘-Q).

Seeking wisdom in your own words

The trouble with the traditional Sherlock command is that it searches only the *names* of your files. If you wrote a 253-page thesis on Wombat Worship Societies, but you accidentally *named* that file "Gift Ideas for Marge," you could search for "Wombat" from now until doomsday without turning up the file.

It would be different, however, if the Sherlock command were smart enough to search for words *inside* your documents. That's exactly what the Contents button does.

Click it, and then, in the empty text box, type *wombat,* or whatever words you're looking for. (They don't have to be together. If you type in *French fries,* Sherlock will also find a file containing a sentence like, "The French electrical committee found that voltage over 14,000 watts often fries the very wires that conduct it.")

Then turn on the checkboxes of the folders you want to search. Usually, your Home folder is all you care about (and, in fact, all you're allowed to search). But if there are other folders worth searching, you can drag them directly into the Sherlock list — yes, right out of whatever windows they're in — and make sure *their* checkboxes are turned on.

Finally, click the green magnifying-glass button (or press Return). The Sherlock window changes to show you a list of the files it found that contain those words, sorted by *relevance.* (If Sherlock finds three occurrences of the word *wombat* in a 50-word document, that's considered more relevant than a 900-word file with only one occurrence.)

Top Ten Word-Processing Tips

1. Select a word by double-clicking — and then, if you keep the mouse button on the second click and drag sideways, you select additional text in complete one-word increments.

2. Never, never, never line up text using the space bar. It may have worked in the typewriter days, but not any more. For example, you may get things lined up like this on the screen:

   1963   **1992**   **2001**
   Born   Elected President Graduated college

   Yet, sure as death or taxes, you'll get this when you print:

   1963   1992   **2001**
   Born   Elected President   Graduated college

   So instead of using spaces to line up columns, use *tab stops.*

3. You can select all the text in your document at once by using the Select All command (to change the font for the whole thing, for example). Its keyboard equivalent is almost always ⌘-A.

4. Don't use more than two fonts within a document. (Bold, italic, and normal versions of a font only count as one.) Talk about ransom notes!

5. Don't use underlining for emphasis. You're a typesetter now, babe. You've got *italics!* Underlining is a cop-out for typewriter people.

6. The box in the scroll bar at the right side of the window tells you, at a glance, where you are in your document.

   By dragging that box, you can jump anywhere in the document.

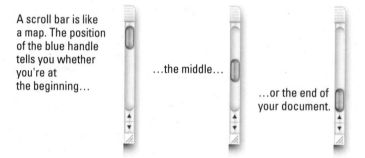

A scroll bar is like a map. The position of the blue handle tells you whether you're at the beginning...

...the middle...

...or the end of your document.

You can move around in two other ways, too:

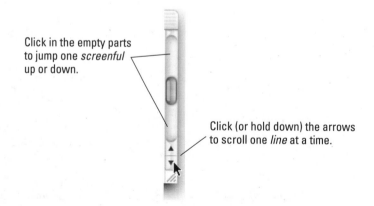

Click in the empty parts to jump one *screenful* up or down.

Click (or hold down) the arrows to scroll one *line* at a time.

7. You've already learned how to *copy* some text to the Clipboard, ready to paste into another place. Another useful technique is to *cut* text to the Clipboard. Cut (another command in the Edit menu) works just like Copy, except it snips the selected text out of the original document. (Cut-and-paste is how you *move* text from one place to another.)

8. It's considered uncouth to use "straight quotes" and 'straight apostrophes.' They hearken back to the days of yore — your typewriter, that is. Instead, use "curly double quotes" and 'curly single quotes' like these.

   You can produce curly double quotes by pressing Option-[(left bracket) and Shift-Option-[for the left and right ones, respectively. The single quotes (or apostrophes) are Option-] (right bracket) and Shift-Option-], for the left and right single quotes, respectively.

   But who can remember all that? Fortunately, decent word processors (AppleWorks, Microsoft Word, and so on) all offer an *automatic* curly quote feature, which is a much better solution.

   (On the other hand, don't type curly quotes into an e-mail message; they come out as bizarre little boxes and random letters at the other end.)

9. If there's an element you want to appear at the top of every page, like the page number, don't try to type it onto each page. The minute you add or delete text from somewhere else, this top-of-the-page information will become *middle*-of-the-page information. Instead, use your word processor's *running header* feature — it's a little window into which you can type whatever you want. The program automatically displays this info at the top of each page, no matter how much text you add or take away. (There's also such a thing as a *running footer,* which appears at the *bottom* of the page.)

10. You know how to select one word (double-click it). You know how to select a line (drag horizontally). You know how to select a block of text (drag diagonally through it). By now, you're probably about to reach Selection-Method Overload.

    But none of those techniques will help when you want to select a *lot* of text. What if you want to change the font size for *ten pages'* worth?

    Instead, try this two-part tip: First, click at the *beginning* of the stuff you want to highlight so that the insertion point is blinking there.

    Now scroll to the *end* of what you want to highlight. Hold down the *Shift key* with one hand and click the mouse button with the other. Magically, everything between your original click and your Shift-click gets highlighted!

1. Click here.

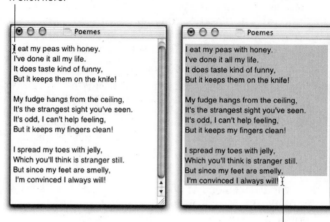

2. Shift-click here.

Chapter 5

A Quiet Talk about Printers, Printing, and Fonts

● ●

In This Chapter

▶ The different kinds of printers and how much they cost

▶ How to hook up and start printing

▶ The truth about fonts

● ●

You, gentle reader, are fortunate that you waited until now to get into the Mac. You completely missed the era of *dot-matrix* printers, whose printouts were so jagged that they looked like Dante's *Inferno* written in Braille.

If you bought a printer, it probably falls into one of two categories: *laser printers* and *inkjet printers*.

Inkjet Printers

The least expensive kind of printer is called an *inkjet*. Hewlett-Packard (HP), Epson, and Canon all make excellent color models. A typical inkjet looks like this:

Tales of dpi

Why have America's scientific geniuses invented all these different kinds of printers?

In a word, they're on a quest for higher *dpi*. That stands for "dots per inch," and it measures the quality of a printout. We're talking about *tiny* dots, mind you — there are about 100 of them clumped together to form the period at the end of this sentence. Clearly, the more of these dots there are per inch, the sharper quality your printouts will have.

Old laser printers manage 300 dpi, and today's generally do 600 dpi. A typical inkjet printer, such as a DeskJet, sprays 720 or even 1,440 dpi onto your paper. Photos printed by a 1,440 dpi printer *look* like photos, let me tell you.

Pretty good, you say? Yeah, well, so's yer ol' man — this book was printed on a *2,400* dpi professional printer!

When you buy one, a critical point is this: *Make sure it's compatible with Mac OS X.* Ask the catalog or computer-store representative specifically. If the printer doesn't have Mac OS X software (or, as the geeks would say, a Mac OS X-compatible *driver*), you're in for a lot of grief.

Inkjet printouts are so good that they almost match a laser printer's. The printers are small, lightweight, and almost silent. You can feed all kinds of nonliving things through them: tagboard, envelopes, sheet metal, whatever. And they can be had for less than $100, even for ones that can print in color. (If you have a color inkjet, and you want to print out photographs, you can buy fancy shiny paper for this — correction: *expensive* fancy shiny paper — that make the printouts look almost like actual photos.)

So what's the catch? Well, they're inkjet printers. They work by spraying a mist of ink. Therefore, the printing isn't laser-crisp if your stationery is even slightly absorbent, and you have to replace the ink cartridges fairly often. Note, too, that plain-paper printouts smear if they get the least bit damp, making them poor candidates for use during yacht races.

Still, inkjet printers are so compact, quiet, and inexpensive that they're hard to resist, especially if you want to print in color.

How to hook up a USB inkjet printer

The term *USB* refers to the kind of connector a printer has — and in the iMac world, USB means U Should B thrilled. Anything you plug into your iMac's USB jack works the first time, every time, with no hassle, no figuring out, and no turning the computer on or off. (And if that sounds perfectly normal to you, then you obviously weren't using computers in the 1980s.)

All modern inkjet printers have USB connectors — but they don't come with the USB *cable* you need to hook them up. You can get one at a computer store, or at a Web site like *www.buy.com*.

Then you're ready to set things up, following the instructions that came with the printer. This process inevitably involves not just connecting the printer to the iMac, but also installing some software from a CD that came with the printer. (Incidentally, if the printer's software for Mac OS X doesn't come on the CD, contact the printer company. You may be able to download the software you need from its Web site.) Jump down to "After All That: How You Actually Print."

Laser Printers

If you can afford to pay something like $400 for a printer, and you don't care about printing photos, some real magic awaits you: *laser printers*.

The printouts are much like photocopies: they're crisp and black, heat-fused to white paper. These laser printers can also print phenomenal-looking black-and-white graphics, like all the diagrams in Macintosh magazines and the weather maps in *USA Today*. They're quick, quiet, and hassle-free; most can print envelopes, mailing labels, and paper up to legal-size (but not tagboard). They're also much bigger and bulkier than inkjets, as you can see by this example.

Just remember that laser printers, while superior to inkjets for *black-and-white* quality, aren't what to buy if you want color. Sure, you can *buy* a color laser printer — for several thousand dollars — but the printouts aren't even as realistic as color *inkjet* printers' printouts.

Inexpensive laser printers connect to your iMac via a USB cable, just like inkjets.

But the more expensive models connect via an *Ethernet* cable. After having collected hundreds of dollars from you, printer companies have charitably recognized that this machine may wind up being *shared* among several different computers. Therefore, many laser printers are designed to be *networked*, as described in Chapter 14.

If you work in an office, then you probably don't care; ask whatever geek is in charge of your office network to connect your iMac to the existing Ethernet wiring system.

If you *are* the geek in charge of all the equipment, life's a little more complicated. All right, a *lot* more complicated:

1. **Connect your laser printer to the Ethernet hub (see Chapter 14). Connect your iMac to it, too.**

   Again, Ethernet *isn't* for dummies — people get advanced degrees in figuring this stuff out — but Chapter 14 should make this step at least somewhat transparent.

2. **Open your Applications folder (Option-⌘-A); open the Utilities folder; open Print Center. Click the Add Printer button.**

   A strange little empty window like this appears:

3. **From the Directory Services pop-up menu, choose AppleTalk.**

   You'll probably get an error message, muttering something about AppleTalk not being turned on. Click the Open Network Preferences button. You've just arrived at the Network panel of System Preferences.

4. **Turn on Make AppleTalk Active, and then click Apply Now. Quit System Preferences.**

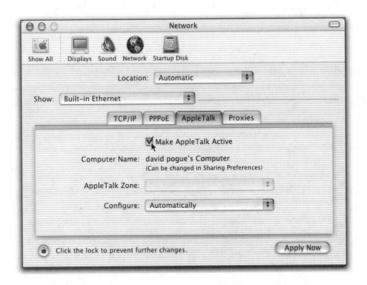

You've just told your computer what language it should use to speak to your printer.

5. **In the Printer List window, click the name of the printer you want to use, and then click Add.**

   After a moment, you return to the main printer list window, where your printer now appears. You're ready to print.

After All That: How You Actually Print

The moment has arrived: You'd actually like to *print* something.

Make sure whatever you want to print is on the screen: the ransom note you prepared in TextEdit, perhaps, or something you've written in AppleWorks (Chapter 9). From the File menu, choose Print. A dialog box appears; it looks different depending on your printer, but this one is typical of what you see if you have a Canon color printer.

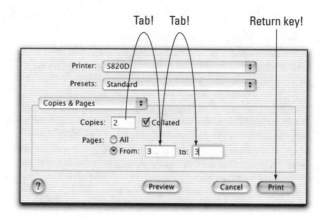

Tab!   Tab!   Return key!

For 95 percent of your life's printouts, you'll completely ignore the choices in this box and simply click the Print button.

For the other 5 percent of the time, the main thing you do in this dialog box is tell the iMac which pages of your document you want it to print. If you just want page 1, type a *1* into *both* the From and To boxes. If you want page 2 to the end, type *2* into the From box and leave the To box empty.

Specify how many copies you want, if you want more than one, by clicking and typing a number in the Copies box.

Using the Tab key in dialog boxes

Now would be a good time, I suppose, to mention what the Tab key does in dialog boxes. Suppose you want to print *two* copies of page 3. Instead of using the mouse to click in each number box on the screen, you can just press Tab to jump from box to box.

Therefore, you'd just type **2** (in the Copies box); press Tab and type **3** (in the From box) and press Tab and type **3** again (in the To box), as shown in the previous illustration. And the mouse just sits there gathering dust.

Anyway, after you're done filling out the options in this box, you can either click the Print button *or* press the Return key. (Remember, pressing Return is always the same as clicking the blue, pulsing button.) The iMac should whir for a moment, and pretty soon the printout will come slithering out of your printer.

This handy shortcut — using the Tab key to move around the blanks and pressing the Return key to "click" the OK or Print button — works in *any* dialog box. In fact, any time you ever see a button with a double-thickness outline, as shown in the preceding illustration, you can press the Return key instead of using the mouse.

Other options

See the Copies & Pages pop-up menu in the previous illustration? Hidden inside is a long list of other commands. Each changes the controls in the Print dialog box itself. The precise options are different for every printer model, but here are a few favorites:

✔ **Layout.** As shown in the following picture, you can save paper and ink or toner cartridges by printing several miniature "pages" on a single sheet of paper.

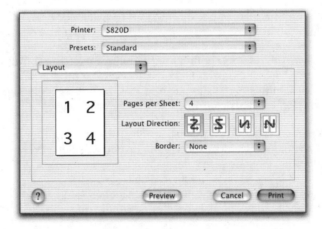

By asking the iMac to print several pages per sheet of paper, you can compare various designs, look over an overall newsletter layout, and so on. Using the Border pop-up menu, you can also request a fine border around each miniature page.

✔ **Output Options.** If you turn on "Save as File," you won't get a paper printout at all. Instead, you'll get a file on your hard drive — a *PDF file,* or *Acrobat file,* as it's known. If you're a novice at this kind of thing, you may not care about PDF files. But in the real world, you'll encounter them fairly often. Each PDF file contains a complete, self-contained computer-language description of your printout, suitable for sending to a print shop, or, indeed, anyone with a computer. They'll be able to open and print your document without requiring the program you used to create it — or even the document itself.

You can click either Preview (to see what the file will look like) or Save (to save the actual PDF document onto your hard drive).

✔ **Quality & Media.** Here's where you tell the printer what kind of paper you've put into it: glossy photo paper, plain paper, whatever.

✔ **Summary.** This command summons a text summary of all of your settings so far.

✔ **Save Custom Setting.** You can make Mac OS X memorize your favorite printing settings just by choosing this command. (The dialog box itself doesn't change when you choose this option.) Thereafter, you can save yourself the hassle of making all the settings just by choosing Custom from the Save Settings or Presets pop-up menu at the top of the window.

Once everything looks good, click Print to set your printer into motion.

Micromanaging your printouts

Most of the time, you'll simply want to print a document and get on with your life.

It's worth noticing, though, that you have a lot of control over the printouts as they're being born. The key is to visit the program called Print Center. It's in the Utilities folder of your Applications folder (you might want to drag Print Center onto your Dock so it's easier to get to).

When you open Print Center, you'll see a list of printers (which, unless you're a particularly wealthy individual, or you work in a corporation), probably contains only one printer.

If you double-click the printer's name *after* you've started printing some things but *before* they're finished being printed, you see them listed here, like this:

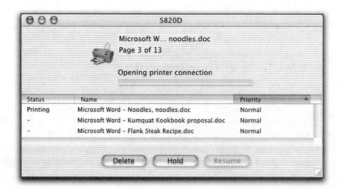

Here are some of the ways in which you can control these waiting printouts, which Apple collectively calls the *print queue:*

- ✔ **Delete them.** By clicking an icon and then clicking the Delete button at the bottom of the window, you remove items from the list of waiting printouts. Now they won't print.

- ✔ **Put them on pause.** By highlighting a printout and then clicking the Hold button, you pause that printout. It won't print out until you highlight it again and click the Resume button. This pausing business could be useful when, for example, you need time to check or refill the printer.

- ✔ **Halt them all.** You can stop all printouts for a specific printer by highlighting its name in the main printer list and choosing Stop Queue from the Queue menu. (Choose Start Queue from the same menu to re-enable printing on this printer.)

Canceling printing

If you want to interrupt the printing process, ⌘-period does the trick — that is, while pressing the ⌘ key, type a period. Several times, actually. Even then, your printer will take a moment (or page) or two to respond.

Top Ten Free Fun Font Factoids

The various *fonts* (typefaces) listed in the Font menus of your programs (such as AppleWorks) or in the Font Panel (of programs like TextEdit) are amazing. They look terrific on the screen and even better when printed, and they're never jagged-looking like the computer fonts of the early days. You may not realize it, but your fonts are a special kind of idiot-proof, jaggy-free, self-smoothing font that looks great on any printer at any size: *TrueType* fonts.

 If you work in the professional printing or graphic design industry, by the way, you may hear about a competing kind of font known as *PostScript* fonts. If you're truly interested in learning about the differences and history of these warring font types, check out a book like *Macworld Mac Secrets;* for now, let's just say that TrueType fonts — the kind that came on your iMac — are easier to manage, handle, and install.

Here are ten examples of the kind of fun you can have with your fonts:

1. Want more fonts? You can, of course, *buy* them. Your friendly neighborhood mail-order joint, like *www.macmall.com* or *www.macwarehouse.com,* are only too happy to sell you CD-ROMs crammed with new fonts.

   Those on a budget, however, can still get tons of great fonts. Dial up America Online or the Internet (see Chapter 6), for example, and help yourself to as many fonts as your typographical taste buds can tolerate. (On America Online, use keyword *filesearch;* on the Internet, try *www.shareware.com.* Either way, search the resulting page for "fonts.")

2. To install a new font, quit all your programs (if you're running any). Open the Macintosh HD icon on your desktop; open the Library folder on it; and drag the font files into the Fonts folder you find there.

   Note to people using the *user-accounts* feature described in Chapter 13: You're allowed to install or remove fonts this way only if you have an *Administrator* account. Still, if the iMac won't let you install new fonts, just thumb your nose, say "nyah, nhah," and open your own Home folder. Open the Library folder you find *there,* and put the fonts into your *own* Fonts folder within. These fonts will show up only when *you* are logged into the computer, but that's probably all you care.

3. If you read the preceding paragraphs carefully, it may have dawned on you that your iMac stores its fonts in two different places. Actually, it's worse than that: your Font menus reflect the contents of at least *three* different places! Each of these Fonts folders serves a different purpose, as you can see here:

Fonts you put into the main Library folder (on your hard drive) are available to everyone who uses this iMac. Only administrators (see Chapter 13) can add or remove these fonts.

Fonts inside the System X folder are for the iMac's own use. Nobody, not even administrators, are allowed to change the contents of this folder.

You have a Fonts folder of your own, too. It's in your Home folder, in the Library folder. You can freely add or remove fonts here — but nobody else with an account on this iMac will see or be able to use these fonts.

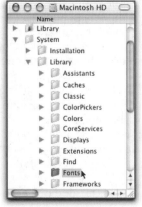

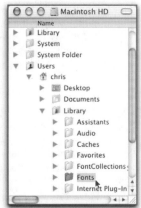

4. To remove a font, quit any programs you're running. Open the appropriate Fonts folder (as described in the previous paragraph). Then just drag the offending font icon out of the window. Put it onto the desktop. Or put it into some other folder — or right into the Trash can. (Can't seem to find a font that you want to delete? Well, for one thing, you're not allowed to remove fonts that the Macintosh uses in its own menus and windows, for example. Other fonts in your Font menus actually reside in a *fourth* Fonts folder: the one in your Mac OS 9 System Folder — a confusing topic that's demystified in Chapter 12.)

5. There are two kinds of people: those who place everything into two categories and those who don't. Among fonts, there are two basic types: *proportional* fonts, where every letter gets exactly as much width as it needs, and *monospaced* fonts, where every letter is exactly the same width, as on a typewriter. What you're reading now is a proportional font; notice that a W is much wider than an I.

   Your iMac comes with two monospaced fonts: Courier and Monaco. All the others are proportional.

   And who the heck cares? You will — the moment somebody sends you, perhaps by e-mail, some text that's supposed to line up, but doesn't. For example, this table that arrived by e-mail:

   ```
   From:     IntenseDude
   To:       pogue@aol.com

   Hello, David! Here are the prices you asked about:

   Item              Features                   Price
   ----              --------                   -----
   Seinfeld Statuette     Removable hairpiece       $25.00
   Baywatch digital watch  Surfboard sweep-second hand  $34.50
   "60 Minutes" bowtie    Mike Wallace autograph       $65.75
   E.R. BandAid Pak™     100 per box              $ 9.85
   ```

   All you have to do is highlight this text and change it to, say, Courier, and everything looks good again!

   ```
   From:        IntenseDude
   To:          pogue@aol.com

   Hello, David! Here are the prices you asked about:

   Item              Features                 Price
   ----              --------                 -----
   Seinfeld Statuette      Removable hairpiece      $25.00
   Baywatch digital watch  Surfboard sweep-second hand  $34.50
   "60 Minutes" bowtie     Mike Wallace autograph     $65.75
   E.R. BandAid Pak™      100 per box            $ 9.85
   ```

6. Only programs that have been written from scratch for Mac OS X — like TextEdit, Stickies, and Mail — offer the Font Panel described earlier in this chapter. That's too bad, because it's a fun little enhancement.

You open it by opening the Format menu, pointing to the Font command, and choosing Font Panel from the submenu. You get this handy column view; if you make the window wide enough, you'll see Collections (font categories) at the left, then Families (actual typefaces), Typefaces (styles like bold and italic), and finally Sizes. (Oblique and Italic are roughly equivalent. So are Bold and Black.)

At the bottom of the Font panel is a small pop-up menu labeled Extras. It offers a few useful tools for customizing the standard Font panel, including a command called Edit Collections, which lets you add to the Collections column. Maybe you want to put certain fonts in groups called Headline or Legal Text, creating smaller groupings of fonts for easier selection in your everyday work.

When you choose Edit Collections, you get this display. Click the + button to create a new entry in the Collections column, whose name you can edit. Click the name of a font, and then click the << button, to add this font's name to your collection. (To remove it from your collection, click its name in the Family column and then click >.) Each font can be in as many different collections as you want. When you're finished, click Done.

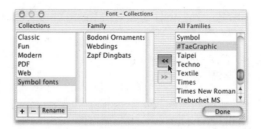

7. Text on your iMac's screen generally looks extra smooth, as though everything you type has been professionally typeset. That's because Mac OS X slightly blurs the edges of every letter.

But at smaller type sizes, some people feel that this text-smoothing business actually makes text *less* readable. Have a look:

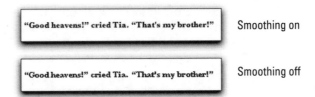

If the smoothing bugs you, open System Preferences (click its icon on the Dock). In the System Preferences window, click the General icon. At the bottom of the window, you'll see an option called, "Turn off text smoothing for font sizes __ and smaller."

Use the Size pop-up menu to designate a different cutoff point. Choose 12 from this pop-up menu, for example, to turn off smoothing for 12-point (and smaller) type. (These settings have no effect on your printouts, by the way — only on screen display.)

8. In Microsoft Word and a few other word-processing programs, you can actually see the names of the fonts in your font menu *in* those typefaces, like this:

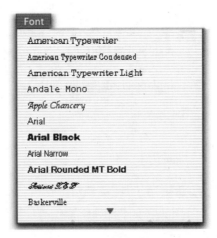

Word is even kind enough *not* to use this feature for *symbol fonts* — fonts where every "letter" is actually a symbol or little picture, like Symbol and Wingdings. (You can also turn off the what-you-see-is-what-you-get Font-menu feature entirely: From the Word menu, choose Preferences. In the list at left, choose General, and then turn off "WYSIWYG font and style menus." Click OK.)

9. Want to look good the next time you're hanging out with a bunch of type geeks? Then learn to bandy about the terms *serif* (pronounced SAIR-iff) and *sans serif* (SANNZ sair-iff).

A serif is the little protruding line built onto the edges of the letters in certain typefaces. In the serif font pictured in the top example here, I've drawn little circles around some of the serifs.

Terrif serifs
Sans-serif

A sans serif font, on the other hand, has no little protuberances, as you can see by their absence in the little square (in the lower example above). Times, Palatino, and the font you're reading are all serif fonts. Helvetica, Geneva, and the headlines in most newspapers are sans serif fonts. And that information, plus 37 cents, will buy you a first-class U.S. postage stamp.

10. This one's techy, but it's good.

When the iMac prints, it matches the placement of each word *exactly* according to its position on the screen. Trouble is, the iMac's screen resolution isn't that good — it's only 72 dots per inch instead of 600 or 1400 dpi (the usual for printers). As a result, you sometimes get weird spacing between words, especially between **boldface** words (see the bottom-left printout in the next illustration).

The solution: When you print, turn on the Fractional Character Widths feature. This makes words look a little bit cramped on the screen (top right in the next figure) but makes your printouts look *awesomely* professional (bottom right).

	Fractional Widths OFF	Fractional Widths ON
On the screen:	**Bullwinkle's Little Secret**	**Bullwinkle's Little Secret**
In the printout:	**Bullwinkle's Little Secret**	**Bullwinkle's Little Secret**

So how do you find this magical feature? In AppleWorks, open the AppleWorks menu, choose Preferences, and choose General from the submenu. You'll see the checkbox called fractional Character Widths.

In Microsoft Word, choose Preferences from the Word menu and click the Print item in the left-side list. You'll see the "Fractional widths" checkbox.

Try keeping it off when you're typing and on when you print.

Part II
The Internet Defanged

The 5th Wave   By Rich Tennant

"It all started when I began surfing the Web for 'Baked Alaska' and frozen custards..."

In this part . . .

The "i" in *iMac* stands for *Internet*.

I know, I know: If you hear *one more person* start droning on about the Internet, the Web, or the Information Superhighway, you'll tie them to a chair and make them watch 18 hours of the Home Shopping Network.

Actually, though, despite the overwhelming abundance of ridiculous, time-wasting chaff in cyberspace, there's also a lot of useful stuff, plus Dilbert cartoons for free. The next few chapters tell you how to get it.

Chapter 6

Faking Your Way onto America Online and the Internet

In This Chapter

▶ The Internet: What and why it is

▶ America Online, the grocery store; Internet, the farmer's market

▶ The iDisk: your free backup disk in the sky

▶ How to hang up — and how to get over downloaded-file hang-ups

*I*f you haven't heard of America Online or the Internet by now, you must've spent the last ten years in some Antarctic ice cave. These days, you can't make a move without seeing an e-mail address on someone's business card, a World Wide Web address (like *www.moneygrub.com*) on a magazine ad, or the glazed raccoon look of the all-night Internetter on a friend's face.

Going online gains you endless acres of features: the ability to send e-mail, instantly and for free, to anyone else who's online; incredible savings when you buy stuff (no middleman!); vast amounts of reading and research material (*Time* magazine, *The New York Times,* and so on, *free*); discussion bulletin boards on 29,000 topics (left-handed banjo-playing nuns, unite!); live, typed "chat rooms" that bring you together with similarly bored people from all over the world; and much more.

Before you begin this adventure, though, a grave warning: Going online is every bit as addictive as heroin, crack, or Presidential sex scandals, but even more dangerous. As you explore this endless, yawning new world, filled with surprises at every turn, you're likely to lose track of things — such as time, sleep, and your family. Take it slow, take it in small chunks, and use these services always in moderation.

Above all, remember that Apple didn't design the Internet. It existed long before the Macintosh. It was invented by a bunch of military scientists in the '60s whose idea of a good conversation was debating things like *TCP/IP, FTP,* and *ftp.ucs.ubc.ca.* As a result, going online is all quite a bit more complicated and awkward than everyday iMac activities.

In other words, if you can't figure out what's going on, *it's not your fault.*

First, the Modem

Your iMac contains a built-in *modem,* the little glob of circuitry that connects your computer to the phone jack on the wall. Fortunately, it's the fastest one money can buy — a so-called *56K* modem, which you can think of as "56 miles per hour."

Now then: When the iMac makes a call, it dials the phone many times faster than, say, a teenager, but ties up the phone line just as effectively. When your iMac is using the modem, nobody else can use the phone. Therefore, you need to figure out how you're going to plug in your modem:

- **Share a single line with the modem.** You can visit your local Radio Shack to buy a *splitter,* a Y-jack, a little plastic thing that makes your wall phone jack split into two identical phone jacks — one for your phone and the other for your iMac. This arrangement lets you talk on the telephone whenever you aren't using the modem and vice versa.

- **Install a second phone line.** This is clearly the power user's method: Give the modem a phone line unto itself.

  Pros: (1) Your main family phone number is no longer tied up every time your modem dials up the latest sports scores. (2) You can talk to a human on one line while you're modeming on the other. (3) If you're in an office with one of those PBX or Merlin-type multiline telephone systems, you have to install a new, separate jack for the modem *anyway.*

  Cons: (1) This option is expensive. (2) It involves calling up the phone company, which is about as much fun as eating sand. (3) You run a greater risk of becoming a serious modem nerd.

- **Don't use a phone line at all.** If you're willing to pay a little extra money each month, you can contact your local cable TV or phone company about installing a high-speed, ultra-rewarding avenue to the Internet known as a *cable modem* or *DSL* (digital subscriber line). These services cost around $35 or $45 per month, and require a visit (and a bill) from a service technician to install. But the results are worth slobbering over: Your iMac is online *constantly,* without even using its built-in modem, and without tying up your phone line. Your iMac gets its own direct umbilical to the Net, at speeds several times faster than even the fastest standard phone-line modem.

  I'll let you and your checkbook mull that one over. For now, it's worth noting that cable modems, DSL, and similar high-speed connections are the wave of the future.

For the rest of this chapter, I'll assume that you plan to go online the way most of the world does it: by connecting to a telephone line. Plug the included telephone wire into the iMac's modem jack. (The modem jack is on the back of the computer, marked by a little telephone icon.) Plug the other end into a telephone wall jack. (If you've equipped your iMac with an AirPort Card, the setup is slightly different; see Chapter 14.)

America Online or Direct to the Internet?

When it comes to visiting the vast, seething world of cyberspace, you have two on-ramps. You can become an America Online member, or you can sign up for a direct Internet account with a company like EarthLink. The geeks call Internet-access companies (like EarthLink) *ISPs,* short for *Internet Service Providers.*

I find the term Internet Service Provider — let alone *ISP* — overly nerdy, like calling a writer a "Literature Service Provider." Unfortunately, you can't crack open a magazine or visit a computer club without hearing people talk about ISPs. ("My ISP only charges $15 a month!" "Really? Maybe I'll change ISPs then.") So, with your permission, I'll refer to the companies who rent you time on the Internet as *ISPs,* just like everyone else does.

In this chapter, I'll show you both methods of getting online. Each route has significant pros and cons, however, which you'll find in the following table. Photocopy, distribute to your family members, and discuss over dinner.

America Online (AOL)	*Internet Service Provider (ISP)*
$24 per month, unlimited access.	$20 per month, unlimited access.
Occasional busy signals between 6 p.m. and midnight.	Busy signals are rare.
Hangs up on you after several minutes of your not doing anything.	Doesn't hang up on you.
The one program on your hard drive — the America Online program — does everything: e-mail, World Wide Web surfing, chat rooms, and so on.	You generally use a separate program for each function.
Generally safe for kids; no pornography on AOL itself.	Adult supervision required.
Very simple, sometimes frustrating; the geeks look down on people with AOL accounts.	More complex, less limiting; nerds admire you for having a "real" Internet account.

America Online (often called AOL) is an *online service.* That is, its offerings are hand-selected by the company's steering committee and sanitized for your protection. Contrast that with the Internet itself, where the offerings constantly change, nobody's in charge, and it's every iMac for itself.

Going onto AOL is like going to a grocery store, where every product is neatly organized, packaged, and labeled. Going onto the Internet, by contrast, is like going to a huge farmer's market that fills a football stadium, filled with whichever vendors happened to show up with their pickup trucks. At the farmer's market, wonderful bargains may await — but it's hard to find anything particular, the turnips may be rancid, and there's no clerk to ask for help.

On the other hand, don't forget that America Online *also* gives you the actual Internet, in addition to its own hand-picked goodies. That is, the AOL grocery store has a back door into the farmer's market.

America Online (AOL), the Cyber-Grocery

If you've decided that AOL is the way to go, your first task should be to install the America Online software for Mac OS X. Lucky for you, Apple stashed it away on your hard drive, in anticipation of exactly this moment.

To find it, open your Applications folder, and then open the Installers folder inside *it.* There you'll see something called Install AOL for Mac OS X. Click it, click Continue, click Install, and otherwise slog through the series of screens that puts the America Online software on your hard drive. (You can install AOL only if you have an *Administrator* account, as described in Chapter 13.)

When the installation is over, you'll find, inside your Applications folder, a soon-to-be-familiar America Online icon. This is the icon you double-click to get started. (You might want to drag this triangular icon onto your Dock.)

Your first online session

The first time you double-click this icon, you'll be guided through a series of setup steps. You'll be asked:

 ✔ For your name, address, and credit-card number. Remember, though, that you get 100 hours of time online (during the first month) for free. Cancel within the first month, and your card is never charged.

 ✔ To choose a local *access number* from a list (and a backup number). Fortunately, AOL has worked out a clever scheme that lets you, as one of 90 percent of Americans living near metropolitan centers, make a *local* call to America Online. Somehow, this system carries your call all the way to Virginia for free. (That's where the actual gigantic AOL computers live.)

 ✔ To make up a "screen name" and a password.

The *screen name* can't contain punctuation. You can use a variation of your name (A Lincoln, MTMoore, Mr Rourke) or some clever CB radio-type handle (FoxyBabe, Ski Jock, NoLifeGuy). Do understand, however, that America Online has about *30 million* members, and *each* of them (including you) can choose up to seven different names, one for each family member. In other words, you can pretty much bet that names like Bob, Hotshot, and Mac Guy were claimed some time in the Mesozoic Era.

If you pick a name that someone has already claimed, the program will make you keep trying — assisted by its own suggestions — until you come up with a name that hasn't been used before.

When all this setup information is complete, your modem begins screaming and making a hideous racket, and you see an AOL logo screen that says things like "Checking Password." Finally, if everything goes well, you're brought to an advertisement screen. Find and click the button that says No Thanks, Cancel, or whatever comes closest to expressing the disgust you must feel at having come so far only to have a slab of crass commercialism thrust into your face. At last you arrive here:

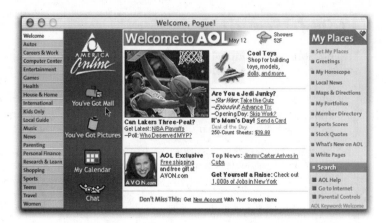

You also get to hear a recording of the famous Mr. Cheerful, the man who says "Welcome!" as though you're *just* the person he's been waiting for all day. If you've got e-mail waiting, he also says "You've got mail!," which he's *really* happy about. (To read the mail, click the "You've Got Mail" icon.)

Exploring by icon

AOL, you'll quickly discover, is a collection of hundreds of individual screens, each of which represents a different service or company. Each day, several of them are advertised on the welcome screen. To jump directly to the advertised feature, click the corresponding icon.

The broader America Online table of contents, however, appears at the left edge of the main screen. Each of *these* buttons takes you to yet another screen, where you can visit related services — for example:

- The *Research & Learn* button lets you consult a dictionary, a national phone book, or a choice of encyclopedias.
- The *Personal Finance* page is stock-market city: You can check quotes, actually buy and sell, get mutual-fund stats, read tax and investing advice, and so on.
- If you click the *Travel* button, you can actually look up plane fares and even make reservations.

Navigating by keyword

If you poked around enough, clicking icons and opening screen after screen, you'd eventually uncover everything America Online has to offer. In the meantime, however, you'd run up your phone bill, develop mouse elbow, and watch four Presidential administrations pass.

A much faster navigational trick is the *keyword* feature. A keyword is like an elevator button that takes you directly to any of the hundreds of features on AOL, making no stops along the way. Just type the keyword of your choice into the strip at the top of the screen (where it says "Type Keyword/Web address"). When you press Return, you're teleported directly to that service.

Here are a few typical AOL services, along with their keywords. Arm yourself with this list so that you make the most of your free month-long trial.

Keyword	*Where It Takes You*
Access	A list of local phone numbers for America Online. Use this before a trip to another city.
Banking	Check your accounts, pay bills, and so on (certain banks only).
Beginners	A collection of help topics for Mac newcomers.
Billing	Current billing info, disputes, and so on.
Encyclopedia	Your choice of several different published encyclopedias. You just saved $900!
Help	Assistance about America Online itself.
Homework	A place for students to get live, interactive help with homework and research.
Macgame	Files, messages, and discussions of Mac games.
Star Trek	*Star Trek.*
Stocks	Check the current price of any stock. You can even see your current portfolio value.

And how, you may well ask, do you find out what the keyword *is* for something you're looking for? Easy — just type in keyword: *keyword!* You'll get a screen that offers a complete list of keywords.

Things to know before entering the Party Zone

If it's your first time in a chat room, you may be nonplused by the gross excesses of punctuation that seem to go on there. Every five minutes, it seems that somebody types {{{{{{{{ Jennifer!!!}}}}}}}} or ****BabyBones!****

Actually, there's nothing wrong with these people's keyboards (or their brains). The braces are the cyberspace equivalent of hugging the enclosed person; the asterisks are kisses. That's how you greet friends who enter the room — online, anyway.

How to find your way back to the good stuff

With several hundred places worth visiting on AOL — and several *million* places worth visiting on the Internet — it'd be nice if there were a way to mark your place. Suppose you stumble onto this *great* English Cocker Spaniel Owners' area, for example, but you've already forgotten which buttons you clicked to get there.

Simple solution: When you're looking at a screen (or Web page) you might someday like to return to, choose Add to Favorite Places from the Window menu (or just press ⌘-+ sign). Thereafter, whenever you want to revisit one of your thus-marked Favorite Places, choose its name from the Favorite Places icon/menu, like this.

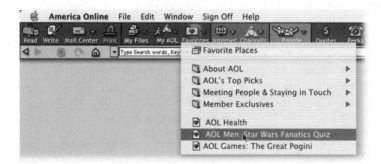

To delete something from this list, choose the very first command (Favorite Places) from the Favorites icon/menu. In the resulting window, just click a place's name once and then choose Clear from the Edit menu.

The e-mail connection

One of the best things about AOL is the e-mail — mainly the sheer, ego-boosting joy of *getting* some.

If, in fact, anybody has bothered to write to you (which you'll hear announced by Mr. "You've got mail!"), click the YOU HAVE MAIL button on the welcome screen to see your messages.

After you've read the message, you can (a) reply to it (by clicking the Reply button); (b) send it on to somebody else (by clicking the Forward button); (c) save it on your hard disk (by choosing Save from the File menu); (d) print it (by choosing Print from the File menu); or (e) close its window without saving it. If you do that, the message hangs around in your Old Mail folder for about a week and then disappears forever.

To *send* a message to somebody, click Write on the toolbar. Type your lucky recipient's e-mail address, a subject, and your message in the appropriate blanks. (Don't forget to press the Tab key to move from blank to blank.) When you're done typing, just press Enter (or click the Send Now button).

If you need to look up somebody's screen name, use this keyword: *members*.

The party line

By far the most mind-blowing aspect of AOL is, of course, the *chat rooms*. In a chat room, you'll find up to 23 people chatting away (by typing). The nutty thing is that everybody's talking at once, so the conversation threads overlap, and hilarious results sometimes ensue.

Nonetheless, the chat rooms are an unusual social opportunity: For the first time, you can be the total belle of the ball (or stud of the studio) — the wittiest, charmingest, best-liked person — without so much as combing your hair.

To get to the chat rooms, choose Chat Now from the People menu/icon on your toolbar. If you click the button called "Find a Chat," you'll discover that dozens of parties are transpiring simultaneously, each founded on a different topic. Double-click a room's name to go there.

Talking behind their backs

What makes the live chats even more fun is that you can whisper directly into the ear of anybody there — and nobody else can hear you. This kind of behind-the-scenes direct communication is called an Instant Message. To send one, choose Send Instant Message from the Members menu (or press ⌘-I). You get a box like this:

As soon as you type your whispered message and click Send (or press Enter), the window disappears from your screen — and reappears on the recipient's screen! That person can then whisper back to you.

Meanwhile, somebody *else* in the room may have been Instant-Messaging *you*.

If you try to maintain your presence in the main window *and* keep your end of all these whispered conversations in *their* little windows, the hilarity builds. *Nothing* makes a better typist out of you than the AOL chat rooms.

P.S. You can also carry on Instant-Message chats with people who aren't America Online members — that is, people who have standard Internet (ISP) accounts instead, as described later in this chapter. They, however, must first download and install a free program called AOL Instant Messenger onto their computers. For details, use keyword: *aim*.

How to find — and get — free software

For many people, the best part of AOL is the free software. Heck, for many people, that's the *only* part of AOL. Just use keyword: *filesearch;* click Shareware; in the Find What? blank, type the name of the file, or kind of file, you're looking for; and click Search.

In a moment, you're shown a complete listing of all files in the AOL data banks that match your search criteria. Keep in mind that roughly 500,000 files hang out on those computers in Virginia, so choose your search words with care.

If you think a file sounds good, double-click its name to read a description. If it *still* sounds good, click Download Now. The iMac asks where you want the downloaded item stashed. If you choose Desktop from the "Where:" pop-up menu before clicking Save, you'll avoid the crisis of "Where did my down-loaded goodies go?" syndrome suffered by 1 in 6 American adults. When you finish using America Online, you'll see the file you received sitting right on the colored backdrop of your iMac (or, as we say in the biz, *on the desktop*).

Your modem then begins the task of *downloading* (transferring) the file to your hard drive. (Make sure that you read the section "When You Can't Open Your Downloaded Goodies," later in this chapter, for a follow-up discussion on downloading stuff.)

Signing Up for an Internet Account (ISP)

If you've decided to sign up for a direct Internet connection (instead of going the AOL route), send a thank-you note to Apple; signing up for such an account on an iMac is as easy as signing up for AOL. In fact, you may have set up your Internet account the very first time you turned the machine on, as described in Chapter 1.

The EarthLink sign-up program

If not, open your Applications folder, open the Utilities folder inside it, and double-click the program called EarthLink (not EarthLink Connect).

Now the EarthLink Total Access sign-up program takes over, showing you a series of screens, asking for your name, address, credit-card number, and so on. (Warning: You're guided through this process by a *voice* that emanates from your iMac's speaker. First time I heard it, it scared the bejeezus out of me.)

Your modem dials an 800 number a couple of times. Along the way, you'll be asked to make up a cybername for yourself (such as *SeinfeldNut83*) and a password that protects your account.

When it's all over, you'll be an official, card-carrying member of the Internet. Now you, too, can have an e-mail address with an @ sign on your business card. Now you, too, can banter at cocktail parties about the ghastly new color scheme on the Microsoft Web site. Now you, too, can slowly drift away from family, job, and reality as you recede into cyberhermitdom.

A little ISP housekeeping

Before you dive headlong into the Internet via EarthLink, you'll thank me later if you take a few minutes to adjust some settings first. The following advice applies *only* to people who dial into the Internet over phone lines — not to the lucky ducks who have cable modems or DSL.

Start by opening System Preferences (click the light-switch icon on the Dock). Click the Network icon. From the Show pop-up menu, make sure it says Internal Modem. Finally, click the PPP tab, so that you see something like this:

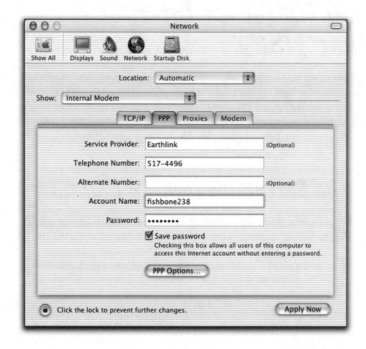

Here you should see, among other things, the EarthLink name and number you'll be using to go online. But at the bottom is a very handy button called PPP Options. It opens a special box that offers an option called "Connect automatically when starting TCP/IP applications." Turn this on, if it's not already checked. (It makes sure that your iMac dials automatically each time you try to check your e-mail or go onto the Web.) You might also want to inspect the "Disconnect if idle for 15 minutes" option, which prevents your iMac from tying up the phone line all day, even after you've wandered away from the machine to do some yard work. You can change the number of minutes, if you like, or turn off the option altogether.

When you're finished inspecting these options, click OK. Now click the Modem tab (shown in the previous picture), turn on "Show modem status in menu bar," and then click Apply Now. (You've just installed a tiny telephone icon on your menu bar, which you can use as a shortcut to go online and offline; more about this in a moment.) Finally, quit System Preferences.

What's on the Internet

In the following pages, you'll read about the various things that you can do on the Internet. As you read, keep in mind that all these features are available to you regardless of whether you have an AOL account or a real Internet (ISP) account.

E-mail

If you have America Online, see "The e-mail connection" earlier in this chapter. If you've signed up for an ISP like EarthLink instead, see Chapter 8. Either way, get psyched for a feature that'll change your life; as a technology, e-mail ranks right up there with cable TV, frequent-flyer miles, and microwave popcorn.

Newsgroups

The next important Internet feature is called *newsgroups*. Don't be fooled: They have nothing to do with news, and they're not groups. That's the Internet for ya.

Instead, newsgroups are electronic bulletin boards. I post a message; anyone else on the Internet can read it and post a response for all to see. Then somebody else responds to *that* message, and so on.

There are about 30,000 different newsgroups, ongoing discussions on every topic — chemists who like bowling, left-handed oboists, Mickey Mouse fans who live in Bali — anything. Here's how you reach these discussion areas:

✔ **On America Online:** Use keyword *newsgroups*. If you then click Read My Newsgroups, you see a starter list of topics; just keep double-clicking topics that interest you until you're reading the actual messages. (To add newsgroup topics to your starter list, use the Search All Newsgroups button.)

After you've read a message, you can respond to it (click the Send New Message button) or just keep reading (click the Next>> button).

✔ **With an ISP:** Mac OS X doesn't come with any software for reading newsgroup messages. But if you've bought Microsoft Office, you can use Entourage, one of its programs, to do so. And if Microsoft Office isn't in your immediate future, go online to a Web site like *www. versiontracker.com* — a massive storehouse of Mac software to download — and download a Mac OS X-compatible newsgroup reader like Halime.

Entourage, Halime, and other newsgroup-reading programs are hairy to set up properly; the assistance of your ISP's cheerful help-line rep is often an important element to your success.

In any case, once you've got the program running, you'll eventually want to pursue a several-prong attack on the newsgroups of the Internet. First, you'll want to download the *list* of those thousands of newsgroups. Then you'll want to search those discussions for something that interests you.

In Entourage, for example, you'll see an icon called *Newsgroup List* (or whatever you called it) at the left side of the screen; double-click it. Entourage asks you if you want to download a list of newsgroups available on that server. Click Yes.

Entourage goes to work downloading the list, which can be quite long — more than 30,000 entries, in many cases — and takes several minutes. Once that's done, though, you won't have to do it again. You *should* occasionally update the list, however, by choosing View⇨Get New Newsgroups.

If you're looking for a particular topic — Macs, say — you can view a list of only those discussions containing *Mac* in the titles by typing in a phrase into the "Display groups containing" field at the top of the window. Entourage hides any newsgroups that *don't* match that text.

To read the actual messages in a newsgroup, click its name in the Folder list at the left side of the window, which reveals the list of messages in the upper-right pane of the window, and Entourage then downloads a list of articles in that newsgroup.

The complete list of discussions — over 30,000 topics. Oy!

Find a discussion by typing keywords into this box.

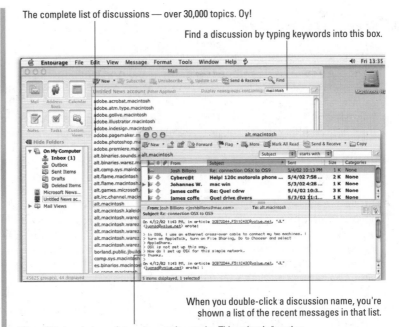

When you double-click a discussion name, you're shown a list of the recent messages in that list.

These little brackets are Internet quotation marks. This writer is "quoting back" a portion of somebody else's message before replying.

Working with newsgroup messages is very similar to working with e-mail messages. You reply to them, forward them, or compose them exactly as described in Chapter 8.

I realize that all of this is about as simple as human genome sequencing, but as I said, nobody ever called the Internet easy.

The World Wide Web

Except for e-mail, by far the most popular and useful Internet feature is the World Wide Web. In fact, it gets a chapter all to itself (the next chapter). For now, all you need to know is this:

✔ **On America Online:** A Web browser is built right into your AOL software. In many cases, you wind up on the Web just by innocently clicking some button within AOL — that's how tightly the Web is integrated with America Online these days. (You can tell when you're visiting a Web page, not an AOL page, when the address in the white strip at the top of the window begins with the letters *http.*)

✔ **With an ISP account:** You use a program called Microsoft Internet Explorer (its icon is already on your Dock). It's described in the next chapter.

How to Hang Up

When you're finished with an AOL session, hanging up is no big deal; just choose Quit America Online from the America Online menu, making your phone line available once again to the other members of your family.

Getting off the Internet if you have a direct Internet account (ISP), however, is trickier. Allow me to propose an analogy: Imagine that you call another branch of your family tree on New Year's Day. You yourself place the call, but then you hand the phone off to various other family members. "And now here's little Timmy! Timmy, talk to Grandma. . . ."

Using the Internet works the same way. Your iMac places the call. But aside from tying up the phone line, your iMac doesn't actually *do* anything until you launch one of the programs you read about in this chapter: an e-mail program or a Web browser, for example. Each of these Internet programs is like one of your family members, chatting with the Big Internet Grandma for a few minutes apiece.

The point here: When you quit your e-mail or Web program, *the phone line is still tied up,* just as though Timmy, when finished talking to Grandma, put the phone on the couch and wandered out to play. When you're finished Internetting, therefore, end the phone call by doing one of the following:

- ✔ Wait. After 15 minutes of your not doing anything online (or whatever time you've specified in the Network panel of System Preferences, as described earlier), your iMac hangs up automatically.

- ✔ Of course, if other people in your household are screaming for you to get off the line so that they can make a call, you can also hang up manually by choosing Disconnect from the little black telephone icon on your menu bar, like this:

- ✔ If, for some reason, you don't see the phone icon on your menu bar, you can also hang up by opening the Internet Connect program (in your Applications folder). Its big fat Disconnect button stares you in the face.

When You Can't Open Your Downloaded Goodies

It's easy to download software — either from AOL or the Internet. Maybe you find something on a Web page worth downloading (see the next chapter). Maybe somebody sends you a family picture as a file that's attached to an e-mail (see Chapter 8). Unfortunately, the first word out of the beginning downloader's mouth, on examining the freshly downloaded loot, is generally this:

"Wha — ?"

In the olden days, the first problem was just *finding* whatever-it-was that you'd downloaded. Fortunately, the iMac makes this a problem of the past. Internet Explorer, America Online, and, most likely, your e-mail program all plop downloaded files right on your desktop.

But that's not the end of the problems. The first thing many people discover when they examine a file they've just downloaded is that it's not what they expected. It has some strange file name suffix like *.dmg* or *.sit* or *.zip,* and definitely doesn't look like the photo/program/document they *thought* they'd downloaded.

Two questions, then: How are you supposed to expand your downloaded file back into usable form? And how are you supposed to make sense of things when you download *one* file and windup with *three* on your desktop?

Problem 1: It's encoded

Almost everything on America Online and the Internet has been especially encoded into a compact format that takes less time to transfer. Despite the inconvenience you're about to read about, you'll eventually appreciate this feature. You can think of the downloading time you save as a result as free minutes tacked onto the end of your life.

You can tell that you've downloaded a compressed file by the final letters of its name, which may be *.sit* (it's been "stuffed" using a program called StuffIt), *.zip* (it's been compressed using a Windows PC), or *.tar* or *.gz* (it's been compressed by a Unix computer).

StuffIt Expander: Free and easy

If your downloaded files decompress and turn into disk images automatically, you have two backstage programs to thank.

First, the program that's responsible for automatically decompressing your files is StuffIt Expander. It's free, thank heaven, and already on board your iMac — in your Applications folder. In general, you can ignore it, because it does its magic behind the scenes and automatically.

This little program can gracefully re-expand just about any geeky Internet file, from *.sit* to *.cpt* and *.hqx*, along with such all-time favorites as *.gz, .z, .ARC, .ZIP,* and *.uu* files, too.

But all StuffIt Expander can do is turn *.gz, .z, .ARC, .ZIP,* and *.uu* files back into ordinary files — which sometimes means those disk images. Now you need a program that can turn disk images into simulated disks on your desktop. And that's why Apple has given you *Disk Copy,* yet another utility program (this one's in your Applications folder, in the Utilities folder).

The only time you'll ever need to know about Disk Copy is when you download some file whose name ends with *.dmg* — and you don't know what to do with it. The answer: Drag its icon *on top of* the Disk Copy program's icon. The *.dmg* file will magically turn into a floppy-disk icon on your screen.

Here's the great news: As an added convenience, both America Online and Internet Explorer unstuff these files *automatically* when you log off the service.

But here's the bad news: It *leaves behind* the original compressed file on your desktop. More on this in a moment.

Problem 2: It's a disk image

After you decompress a program you've downloaded, it still may not be usable. You may now wind up with a file whose name ends in *.dmg.*

Now you've got yourself a *disk image,* which is a simulated CD or floppy disk, containing an installer for the program you downloaded.

Once you've unstuffed (or untarred) a downloaded program, it often takes the form of a disk image, whose name ends with the letters *.dmg.* All you have to do is double-click the .dmg icon. After a moment, it magically turns into a floppy-drive icon on your desktop, which you can work with just as though it's a real disk. *Finally,* you've found the icon that actually contains the software you thought you were downloading.

Here's a step-by-step example.

Phase 1:
Your downloaded goodies probably
resemble one of these compressed files.

Phase 2:
Your Mac automatically turns the
compressed file into a "disk image."
Double-click it.

Phase 3:
The disk image turns into a phantom
floppy disk. Double-click it.

Phase 4:
At last, you see the actual software you
intended to download. It's sometimes
a file that you can drag to your hard drive
or Home folder, and sometimes an
installer that you double-click to begin.

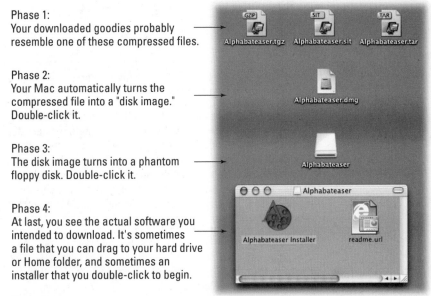

Phase 5:
After the installation, you can discard the files from Phases 1 and 3. You may want to hang
onto the Phase 2 (.dmg) file, though, in case you ever want to install the software again.

When you're finished working with the simulated floppy drive, you can
remove it from your desktop by pressing the Eject key on your keyboard,
dragging it to the Trash (whose icon turns into a big silver Eject key as you
drag), or highlighting it and choosing Eject from the File menu. (You've still
got the original .dmg file you downloaded, so you're not really saying good-
bye to the disk image forever.)

Problem 3: Wrong format

Bill Gates, as you may have heard, is the wealthiest human being in the history of everything. He got that way by foisting something called Windows
onto all the office computers of the world.

Fortunately, you've got something that works better: an iMac. Unfortunately,
sooner or later, you'll encounter files on the Internet intended for Windows
people — or files that are meant to be used by *both* Macintosh and Windows.
In both cases, you may be befuddled.

The giveaway is the three-letter suffix at the end of a downloaded file's name. As described in the previous section, suffixes like *.sit, .hqx, .zip, .uu,* and others mean that the file is compressed. But sometimes, even *after* being decompressed, a three-letter suffix remains, such as the common ones revealed in this table:

Suffix	How to Open It
.doc	You've got yourself a Microsoft Word file, the most common word-processing format in the world.
	If you *have* Microsoft Word (you'd probably remember having spent $300 for it), double-clicking a .doc file opens it automatically. If not, double-clicking this kind of document opens into AppleWorks, described in Chapter 9. (If you get, instead, a dialog box that says, "There is no application available to open this document," click the Choose Application button, and then navigate to, and choose, the AppleWorks 6 program. The iMac will convert the Microsoft Word file into AppleWorks format automatically.)
.exe	An *executable* file — in other words, a Windows program. By itself, your iMac can't run Windows programs, just as Windows computers can't run Macintosh programs. All is not lost, however: If you buy and install a program like VirtualPC (*www.connectix.com*), your iMac *can* run Windows programs.
.jpg or .gif	You've downloaded yourself a photograph! When you double-click it, it will open up into the iMac's little picture-viewer program called Preview.
	If you want to make changes to the photo, you need a photo-*editing* program like Photoshop or even AppleWorks.
.pdf	This downloaded item is probably a manual or brochure. It came to you as a *portable document format* file, better known as an Adobe Acrobat file. To open it, you need a free program called Acrobat Reader. Lucky you: This program, too, came with your iMac. It's in the Utilities folder, in your Applications folder, although you probably won't ever have to worry about that; just double-clicking a file whose name ends with *.pdf* should open the Acrobat Reader program automatically and show you its contents.
.html	A file whose name ends in *.html* or *.htm* is a Web page. In general, Web pages hang out only on the Internet. Every now and then, however, you may find that you've downloaded one to your iMac's hard drive. When you double-click it, Internet Explorer, the Web browser, opens automatically and shows it to you.

The Internet as Giant Backup Disk

As described in Chapter 4, *backing up* means making a safety copy of your work. Some iMac fans buy disk drives for this purpose. Others burn CDs or send files to themselves as e-mail attachments (see Chapter 8). But one of the cheapest and most convenient ways to back up your iMac is to use the *iDisk,* which is a simulated backup disk that Apple has given you as a thoughtful bonus gift.

If you'd like to have a look at yours, here's how to go about it.

1. **Open System Preferences (click the light-switch icon on your Dock), and in the System Preferences window, click Internet.**

   You see a screen like this:

2. **Click Sign Up.**

   Your iMac goes online, if it wasn't already, fires up Internet Explorer, and takes you to a special iTools "Getting Started" Web page.

Apple may change the signup ritual from time to time, but it probably goes something like this:

3. Click the big red Start button.

Internet Explorer automatically downloads a program called iTools Installer onto your desktop. Hide Internet Explorer, if you like (choose Hide Explorer from the Explorer menu), and then go on.

4. Double-click the iTools Installer icon on your desktop.

The iMac whirs for a minute and installs some software. When it's finished, you go back to Internet Explorer, where you see an application form.

5. Fill in your name, address, a screen name and password you'd like to use, and so on.

Remember: You can press the Tab key to jump from box to box.

6. Click Continue when you're finished.

If the nickname you made up is already in use, you'll be asked to choose a different one. Finally, you arrive at a summary screen. Quit Internet Explorer, if you like. You can also throw away the iTools Installer icon on your desktop.

System Preferences is probably still open behind it, waiting for you to fill in your iTools Member Name and password.

7. Fill in your newly created iTools nickname and password, and then close the System Preferences window.

Your iDisk is ready to use!

Now, when you want to back up some files from your iMac, go online, open the Go menu, and choose iDisk. After a while — sometimes a *long* while —

you'll see a special disk icon appear at the right side of your screen, and a window showing its folder contents, like this:

The folders include a mirror image of the folders in your own Home folder — Documents, Music, Pictures, and so on. You'll also find a Software folder, which is filled with great Mac OS X-compatible programs for you to try. There's even something called a Public folder. It's a handy convenience: Anything you put in here can be downloaded by other Mac fans — people who themselves have signed up for free iTools accounts — without your having to tell them your password. (Tell them to go to *www.apple.com/itools,* sign in with their *own* name and password, click the iDisk icon, and then type *your* account name into the Open Public Folder box.)

To back up some files from your hard drive, just drag them into one of those folders. You can't drag stuff onto the iDisk icon itself, nor loose in its window — only into one of the *folders* on it. Remember, too, that the iDisk holds only 20 megabytes of your stuff. That's plenty for word-processing files, graphics, and so on, but probably not enough for movies.

Copying files to the iDisk takes a long, long time; it's times like these that make you glad you keep a stack of magazines next to the computer. Sooner or later, though, the job is done. You can sleep well, secure in the knowledge that even if your iMac blows up, your house gets razed to the ground, and your entire neighborhood gets swallowed up by a sinkhole, your files are safe, thousands of miles away on one of Apple's computers.

(If all of that actually *happens* to you, by the way, just open the folders on your iDisk and copy your stuff back *into* your Home folder.)

When you're finished performing your backup, drag the iDisk crystal-ball icon to the Trash.

Top Ten Best/Worst Aspects of the Net

No question: The Internet is changing everything. If you're not on it now, you probably will be within a few years. Here's what to look forward to:

1. Best: Everyone is anonymous, so everyone is equal. It doesn't matter what you look, sound, or smell like — you're judged purely by your words.

2. Worst: Everyone is anonymous, so everyone is equal. You can pretend to be someone you're not — or a *gender* you're not — for the purposes of misleading other Internet surfers.

3. Best: The cost — $20 a month for unlimited access, or about twice as much for a high-speed connection like a cable modem or DSL.

4. Worst: That's a lot of money.

5. Best: The Internet connects you to everyone. You're only an e-mail or a Web page away from anyone else on the planet.

6. Worst: The Internet *disconnects* you from everyone. You become a hermit holed up in your room, as family, friends, and relationships pack up and leave.

7. Best: The Internet is drawing people away from TV. Statistics show that as more people discover the Web, they spend less time in front of the boob tube.

8. Worst: The Internet is drawing people away from TV. The TV industry is going crazy wondering what to do.

9. Best: The Internet is complete freedom of speech for everyone. No government agency looks over your shoulder; the Net is completely unsupervised and uncontrolled.

10. Worst: The Internet is complete freedom of speech for everyone, including pornographers, neo-Nazi groups, and others you may not want your 10-year-old getting chummy with.

Chapter 7

The Weird Wide Web

In This Chapter

▶ The who, where, what, and why of the World Wide Web

▶ Microsoft Internet Explorer

▶ Tips and tricks for faster, better, cookie-free browsing

*T*he most popular part of the Internet is the World Wide Web — you can't help hearing about this thing. Fourth graders run around urging schoolmates to "check out their Web pages." Web addresses show up everywhere — on business cards, in newspaper ads, on TV. (Have you noticed *www.sony.com* or *www.spam.com* flashing by at the end of movie ads and car commercials? Those are Web addresses.)

The Web has become incredibly popular for one simple reason: It *isn't* geeky and user-hostile, like the rest of the Internet. It looks friendly and familiar to actual humans. When you connect to the Web, you don't encounter streams of computer codes. Instead, information is displayed attractively, with nice typesetting, color pictures, and interactive buttons.

Getting to the Web via America Online

To get to the Web once you're online with America Online, choose "Go to the Web" from the Internet icon, as shown here.

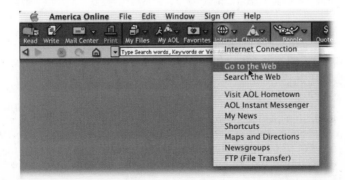

If you've been given a particular Web address to visit (such as *www.hamsters. com*), you can also treat it as a keyword. That is, type in that Web address into the Keyword box (or the strip at the top of the AOL screen). When you press Enter or Return, it'll automatically open up a Web window and take you to the appropriate page.

Getting to the Web via an ISP

If you've signed up for a direct Internet account (such as EarthLink, as described in Chapter 6) instead of America Online, you'll be using a special program for browsing the Web — called, with astounding originality, a *Web browser*.

There are several good ones kicking around out there — Netscape Navigator, iCab, Opera — but the one that came installed on your iMac, and the one that most people use, is Microsoft Internet Explorer.

To go a-browsing, launch your Web browser. (It's the big lowercase *e* logo on your Dock, and it's also in your Applications folder.) If you have, in fact, signed up for an Internet account (see Chapter 6), the iMac dials the phone automatically, hisses and shrieks, and finally shows you a Web page.

Internet Made Idiotproof: Link-Clicking

Navigating the Web requires little more than clicking buttons and those underlined blue phrases, which you can sort of see in the following figure.

When you click an underlined phrase, called a *link,* you're automatically transported from one Web page (screen) to another, without having to type in the usual bunch of Internet codes. One page may be a glorified advertisement; another may contain critical information about a bill in Congress; another might have been created by a nine-year-old in Dallas, to document what her dog had for lunch.

Unfortunately, all of this amazing online multimedia stuff stresses your modem nearly to the breaking point. Even with your iMac's 56 Kbps modem, the fastest standard modem there is, you still wait five or ten seconds for each Web page to float onto your screen.

That's why more and more people are signing up (and ponying up) for *cable modems,* provided by your cable TV company, or *DSL* service, provided by your phone company. Each is a box that not only delivers the Internet at 50 times the speed of a dial-up modem, but is online all the time. You're spared the minute of connecting and disconnecting before and after each Web or e-mail session.

Where to Go, What to Do on the Web

Once you're staring at your first Web page — whether via America Online or an Internet access company — getting around is easy. Just *look* at all the fun things to see and do on the Web!

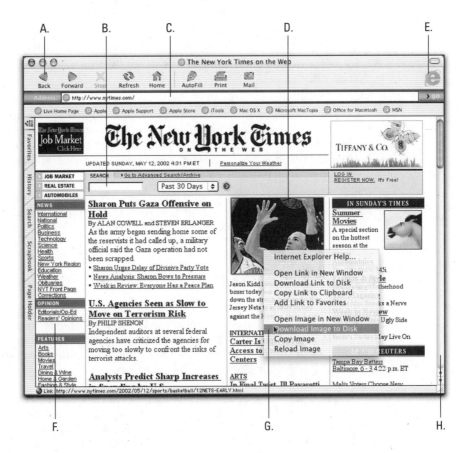

A. Click the Back button to revisit the page you were just on — or the Forward button to return to the page you were on *before* you clicked the Back button. (Does that make sense?)

B. Click in a Search blank and type what you're looking for. (Click the Search or > button when you're finished typing.) Similar blanks appear when, for example, you're asked to fill out a survey, type in your mailing address, and so on.

C. Type a new Web page address into the thin horizontal strip at the top of the browser window and press Return to go to the site. A Web address, just so you know, is known by the nerds as a *URL* — pronounced "U. R. L."

And where do you find good Web addresses? From friends, from articles, on television, and so on. Look for *http://* or *www* at the beginning of the address — a guaranteed sign that the address points to a Web page.

D. Clicking a picture or a button often takes you to a new Web page.

E. Enjoy the little animated Internet Explorer logo in the upper-right corner. It means "Wait a sec, I'm not done painting this Web page picture for you. As long as I'm animating, you'll just have to wait."

F. Clicking blue underlined phrases (called *links*) *always* takes you to a different Web page. (As a handy bonus, these links change to some other color when you see them next. That's to remind you that you've been that way before.)

G. When you see a picture you'd like to keep, point to it, hold down the mouse button, and watch for a pop-up menu to appear at your cursor tip. From this pop-up menu, choose "Save this Image As" (in Navigator) or "Download Image to Disk" (in Explorer). After you click the Save button, the result is a new icon on your hard drive — a graphics file containing the picture you saved.

H. Use the scroll bar to move up and down the page — or to save mousing, just press the space bar each time you want to see more. (If that space bar trick doesn't work, first click any blank area of the Web page.)

Ways to search for a particular topic

Suppose you're looking at the Kickboxing Haiku Web page. But now you want to check the weather in Detroit. Because the World Wide Web is indeed a big interconnected web, you could theoretically work your way from one Web page to another to another, clicking just the proper blue underlined links, until you finally arrived at the Detroit Weather page.

Unfortunately, there are several hundred million Web pages. By the time you actually arrived at the Detroit Weather page, the weather would certainly have changed (not to mention Detroit). Clearly, you need to be able to *look something up* — to jump directly to another Web page whose address you don't currently know.

For this purpose, the denizens of the Web have seen fit to create a few very special Web pages whose sole function is to search all the *other* Web pages. If you're on the Web, and don't know where to look for, say, information about Venezuelan Beaver Cheese, you can use the Find commands at sites like these:

- *www.google.com*
- *www.yahoo.com*
- *www.altavista.com*

All of these search pages work alike, but most people find Google to be the fastest and most accurate. Here, for example, is what it would look like if you used Google to find information about dolphins.

After clicking the Search button, you'd be shown a brand-new Web page listing *hits* — that is, Web pages containing the word "dolphin."

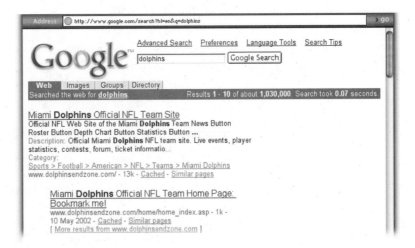

See how useful a search page is? This handy Google thing narrowed down our search to a mere *1,030,000 Web pages!* You're as good as home!

Not. You can see here, in a nutshell, the problem with the Web: There's so much darned stuff out there, you spend an *awful* lot of your time trying to find exactly what you want. In this case, most of the matches you've found have to do with the *Miami* Dolphins football team — probably not exactly what your Marine Mammals 101 instructor had in mind.

In this case, you probably should have clicked the little Search Tips button on the main Google screen. It would have told you that to find a page containing the word "dolphins" *without* "Miami," you should have put a minus sign just before the word Miami, like this: *dolphins –Miami.* That would have ruled out all the "hits" containing "Miami."

Who ever said these things were user-friendly?

Searching using Sherlock

When trying to locate a certain piece of information on the Web, most of the world's citizens use a searching Web page like Google or Yahoo. As a Mac owner, however, you are more fortunate. You can search for stuff on the Web exactly the way you search for files on your own hard drive: by using the machine's built-in Find feature, better known as Sherlock.

Searching the Web

It works exactly the way you'd expect: Click the Sherlock icon on your Dock (the detective-hat-and-magnifying-glass icon). When the Sherlock window opens, click the globe icon, which looks like this:

As you'll quickly discover, an advertisement appears at the bottom of this window. On one hand, you may find that the ad slightly dampens the pure giddy joy of searching the Web with such ease. On the other hand, now you know why the Sherlock service is free.

In the lower part of the window, you'll see an assortment of *search engines* (geek-speak for "Web pages that search the Internet"). If you were stranded in a desert condominium without Sherlock, you'd have to search each of these Web sites individually. Thanks to Sherlock, however, you can search several search engines simultaneously for a certain morsel of info. Just turn on the appropriate checkboxes, as shown in the illustration above.

Type what you're looking for — in plain English — and then click the green magnifying-glass icon (or press Enter or Return).

Your iMac now connects to the Internet (if it wasn't already online), sends your request to the search engines you selected, and displays, in a new window, a list of Web pages that match your search, like this:

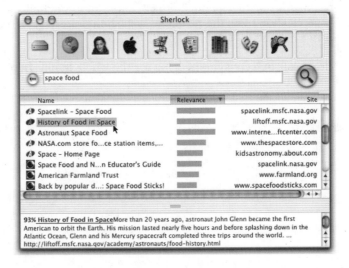

At this point, you can proceed in any of several ways:

- ✔ Click one of the results *once* to read, in the lower pane of the window, the first several lines' worth of text from that Web page. Doing so gives you a quick insight into whether or not the Web site Sherlock turned up is actually what you were looking for.

- ✔ *Double-click* one of the results to launch Internet Explorer, which opens directly to the corresponding Web page.

- ✔ Drag a row of the results directly out of the window and onto your desktop, strange as that gesture may feel.

  The iMac automatically creates an icon on your desktop. At any time in the future, you can double-click this icon to open the corresponding Web page. *Handy hint:* Create a folder full of these icons, each representing one of your favorite Web sites. Leave this folder either sitting on your desktop for easy access — or better yet, drag it to your Dock for quick and easy access at any time.

Specialized Web searches

Each icon button at the top of the window searches the Internet for a different *kind* of information. (Apple calls these icon buttons *channels;* I call them *icon buttons.*) When you click the twentysomething brunette's head, for example, you can actually type in a person's name; Sherlock searches the Internet for that person's e-mail address or phone number. (In theory, this icon button gives you a worldwide White Pages right on your screen. In practice, Sherlock often comes up empty-handed. Could be that it's wired only to find twentysomething brunettes.)

Another example: Click the shopping cart button to search shopping Web sites for a particular item. Note, as you click the various icon buttons, that the columns of information in the results window actually change. When Sherlock shows you the results of Web shopping sites, for example, you get a Price column that doesn't normally appear.

Sherlock 2, in fact, is hours of fun for the whole family. Here's what each of the icon buttons does:

Search your hard drive

Search for phone numbers and e-mail addresses

Search shopping and auction sites

Search dictionaries and encyclopedias

Make your own collection of search sites (by dragging checkboxes here from the other "channels")

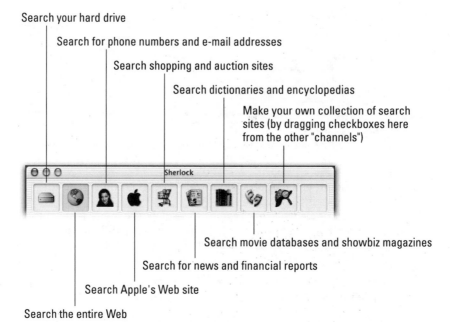

Search movie databases and showbiz magazines

Search for news and financial reports

Search Apple's Web site

Search the entire Web

When you click the rightmost (Sherlock hat) icon, you get an empty list of Web search pages. That's because this "channel" is one that you're supposed to build yourself. Click the News icon button, for example; *drag* the CNN item in the checkbox list up and to the right, until your cursor is _on top of_ the Sherlock hat. You've just installed that search page onto your very own customizable list.

Useful Web pages: The tip of the iceberg

But there's more to the Web than getting meaningful work done, as millions of American office workers can attest. Here are some good starting places for your leisure hours.

Note, by the way, that their addresses generally begin with _http://www_ and end with _.com._ But anyone who actually takes the time to type all that is a sucker. Whenever you spot an address that takes that form, all you have to type into your browser is the _middle_ section, omitting the _http://www_ and _.com_ portions. Internet Explorer supplies those letters automatically when you press Enter.

(**_Disclaimer:_** Web pages come and go like New York City restaurants. I guarantee only that these pages existed the day I typed them up.)

- _www.louvre.fr_ — The Louvre museum home page, where you can actually view and read about hundreds of paintings hanging there.

- _amazon.com_ — An enormous online bookstore, with five million books available, most at a 30 percent discount. Reviews, sample chapters, the works. Don't freak out about typing in your credit-card number online; you're far more likely to be ripped off by handing your Visa card to the gas-station attendant or restaurant waiter.

- _www.dilbert.com_ — Today's Dilbert cartoon. And a month of past issues.

- _www.clicktv.com_ — Free TV listings for your exact area or cable company. You can customize it to color-code various kinds of shows, to hide the channels you don't want, and so on.

- _www.shopper.com, www.dealtime.com, www.mysimon.com_ — Comparison-shopping sites that produce a list of Web sites that sell the particular book, computer gadget, PalmPilot, or other consumer good you're looking for. This quick, simple research can save you a _lot_ of money.

- _efax.com_ — An amazing free service that gives you a private fax number. When anybody sends a fax to your number, it's automatically sent to you by _e-mail._ You read it on your iMac screen with a special free program called EfaxMac, delighted that you've saved the cost of a fax machine, phone line, paper, ink cartridges, and the Brazilian rain forest.

- _http://terraserver.microsoft.com_ — Satellite photographs of everywhere (your tax dollars at work). Find your house!

- ✔ *www.yourdictionary.com* — A web of online dictionaries.

- ✔ *www.homefair.com/homefair/cmr/salcalc.html* — The International Salary Calculator.

- ✔ *www.imdb.com* — The Internet Movie Database: an astoundingly complete database of almost every movie ever made, including cast lists, awards, and reviews by the citizens of the Internet.

- ✔ *www.____.com* — Fill in the blank with your favorite major company: Microsoft, Apple, Honda, Sony, CBS, Palm, Symantec, NYTimes, Disney, DavidPogue, and so on. If it's a big company, you can probably guess its Internet address.

Internet Explorer Tip-O-Rama

If that tip about leaving off the *http://www* and *.com* business left you patting moist towelettes onto your forehead, you'll really love these other browser tips.

More address shortcuts

When you begin to type into the Address bar, Internet Explorer's AutoComplete feature compares what you're typing against a list of Web sites you've recently visited, and displays a list of Web addresses that seem to match what you're typing, like this:

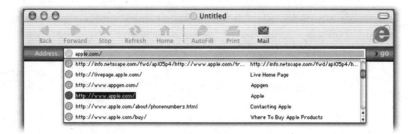

To spare yourself the tedium of typing out the whole thing, just click the correct complete address with your mouse, or use the down arrow key to reach the desired listing and then press Enter. The complete address you selected then pops into the Address bar.

Even less typing

Internet Explorer can also remember user names, passwords, and other information you have to type into Web page text boxes *(forms)* over and over again.

From the Explorer menu, choose Preferences, and then click the AutoFill Profile icon at the left side. Then fill in your name, address, and so on. Click OK when you're finished.

Next time some Web site is staring you in the face, asking for you to type in your information for the 11,000th time, just choose AutoFill Forms from the Tools menu. *Bam* — Internet Explorer fills in all the blanks, like this:

Go get the plug-in

Web browsers can show you text and pictures. But every now and then, you'll stumble onto some page where a *sound* or a *movie* is the main attraction. Unfortunately, Internet Explorer doesn't know how to play these multimedia morsels — but they know somebody who does!

What I'm driving at is *plug-ins* — small add-on programs that, after installed in the Plug-Ins folder on your hard drive, teach Explorer how to play those extra goodies like sounds and movies. Plug-ins are free; you just must know where to go to get them on the Web. Lucky you: I'm about to tell you.

Go to the Web address *www.plugins.com*. There you'll find all the little plug-ins looking for a home on your iMac. The ones you'll need most often are the Real plug-in (for listening to Internet radio broadcasts), which you can also get from *www.real.com,* and the Shockwave Player plug-in (for animations and games), which is at *www.macromedia.com.*

I'm not saying you can't live a long, healthy, fulfilling life without any of this stuff. I'm just pointing them out in case you try to visit some Web page and get nothing but an error message saying something like, "Sorry, you can't visit this page until you spend all afternoon downloading and installing Such-N-Such plug-in."

Where's home for you?

Every time you sign onto the Web, your browser starts by showing you the same darned starting page — let me guess: a very complex and daunting-looking Apple page. Wouldn't it be great if you could change the startup page?

You can! From the Explorer menu, choose Preferences. Click the icon at the left side of the screen that says Browser Display, as shown here.

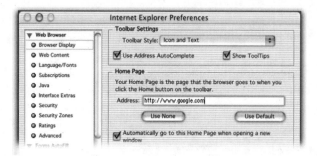

Now just change the Web address in the Home blank to a more desirable starting point. For example, you might prefer *www.dilbert.com*, which is a daily comic strip . . . or *www.macintouch.com*, which is daily news about the Mac . . . or even your own home page, if you've made one.

Faster — please, make it faster!

If the slug-like speed of the Web is making you sob quietly into your late-night coffee, despair no more. You can quadruple the speed of your Web surfing activities — *by turning off the pictures.*

Yes, I realize that graphics are what make the Web look so compelling. But all those pictures are 90 percent of what takes Web pages so darned long to arrive on the screen! You owe it to yourself to try, just for a session or two, turning graphics *off*. You still get fully laid-out Web pages; you still see all the text and headlines. But wherever a picture would normally be — wherever you would have had to wait for eight seconds — you'll see an empty rectangle containing a generic "graphic goes here" logo, often with a label that tells you what picture belongs there. Here, for example, is the CNN page (*www.cnn.com*, of course) with all its graphics gone. See? It's really not so bad.

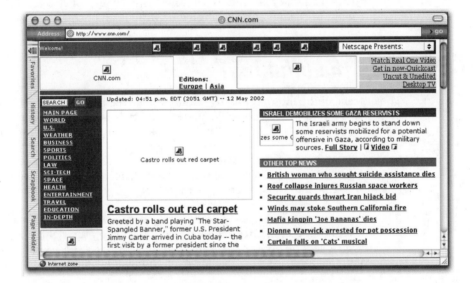

If you like the sound of this arrangement, here's how to make it so. From the Explorer menu, choose Preferences. Click the words Web Content (at the left side of the list) and then turn off Show Pictures.

The speed you gain is incredible. And if you wind up on a Web page that seems naked and shivering without its pictures, you can choose to summon them all — just on this one page — by choosing Load Images from the View menu.

Bookmark it

When you find a Web page you might like to visit again, you're not condemned to writing the address on the edges of your monitor, like some kind of geeky bathroom graffiti. Instead, just choose Add Page to Favorites from the Favorites menu (or press its keyboard shortcut, ⌘-D).

You're rewarded by the plain-English appearance of that page's name in the Favorites menu! Thereafter, the *next* time you want to visit that page, you're spared having to remember *http://www.madonnahairstyles.com* or whatever; you can just choose the page's name from your Favorites menu.

To get *rid* of something in your Favorites menu, choose Organize Favorites from the Favorites menu itself. Click the little bullseye next to a page's name (*not* the name itself), and then press the Delete key. Click OK to confirm that you're sure.

While this bookmark-organization window is open, you can also rearrange (by dragging) or rename (by clicking) your various favorites.

Stop the blinking!

The citizens of the Internet quietly endure the advertising that fills the top inch of almost every Web page. We understand these ads pay for our free TV listings, free *New York Times,* free Internet backup storage, and so on.

But there's a big difference between a calm banner across the top of the screen and a seizure-inducing, blinking, flashing, looping, *animated* advertisement that's so distracting, you can't read the actual Web page itself.

If blinking ads make you, too, itch for a sledgehammer, choose Preferences from the Explorer menu. Click the Web Content icon; on the right side of the screen, you'll see the options for Animated GIFs. Turn off the Looping option to prevent animated ads from cycling over and over again; turn off Animated GIFs to play *no* animated ads.

Open a new window

Usually, clicking a link is like changing the TV channel: A new image fills the same window you've been watching.

If you click a link while pressing the ⌘ key, however, you open up a *second* browser window in front of the first. That's an especially useful tactic when you're browsing a list of Web sites — the results of a search, for example — that you want to investigate one by one. Just ⌘-click the first one to open it into a new window; check it out; then close that window to return to the one containing your list. ⌘-click the second one in the list, and so on.

The Complete Cookie Cookbook

Spend enough time in the 21st century, and you're bound to hear people talk about their fear of *cookies*. Unless they're avid dieters, they're probably talking about *Web* cookies.

Cookies are something like Web page preference files. Commercial Web sites (Amazon.com, for example) deposit these tiny, mostly invisible preferences onto your hard drive, so that they'll remember your name, address, and other information the next time you visit. If Amazon.com greets you, "Welcome, Rhoda!" (or whatever your name is), you have a cookie to thank.

Most cookies are perfectly innocuous — and, in fact, are extremely helpful, because they spare you the effort of having to type in your name, address, credit card number, and so on, every single time you visit these Web sites.

But in this age of privacy paranoia, plenty of people worry that sinister cookies may be tracking your movement on the Web. If you're worried, Internet Explorer is ready to protect you.

In Internet Explorer, choose Preferences from the Explorer menu, and then click the Cookies button at the left side. The "When receiving cookies" pop-up menu lets you control just how careful you want to be: You can choose "Never ask" (accept *all* cookies), "Ask for each site" (ask once per Web site), "Ask for each cookie" (ask permission to download each individual cookie), or "Never accept."

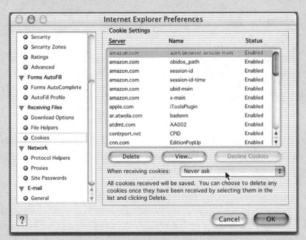

If you choose "Never accept," you create an acrylic shield around your iMac. No cookies can come in, and no cookie information can go out. You'll have absolute privacy, but you'll also find that the Web is a very inconvenient place, because you'll have to re-enter your information upon every visit, and some Web sites may not work properly.

Extreme browsing

All those toolbars at the top of your screen are handy, but they eat into your Web-page space like taxes into your paycheck. If you choose Collapse Toolbars from the View menu (or just press ⌘-B), though, they all retreat to the side, like this, making room for much more of the Web you're paying for:

As you can see, the important buttons like Back, Forward, and Stop are still available (as tiny icons in the upper-left corner). But if you miss the toolbars, just press ⌘-B again to bring them back.

Learn to love history — and the Scrapbook

The little "tabs" at the left edge of your browser window are handy, clickable buttons. Each produces a narrow panel filled with useful information, like this:

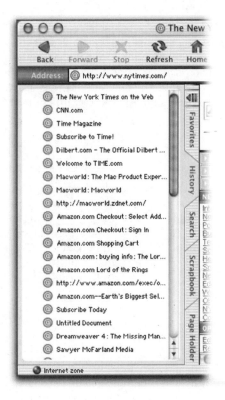

Here's what they do:

- The **Favorites** list is just a duplicate of your Favorites menu.

- The **History** list offers a handy hierarchical record of every Web site you've visited recently — and it's a great help if you can't remember the address for a Web site that you remember having visited, say, yesterday.

  To specify how far back Internet Explorer's memory goes, choose Explorer⇨Preferences. Click the Advanced icon at the left side. Change the number in the "Remember the last __ places visited" box. The more days IE tracks, the easier it is for you to refer to those addresses quickly.

  And if you find it creepy that Internet Explorer maintains a complete list of every Web site they've seen recently, right there in plain view of any family member or coworker who wanders by, click the Clear History button — and then set the "Remember the last __ places visited" number to 0. (After all, you might be nominated to the Supreme Court some day.)

✔ **Search** is yet another way to find specific Web pages. (Google is better.)

✔ **Scrapbook** is a sensational way to sock away important Web pages for future reference: receipts for stuff you order online, articles you want to save, and so on. That's important, because the Web is constantly changing, and every Internet citizen has experienced the heartbreak of finding that some important Web page has disappeared overnight.

Once the page you want to save is on the screen, open the Scrapbook tab and click the Add button. That's all there is to it. Internet Explorer stores that page, complete, somewhere on your hard drive — and whenever you want to retrieve it, just double-click its name in the Scrapbook list.

✔ **Page Holder** is a temporary holding place for pages — usually search-results pages — whose links you want to check out, one at a time. For example, suppose you've just done a search on Amazon.com for bass-fishing books. Click the Add button on this panel. Now all of the Amazon search results are listed in this panel. You can click one link at a time, visiting the corresponding page in the main portion of your window, without having to mess with the Back button or juggling multiple open windows.

Chapter 8

E-mail for He-males and Females

In This Chapter

▶ How to get, read, and write e-mail

▶ How to enjoy getting, reading, and writing e-mail

▶ The Anti-Junk-Mail Handbook

*I*f you have any intention of getting the most from your expensive high-tech appliance, you *gotta* get into e-mail. E-mail has all the advantages of the telephone (instantaneous, personal) with none of the disadvantages (interrupts dinner, wakes you up). It also has all the advantages of postal mail (cheap, written, preservable) with none of its drawbacks (slow speed, paper cuts).

Chapter 6 covers the glorious world of e-mail on America Online. If you're on the Internet courtesy of an Internet access company (an ISP) like EarthLink, however, read on.

Getting into E-Mail

To read and write electronic mail, you need an e-mail *program*. A free Apple program called Mail, for example, is sitting right there on your iMac's hard drive (in the Applications folder), and its icon already appears on your Dock. Your Web browser (Internet Explorer) also includes a Mail function, but Mail is a much superior e-mail program.

The grisliest part of joining the e-mail revolution is setting up your account for the first time. The good news is that if you signed up for an EarthLink account using the automatic set up program described in Chapter 6, all the blanks should be filled in for you. You're all ready to go a-mailing.

If you *didn't* use that automated setup program before trying to use Mail, the program asks you to fill in a bunch of evil-looking blanks — things like SMTP Server, POP3 Server, and so on — the first time you open it. Don't say I didn't warn you. Call up your ISP company and ask for help filling them in.

After asking you to fill in the blanks, Mail offers to import your e-mail collection from whatever e-mail program you used to use. In your case, that may be a courteous but irrelevant request; you probably *have* no previous e-mail collection on this iMac. Click the No button.

At last you arrive at the main Mail screen, which looks something like this:

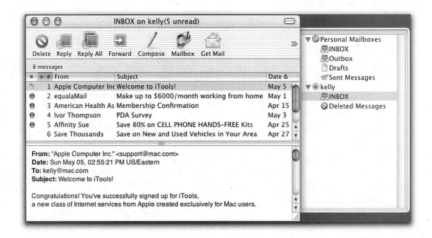

Sending e-mail

To write an e-mail, click the Compose (pencil) icon on the toolbar. An empty e-mail message appears, filled with blanks to fill out. (The To, Subject, and message areas are the only mandatory ones.) Here's how to fill them out, keeping in mind that, as anywhere else on the Mac, you can press the Tab key to jump from box to box:

These people get copies.

This person gets the message.

Click here when you're finished.

Click here to save this, without sending it yet, into your Drafts "mailbox."

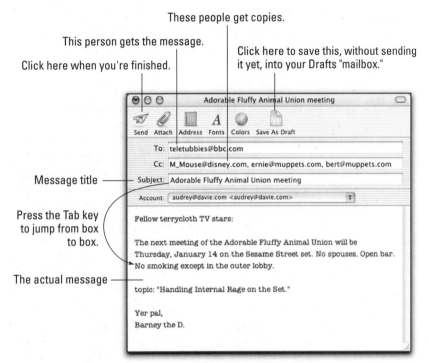

Message title

Press the Tab key to jump from box to box.

The actual message

1. **Type the e-mail address of the recipient into the To field.**

   If you want to send this message to more than one person, separate their addresses with commas: *sarah@earthlink.net, billg@microsoft.com, george@bush.com*. As you'll quickly discover, e-mail addresses can't include any spaces, always have an @ symbol in them, and must be typed *exactly* right, even if they look like *cc293fil@univ_amx.intermp.com*. Capitals don't matter.

   You don't have to remember and type those addresses, either. If somebody is in your address book (click the Address book icon on the toolbar), just type the first couple letters of his name; Mail automatically completes the address. (If the first guess is wrong, just type another letter or two until Mail revises its proposal.)

2. **To send a copy of the message to other recipients, enter the e-mail address(es) in the Cc field.**

   Cc stands for *carbon copy*. Getting an e-mail message where your name is in the Cc line implies: "I sent you a copy because I thought you'd want to know about this correspondence, but I'm not expecting you to reply."

3. Type the topic of the message in the Subject field.

To demonstrate your fine breeding and etiquette, put 1.5 seconds of thought into the Subject line. Use "You left your gloves here" instead of "Yo," for example.

4. Specify an e-mail format.

There are two kinds of e-mail: *plain text* and *formatted* (which Mail calls Rich Text). Plain text messages are faster to send and open, are universally compatible with the world's e-mail programs, and are greatly preferred by many veteran computer fans.

Formatted messages, for their part, take longer to download, take longer to open, and introduced the risk that you might design something tacky looking.

To control which kind of mail you're about to send, open the Format menu and choose either Make Plain Text or Make Rich Text. (You can also tell Mail what you'd like to use most of the time. From the Mail menu, choose Preferences. Click the Composing icon, and make a selection from the "Default message format" pop-up menu.)

5. Enter the message in the message box.

You can use all the standard editing techniques, including text drag-and-drop, the Copy and Paste commands, and so on. If you selected the Rich Text style of e-mail, you can even use the Fonts and Colors button to dress up the message, like this — well, *not* like this:

As you type, Mail checks your spelling, using a dotted underline to mark questionable words. Fortunately, you're not expected to know the correct spelling — the computer is perfectly happy to supply that for you. While pressing the Control key, click the underlined word; a list of suggestions appears in the resulting pop-up menu. Click the word you really intended.

6. **Attach any files that you want to send along for the ride.**

    Fortunately, there's more to e-mail than just sending typed messages back and forth. You can also send files from your hard drive — in the form of *attachments* to your e-mail messages. Companies use this method to exchange design sketches, movie clips, and spreadsheets. Authors turn in chapters (written in Microsoft Word or AppleWorks) to publishers this way. And families send baby pictures this way, to the eternal boredom of most recipients.

    To pull this off, make sure that your message makes reference to the attachment, so that your recipient doesn't miss it (for example: "By the way, I've attached an AppleWorks file. It's a drawing little Cindy did of a tobacco-company executive in a paroxysm of self-loathing and doubt.").

    Then locate the icon of the file you want to send — in your Home folder, for example. This may entail adjusting the windows on your screen so that you can see *both* your e-mail message *and* the icon of the file you want to send, like this.

Alternatively, click the Attach icon on the toolbar. The usual Open File dialog box appears, so that you can navigate your hard drive and find the files you want to include. As in the preceding figure, the icons show up at the bottom of the window to indicate that your dragging was successful.

(Caution: Don't attach big files like movies or photos that you haven't manually scaled down to a smaller size, as described in Chapter 10. Files like these are too big to send, and too big to receive — you'll probably spend half an hour waiting for them to upload, only to find that your recipient never even got them. Instead, you'll receive an error message by e-mail telling you that you overwhelmed the size limitations of that person's e-mail box.)

7. **Click Send (the paper-airplane icon on the toolbar).**

If everything's set up right, your modem now dials, connects to the Internet, and sends your e-message.

Sending files to Windows people

As you may have heard, Windows is a more technical computer system than Macintosh. Therefore, the following discussion is by far the most technical one in this book. Fear not, however: This page has been reinforced with invisible microfilaments for added strength.

When you're sending files to Windows PCs, you have to worry about three conditions. First, *you must send a file Windows can open.* Just as Betamax VCRs can't play VHS tapes, so Windows programs can't always open files from your iMac. Here are some kinds of files that Windows *can* open: documents created by Microsoft Word, Excel, or PowerPoint; graphics in JPEG or GIF formats; Web pages (.html or .htm to files) you've created or downloaded; FileMaker and Photoshop files; and other files where the same application is sold in both Macintosh and Windows formats.

Windows PCs probably *can't* open AppleWorks documents, by the way. If you want to send an AppleWorks document, convert it to Microsoft Word format before sending. To do that, choose Save As from the File menu in AppleWorks; from the File Format pop-up menu, choose "Word Windows 97, 2000, XP 2002" before clicking the Save button.

The second consideration is that *every file on every Windows computer has a three-letter suffix* that tells the computer what sort of file it is. Without this code, your poor suffering Windows friends won't be able to open what you send them. A Microsoft Word file might be named Thesis.doc, a photo might be called Mama.jpg, and so on.

Fortunately, every Mac OS X program automatically adds the proper three-letter suffix to the files named even though you can't see it. (Apple hides these suffixes when they're on the Mac, to avoid making the computer look too computery.) You do, however, have to worry about adding these filename suffixes when you've switched your iMac into Mac OS 9, as described in Chapter 12.

The third consideration: *You must send your file in a format Windows e-mail programs can understand.* The Internet, technically speaking, can't transmit files at all — only pure typed text. Behind the scenes, anything else that you transmit, such as photos or AppleWorks documents, must first be converted into a stream of text gibberish that's reconstructed at the other end.

Fortunately, the iMac's Mail program automatically uses an encoding scheme that both Macs and Windows PCs can understand.

America Online, unfortunately, is a different story. If you try to attach more than one file to a single outgoing message, America Online compresses them using the StuffIt format, which Windows users can't read. Your only option is to send files one at a time, making sure that the "compress Attachments" checkbox *isn't* selected after you click the Attach File icon.

Five tips for sending mail

Just sending feeble little ordinary messages is a great start, but six weeks from now, you'll surely begin to feel pangs of desire for a little further personal growth. Mastering these tips is just the ticket:

✔ If you're interrupted halfway through composing some masterful message, click the Save as Draft button on the toolbar. You've just saved the message in your Drafts folder. (The Drafts folder is in a special, side-of-the-window, slide-out panel called the mailbox drawer. To see it, click the Mailbox icon on the toolbar.) To reopen a saved draft later, click the Drafts icon in the mailbox drawer, and then click the draft that you want to work on.

✔ If it's taking you 20 minutes to write each piece of e-mail, you'll drive yourself crazy waiting for the modem to connect to the Internet over and over again, once per message. Fortunately, there's a way to write a bunch of messages without ever going online — and then send them all at once when you're good and ready.

The trick is to open up the Mailbox menu and choose Go Off line. Now, whenever you write a message and then click Send, Mail won't actually attempt to connect to the Internet. When you're finally ready to send the batch of messages you've written, choose Go Online from the Mailbox menu.

✔ A *blind carbon copy* is a secret copy, sent to a secret recipient. None of the main addressees will even be aware that your message was surreptitiously copied to a third party.

Suppose, for example, that you've addressed a message to your co-worker that says, "Frank, you seem to have fallen into the habit of pouring your unfinished soda into the vents of the computers, and I'm concerned that it may not be the best thing for the electronics." You might send a blind carbon copy to your boss, so that Frank won't think you're squealing on him.

To open up the box where you can type in a Bcc address, open the Message menu and choose Add Bcc Header. Type a secret address into the new address box that appears in your outgoing message.

✔ *Signatures* are bits of text that get stamped at the bottom of your outgoing e-mail messages. A signature may contain a name, postal address, or some cute quote from *Friends*.

To compose your signature, open the Mail menu and choose Preferences. In the resulting dialog box, click the Signatures icon. Now click the Create Signature button, which opens an editing window in which you can type your new signature (and define a name for it). Click OK when you're done.

Back in the Mail Preferences dialog box, use the Select Signature pop-up menu to choose the signature you just made. Then close the dialog box.

From now on, Mail automatically stamps that signature at the bottom of every message you write. (You can always delete the signature on a message-by-message basis — a handy feature when, for example, you're sending a message to your grandmother, and your signature is "Party hearty, dudes!")

Checking Your Mail

If the messages you send out to your friends are witty and charming enough, you may actually get a few responses.

To check your e-mail, click the Get Mail icon on the toolbar. In a spasm of shrieking, your modem then dials cyberspace's home number and fetches any waiting mail. You'll see it in a list, as shown here.

Three ways not to be loathed online

Like any foreign country, the Net has its own weird culture, including rules of e-mail etiquette that, if broken, will make nasty comments and snideness rain down upon the offender. If you want to be loved online, read up:

✔ Don't type in ALL CAPITALS. They'll *murder* you for that.

✔ Don't ask what LOL means. It stands for "laughing out loud." And while we're at it: IMHO is "in my humble opinion," ROTFL is "rolling on the floor laughing," and RTFM is "read the freakin' manual."

✔ Quote what you're responding to. If someone e-mails you with a question, don't just write back, "No, I don't think so." The question-asker may have long since forgotten his/her own query!

Instead, begin your reply with the question itself. (On the Net, people generally put this quoted portion in <brackets>, like this.) *Then* follow it with your actual answer.

Oh, yeah, one more thing: You'll see these little guys all over the place:

:-)

Turn your head 90 degrees to the left, and you'll see how it makes a little smiley face. That's to indicate, of course, the writer's facial expression (which you can't otherwise see). A thousand variants of that punctuation-face are available — and an equally large number of people who absolutely can't stand those little smileys.

Drag this divider to adjust the column width.

Click a column heading to sort the list by that criterion.

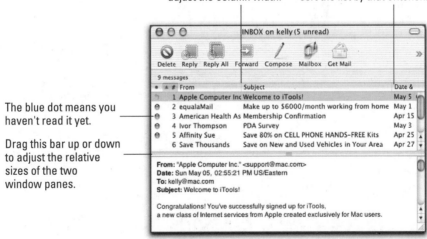

The blue dot means you haven't read it yet.

Drag this bar up or down to adjust the relative sizes of the two window panes.

As a bonus, you'll see a bright red starburst on the Mail icon on your Dock, showing the number of unread messages that await your inspection. These new messages are also indicated by what looks like colorful globs of hair gel in the main list.

To read one of your messages, just click its name once (to view the incoming memo in the lower pane of the main window) or twice (to open it into its own, larger window).

Listening to your mail

Of course, you may prefer to have your computer read your e-mail *to* you, as you sit back sipping your lemonade. To make Mail talk, hold down the Control key, click the text of the e-mail message, and, from the Speech submenu, choose Start Speaking.

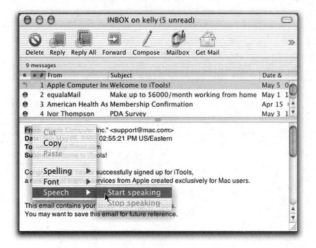

When you've had enough of the computerized voice, Control-click again, this time choosing Stop Speaking from the Speech menu. (Let's see your friends try *that* on a Windows PC!)

Processing a message you've read

When you're finished reading an e-mail, you have a number of choices:

> ✔ **Write a reply.** To do so, click the Reply button on the toolbar. Now you're back into I'm-Writing-An-E-mail-Message mode, as described ear-lier in the chapter. (Mail thoughtfully pretypes the e-mail address of the

person you're answering — along with the date, time, and subject of the message. If I had a machine that did that for my *U.S.* mail, I'd be a much better paper correspondent.)

You may notice that Mail automatically pastes the original message — the one you're answering — at the bottom of the window, denoted by brackets or lines. This common Internet technique helps your correspondent grasp what the heck you're talking about, especially since some time may have passed since he or she wrote the original note.

✔ **Forward it.** If you think somebody else in your cyber-world might be interested in reading the same message, click the Forward button at the top of the window. A new message window opens up, ready for you to address, that contains the forwarded message below the notation, "Begin forwarded message." If you like, you can type in a short note of your own above that line ("Marge — thought this might annoy you") before clicking the Send button.

✔ **File it.** If you don't see the mailbox *drawer* at the side of your main window, as shown in the following picture, click the Mailbox icon.

But once the drawer is visible, you can make new mailbox folders to hold your messages. You might create one for important messages, another for unimportant ones, and another for jokes. You can even create mailboxes *inside* these mailboxes, a feature beloved to Type A personalities worldwide.

To create a new mailbox folder, begin by clicking the mailbox in the drawer that will *contain* it. For example, click Personal Mailboxes if you want to create a new mailbox within it, or click Inbox if you want to create folders inside *it*. Now open the Mailbox menu and choose New Mailbox. The iMac asks you to title the new mailbox; once you've done so, a new icon appears in the mailbox drawer, ready for use.

Then, to move a message (or group of messages) into your newly created folder, just drag its name, like this:

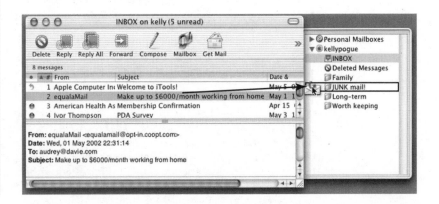

Later, whenever you want to see the contents of one of these folders, just click it.

✔ **Print it.** From the File menu, choose Print.

✔ **Add the sender to your Address Book.** If you choose, from the Message menu, Add Sender To Address Book command, Mail memorizes the e-mail address of the person whose message is on the screen. In fact, you can highlight a huge number of messages and add them all simultaneously using this technique.

Thereafter, you'll be able to write new messages to this person just by typing the first couple letters of the name. Your computer, ever humble, attempts to complete the rest of the address, saving you that much effort.

✔ **Open an attachment.** Just as you can attach files to a message, so people often send files to *you*. Only the presence of the file's icon in the message body tells you that there's something attached.

The easiest way to rescue an attached file from the message that's holding it hostage is to drag the file's icon directly out of the message window and onto any visible portion of your desktop, like this:

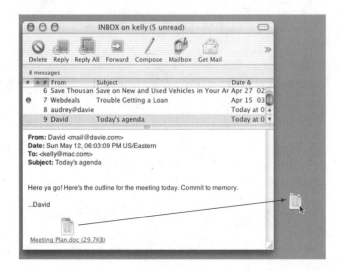

You can also double-click the attachment's icon in the message. If you were sent a document (such as a photo, Word file, Excel file, and so on), it now opens in the corresponding program (Preview, Word, Excel, or whatever). *Important:* At this point, you should *use the Save As command* in the File menu to save the file into a folder of your choice. Otherwise, your iMac won't preserve any changes you make to the document.

✔ **Trash it.** Highlight a message in the list. Press the Delete key, or click the Delete button on the toolbar, to send the message to the great cyber-shredder in the sky.

Well, sort of. Actually, you've just moved the message to the Deleted Items folder, which works like the iMac's Trash. If you like, you can click this icon to view a list of the messages you've deleted. You can even rescue some by dragging them into any other mailbox (such as right back into the Inbox).

Mail doesn't truly nuke the messages in the Deleted Items folder until you "empty the trash." To do that, open the Mailboxes menu and choose Empty Deleted messages. Alternatively, wait about a week — Mail will vaporize those messages automatically.

The Anti-Spam Handbook

No doubt about it: Unsolicited junk e-mail, better known as *spam,* is the ugly underbelly of e-mail paradise. You'll know it if you've got it — wave after wave of daily messages like "MAKE EZ MONEY AT HOME CARVING TOOTH-PICKS!" and "SEXXXY APPLIANCE REPAIRMEN WAITING FOR YOUR CALL!"

Unfortunately, we can't hunt down the lowlife scum that send out these billions of junk e-mails. Their e-mail doesn't include a phone number or postal address; you're generally expected to visit a Web site or respond by e-mail. Meanwhile, our e-mail boxes fill up with useless crud that makes it harder to find the *real* messages among them.

Whatever you do, *never reply* to a piece of spam e-mail — even if the message says that you can get *off* the e-mail list by doing so! Ironically, your response to the e-mail will simply flag your e-mail address as a live, working account manned by somebody who takes the time to *read* the stuff. Your name will become much more valuable to junk e-mailers, and you'll find yourself on the receiving end of a new wave of spam.

You may have wondered: How did you wind up on these junk lists to begin with? Answer: They get your e-mail address from *you.* Every time you post a message on an online bulletin board, fill in a form on the Web, or do a chat in a chat room, you've just made yourself vulnerable to the spammers' software robots. These little programs scour America Online, newsgroups, and the Web, looking for e-mail addresses to collect.

"But if I can never post messages online," I can hear you protesting, "I'm losing half the advantages of being online!"

Not necessarily. Consider setting up a second mailbox — that is, a second e-mail address for your same America Online or Internet account. (That's easy to do on AOL; go to keyword *names* to set up a new one. If you have an Internet account, call your ISP's help line to arrange an additional mailbox. Or sign up for iTools, as described in Chapter 6, and use the e-mail address Apple issued you — *yourname@mac.com,* for example.)

Thereafter, the game is easy to play: Use *one* e-mail address for public postings, chats, and so on. Use your second, private one *for e-mail only*. Spam robots can't read private e-mail, so your secret e-mail address will remain virginal and spam-free.

Part III
Software Competence

In this part . . .

The next few chapters introduce you to the *software* that came with (or can be added to) your iMac. These remarkable programs include iPhoto (for mastery of digital camera photos), iTunes (for mastery of digital music files), iMovie (for mastery of camcorder video editing), and AppleWorks (a terrific all-in-one word processor/spreadsheet/database/presentation program that shouldn't feel left out just because it doesn't start with a lowercase *I*).

After all, without software, your iMac is little more than an art object — cool-looking and futuristic, to be sure, but not much help when it's time to write a letter.

Chapter 9

Faking Your Way through AppleWorks

- -

In This Chapter

▶ Simulating mastery of the database and word processor

▶ Pretending you know how to create art

▶ Feigning wisdom with the spreadsheet

▶ Appearing to know what you're doing when it comes to slide-show-type presentations

- -

Your Personal Software Store

Your iMac came with a gold mine of software programs that, if purchased separately, would have cost you literally dozens of dollars.

Now, history has shown that Apple giveth and taketh away as the years go by; what came on your iMac may not exactly match the list here. But this is what the original flat-screen iMacs came with:

✔ **Chess** — Not just chess, but 3-D, gorgeous, computer chess. When you start the program, you're presented with a fresh, new game that's set up in Human vs. Computer mode — meaning that you (the Human, with the white pieces) get to play against the Computer (your Mac, on the black side). Drag the chess piece of your choice into position on the board, and the game is under way.

If you open the Chess menu and choose Preferences, you'll find the controls that let you make the game more or less difficult, switch colors with the Mac, or even pit the iMac against itself!

✔ **Quicken 2002** — This famous program started out as a simple electronic checkbook, and grew over time to become the Mother of All Personal Finance programs. It can track your stocks, churn out reports for your taxes, and even show you your net worth, if any. If you're feeling particularly forward-thinking, you can even connect to your bank via the Internet, so that paying your bills involves only clicks, not licks (on envelopes and stamps). It's a glorious arrangement that can save you a lot of time, money, and paper cuts.

✔ **Otto Matic** — As the instructions put it: "You are Otto Matic, the robot who is given the job of saving Earth from the clutches of The Giant Brain from Planet X." All right, as computer games go, this one isn't exactly Barbie Meets Ken.

As with most sophisticated, high-speed video games, there are enough keyboard controls, rules, and permutations to keep a 13-year-old up in his room for weeks (see the top of the following illustration). The basic idea, though, is that you press the arrow keys on your keyboard to move your guy around, the space bar to jump, the Option key to punch, and the ⌘ key to shoot your weapon. The object of the game is to find humans, touch them to teleport them to safety, and demolish your enemies.

✔ **World Book Encyclopedia** — I can still remember my parents sacrificing a whole lot of hard-won bucks for the famous 26-volume book set of this encyclopedia. Guess I'd better not mention to them that these days, the whole thing, now enhanced with movies, music, and color pictures, comes free inside every specially-marked package of iMac.

Anyway, the World Book program is in your Applications folder, in the World Book folder. Once you've opened the program, click the Topics button, and then type what you're looking for into the "Enter search words" box — and click Go. The program (previous illustration, bottom) instantly shows you a list of matching articles in the encyclopedia, which you can click to read. There's a dictionary, a "highlighter" pen, an atlas, a timeline, and a number of other ways to explore the world of knowledge that's on your hard drive.

✔ **iPhoto, iMovie, iTunes** — Patience, grasshopper. These programs are described in the next couple of chapters.

For most people, though, the most important program that comes with the iMac is AppleWorks. It's the Swiss Army Knife of software. Just look at all you get, even if you don't know what they are yet: a word processor, a database, and a spreadsheet. But wait — you also get a graphics program that can even serve as a basic page-layout system. And if you order now, you even get a little telecommunications program — absolutely free!

All these modules are neatly bundled into a single integrated program, which came on your iMac's hard drive at no extra charge. You can write a letter and put a graphic in it, or design a flyer that has a little spreadsheet in it, and so on. Chances are good that you and AppleWorks will get to know each other very, very well in the coming months — and the following pages are designed to point you in the right direction.

AppleWorks

To start up AppleWorks, click its icon on your Dock, shown here at top:

After the logo disappears, the Starting Points dialog box, shown previously at bottom, asks you what you want to accomplish. Because you'll face this decision every time you use this program, a rundown may be in order here. If my Executive Summaries don't quite do the trick, don't sweat it; you'll be introduced to each of these modules in this chapter.

- ✔ **Word Processing:** You know what a word-processing document is: something that you type: a memo, a novel, a ransom note.

- ✔ **Spreadsheet:** A computerized ledger sheet designed to help you crunch numbers: You can use it to calculate your car's mileage per gallon, your bank account, how much of the phone bill your teenage daughter owes, that kind of thing.

- ✔ **Database:** An electronic index-card file. You type in your lists — household expenditures; record collections; subscriber list to *Survivor* magazine — and the program sorts them, prints them, finds certain pieces of info instantly, and so on.

- ✔ **Drawing:** This is a *drawing program*. In this kind of document, you toy around with lines, shapes, and colors to produce such important visuals as logos, maps, and Hangman diagrams.

- ✔ **Painting:** This is a painting window. *Painting* is another way of making graphics. But unlike the Drawing mode, where you can create only distinct circles, lines, and squares, the Painting tool lets you create shading, freeform spatters, and much more textured artwork. If you have a scanner or a digital camera, you can use this program to touch up the photos.

- ✔ **Presentation:** Slide shows, baby! Not family photos — we're talking boardroom presentations, "Earnings Trends — 4th Quarter," that kind of thing.

To make AppleWorks strut its stuff, I'll start by showing you how to create a thank-you letter. But not just *any* thank-you letter — this is going to be the world's most beautiful and personalized *form letter*. You're going to merge a list of addresses into a piece of mail, creating what appear to be individually composed letters; thus the technoid term for what you're about to do is *mail merge*.

Even if form letters aren't exactly what you bought a computer to create, follow along. This exercise will take you through most of AppleWorks, and you'll brush up against some features that *will* be useful to you.

Your first database

Suppose that you just got married. You were showered with lovely gifts. And now it's your task to write a charming thank-you note to each of your gift givers. You'll begin by typing a list of the gift givers. The ideal software for organizing this kind of information is a *database*. Therefore, click the word Database, as shown in the previous illustration.

Don't be alarmed. The screen that now appears may look complicated, but it's actually not so bad — it simply wants to know what blanks you'll be wanting to fill in for each person in your list (name, address, gift type, and so on).

You're about to type names for these blanks (which the program calls *fields*). As always, if you make a typo, just press the Delete key to backspace over it. Here we go:

1. **Type *First Name* and press the Return key.**

   Pressing Return is the same as clicking the Create button.

2. **Type *Last Name* and press Return.**

3. **Type *Address* and press Return.**

   See how you're building a list?

4. **Type *Gift* and press Return.**

5. **Type *Adjective* and press Return.**

   In this blank, you'll eventually type a word that describes the glorious present that this person gave you.

6. **Finally, type *Part of House* (you'll see why in a moment) and press Return.**

   Your masterpiece should look something like this.

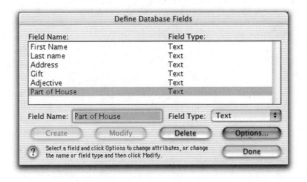

7. **Click the Done button in the lower-right corner.**

   The dialog box goes away.

Accent heaven

Ah, mais oui, mon ami. C'est vrai, c'est la vie, c'est le résumé.

I know what you're thinking: What a smooth, sophisticated guy to be able to speak French like that! Thank you.

But you're also thinking: How did he get those cool accent marks? Very easily — and you, having been smart enough to choose an iMac over all its inferior competitors, can do it, too.

The iMac has a ton of these special characters. Look at your keyboard — I bet you don't see © or ™, or •, or ¢, or any other useful symbols that Mac people use all the time. That's because they're hidden. The secret that unlocks them is . . . the Option key.

It works like the Shift key: While pressing Option, you type a key. Here are some popular ones:

To Get This . . .	Press Option and Type This . . .
©	g
™	2
ç	c
¢	4
¡	1
£	3
•	8
®	r
†	t

What's nice to know is that you have a complete built-in cheat sheet that shows these symbols' locations on the keyboard. It's the Key Caps program, which is in your Applications folder, in the Utilities folder.

Open it up and take a look. Now try pressing the Option key.

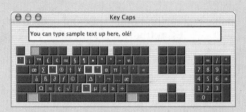

So that's where all those little critters live!

Anyway, there's one more wrinkle to all this. A few symbols, called *diacritical marks* (that's not a computer term; it's a proofreading one, I think) can be placed over any letter. They include the markings over this ü, this é, this è, and so förth. Because the iMac doesn't know ahead of time which vowel you're going to type, creating these marks is a two-step process:

1. While pressing Option, type the key as shown here.

To Get This . . .	Press Option and Type This . . .
é	e
ü	u
è	`
ñ	n
î	i

When you do this, nothing will happen. In other words, no marking appears on the screen — until you do Step 2.

2. Type the letter you want to appear under the diacritical marking.

Only now does the entire thing — letter and marking — appear on the screen. So if you think about it, typing the six-letter word résumé requires eight keystrokes. *C'est formidable, ça!*

When you see what you've created, things should make a little bit more sense. You've just created the blanks (oh, all right, *fields*) to fill in for each person in your list.

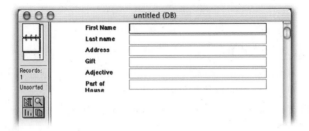

Data entry time

This is important: To fill in the fields of a database (like this one), just type normally. To advance from one field to the next — from First Name to Last Name, for example — *press the Tab key.* Do *not* press the Return key, as every instinct in your body will be screaming to do. You'll discover why in a moment. (You can also move to a new field by clicking in it, but the Tab key is quicker.)

So here goes:

1. **Make sure that you can see a dotted-line rectangle for each field, like the ones in the preceding figure; if not, press the Tab key.**

   The little blinking cursor should be in the First Name blank. (If it's not, click there.)

2. **Type *Josephine* and then press the Tab key to jump to the Last Name field.**

3. **Type *Flombébé* and, again, press Tab.**

   (See the sidebar "Accent heaven" to find out how you make those cool little accents.) Now you're in the Address blank.

4. **Type *200 West 15th Street.***

   Ready to find out what the Return key does? Go ahead and press Return. Notice that you don't advance to the next blank; instead, the program thoughtfully makes this box bigger so that there's room for another line of address.

   If you ever hit Return by *mistake,* intending to jump to the next blank (but just making this blank bigger), press the Delete key.

First Name	Josephine
Last name	Rombébé
Address	200 West 15th Street New York, NY 10010
Gift	
Adjective	
Part of House	

5. **Go ahead and type** *New York, NY 10010* **and then press Tab.**

   And don't worry that the second line of the address immediately gets hidden. The information you typed is still there.

6. **Type** *acrylic sofa cover* **(and press Tab);** *practical* **(and press Tab); and** *living room* **(and stop).**

You've just filled in the information for your first gift sender. So that this won't take all day, let's pretend that it was what they call an *intimate* wedding, and you received gifts from only three people.

But let's see — we need a new set of fields, don't we? Come to think of it, wouldn't life be sweeter if there were a computer *term* for "set of fields"? By gumbo, there is! A set of fields is called a *record*.

I wouldn't bother with that term if it didn't crop up in the next instruction:

1. **From the Edit menu, choose New Record.**

   A new record ("set of fields") appears, just below the first set. You're to type the second person's information.

2. **Type anything you want, or copy the example below, but remember to press Tab at the end of each piece of information.**

   (Oh, and if you want a second line for the address, press Return.) Make up a town and state; you're a creative soul.

First Name	Suzie
Last name	Khiou
Address	1 Doormouse Ave.
Gift	Harley
Adjective	expensive
Part of House	garage

3. **Choose New Record from the Edit menu again and type a third set of information, perhaps typing** *Ming vase* **as the name of the gift.**

   Fabulous! You're really cooking now.

4. **As a final wise step, open the File menu, choose Save, and type *Gift List* as the name of your database into the Save As text box.**

   Note that AppleWorks proposes putting the *.cwk* filename suffix on. Let it do that. You won't see this geeky-looking suffix when you're working with files in your folders, but it will help the Mac keep its documents straight.

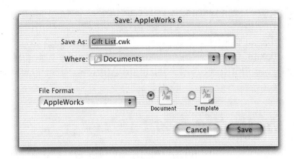

5. **Click the Save button to preserve your database on the hard disk.**

Finding and sorting in AppleWorks databases

After you've got some data typed into an AppleWorks database, you can manipulate it in all kinds of fun and exciting ways. From the Layout menu, choose Find to get what appears to be a blank record. Type what you're looking for into the appropriate blanks. For example, if you're trying to find everybody who lives in zip code 90210, you'd fill out the Find dialog box as shown in the figure below.

Then click the Find button. After about one second, you'll be returned to normal view, where you'll see the results of your search. This is important — AppleWorks is *hiding* the records that *didn't* match your search requirements. You haven't lost them; they're just out of sight until you choose Show All Records from the Organize menu. You can prove this to yourself by consulting the little book at the left side of the screen. It will say "Records: 22 (194)." That means that AppleWorks still knows there are 194 addresses in your mailing list, but only 22 have zip code 90210.

First Name	
Last name	
Address	90210
Gift	
Adjective	
Part of House	

You've just created your first database (it's in the Documents folder of your Home folder, as it should be). Note that it now has several records; see the tiny flip-book icon at the upper-left corner of the window? You can flip through the different "cards" in your file by clicking the pages, or by dragging the little yardstick that seems to be sticking out of the book.

Having gone through the tedium of typing in each little scrap of information the way the iMac wants it, you can now perform some stunts with it that'd make your grandparents' jaws drop. You can ask the iMac to show you only the names of your friends whose last names begin with Z. Or only those who live in Texas. Or only those whose gifts you've categorized as *fabulous*. See the sidebar "Finding and sorting in AppleWorks databases" for details.

Forming the form letter

Next, you're going to write the thank-you note. At each place where you want to use somebody's name (or other gift-related information), you'll ask AppleWorks to slap in the appropriate info.

1. **Close your database window by clicking its upper-left red gel dot.**

   You're back at the Starting Points window. You always return here if no other windows are open.

2. **Click Word Processing.**

   You get a sparkling new sheet of electronic typing paper. You'll start the letter with the address, of course. Yet the address will be different on each letter! This is where mail-merging comes in handy.

3. **From the File menu, choose Mail Merge.**

   When the Choose a File window appears, you'll see your database name, Gift List, prominently displayed among the other files in your Documents folder.

4. **Double-click Gift List to tell AppleWorks that it's the database you want to work with.**

   Now a strange-looking window appears — the gray one shown in the next illustration.

   The scrolling list shows the *Field Names* from your database. Here's how it works.

5. **Point to First Name and double-click.**

   See what happened? The program popped a placeholder for the First Name right into your letter. When you print, instead of *<<First Name>>*, it will say *Josephine*.

6. **Type a space; in the Mail Merge window, point to** *Last Name* **and double-click; press Return to begin a new line of the address; then point to the Mail Merge window again and double-click** *Address.*

Before you continue typing, you may want to drag the little Mail Merge window off to the right of your screen as best you can. (To move the window, drag its title bar.) You're going to want to see both it and your typing simultaneously.

7. **Press Return a couple of times and then type** *Dear,* **followed by a space.**

8. **Point to the words** *First Name* **in the Mail Merge window, as you did a moment ago; double-click; then type a comma.**

Your letter should look something like this.

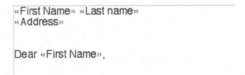

This is where it gets good.

9. **Press Return a couple of times and then type** *I nearly cried when I unwrapped the incredible,* **followed by a space.**

10. **Double-click the word** *Gift* **in the Mail Merge window.**

11. **Continue typing the following:** *you gave me for my wedding. It is far and away the most* **(and now double-click** *Adjective* **in the Mail Merge window)** *gift I will ever receive.*

«First Name» «Last name»
«Address»

Dear «First Name»,

I nearly cried when I unwrapped the incredible «Gift» you gave me for my
wedding. It is far and away the most «Adjective» gift I will ever receive.

Are you getting the hang of this? At each place where you want
AppleWorks to substitute a piece of information from your Gift List
database, you insert a little <<*placeholder*>>.

Finish the letter as follows.

12. Type *It will look sensational in the* (double-click *Part of House* in
the Mail Merge window) *of our new home.*

13. Press the Return key twice and finish up like this: *I had to write this
personal note to you and you alone, so you'd know how much I
treasure your gift above all the others. Love, Marge*

«First Name» «Last name»
«Address»

Dear «First Name»,

I nearly cried when I unwrapped the incredible «Gift» you gave me for my
wedding. It is far and away the most «Adjective» gift I will ever receive.

It will look sensational in the «Part of House» of our new home.

I had to write this personal note to you and you alone, so you'd know
how much I treasure your gift above all the others.

Love,
Marge

Miss Manners would go instantly bald in horror if she thought you were
about to send out a letter that says *Dear First Name*. But through the miracle
of computers, when these letters are printed, it'll be impossible to tell that
each one wasn't typed separately.

From the File menu, choose Save. Type *Thank-You Letter* in the Save As text
box and click Save. A new icon in your Documents folder is born.

The graphics zone: Designing a letterhead

To show you how AppleWorks can tie everything together, let's whip up a
quick letterhead in the Drawing module.

Specifying your favorite type

Wherever the Intergalactic Committee for Frequently Asked Questions keeps its master list, I'll bet that the first item on the list is this: "I hate having to set up my favorite type style and size every time I open a new AppleWorks word-processing document. How do I specify my favorite font once and for all?"

The answer is easy, although you'd never figure it out on your own. From the File menu, choose New; in the Starting Points dialog box, double-click Word Processing. Now, from the Format menu, choose the font, size, and style you prefer. (If you're into such advanced kinky stuff

as double spacing, margin adjustments, a logo in your header, and so on, you can make these changes now, too.)

Finally, from the File menu, choose Save As. Click the Template button. Type this name exactly — *AppleWorks WP Options* — and then click Save, and finally click OK.

From now on, every time you indicate that you'd like to begin a new word-processing document, your preferred font (and other formatting choices) will be in place before you even type a word.

Close your thank-you letter *and* the Gift List database, if it's open, so that the Starting Points window reappears. This time, double-click the word Drawing.

AppleWorks shows you its drawing window. The grid of dotted lines is there to give things a nice architectural look; it won't appear in the finished printout.

1. **Click the Text tool — it looks like a letter A, and it's the upper-left icon on the tool palette — and release the mouse button. Then move your cursor onto the drawing area and drag across the screen, as shown here.**

Click the Text tool.

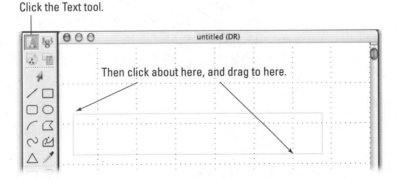

2. **Open the Text menu; from the Font command, choose Apple Chancery. Open the Text menu again, and this time use the Size menu to choose 36 Point.**

3. **Type — *A Very Personal Note* — .**

   You make a long dash by pressing the Shift and Option keys together; while they're down, type a hyphen.

4. **Press the Enter key so that handles appear around your text. Using the Alignment submenu of the Format menu, choose Center.**

—A Very Personal Note— ·

Finally, you'll add that elegant white-lettering-against-black look that shows up on so many corporate annual reports. At the left side of your screen, there's a set of odd-looking icons.

5. **Click the third-from-bottom icon on the palette, as shown here by the letter A.**

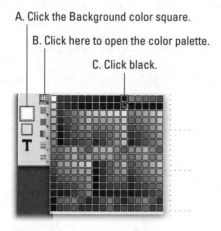

A. Click the Background color square.

B. Click here to open the color palette.

C. Click black.

You've just told AppleWorks that you want to change the *background* color of the text box.

6. **Click the little color-checkerboard palette to its right; from the pop-out color palette, click black (previous illustration, labeled B and C).**

You've just used the Fill palette to color in the entire text block with black. Which is just great, except that now the text is a solid black rectangle! To fix the problem, you need to make the text *white*.

7. **Open the Format menu. In the palette that pops out from the Text Color submenu, click the white square.**

Ah, much better!

Of course, while you're in the Drawing mode, you could actually do some graphics . . . you could use any of the other drawing tools to dress up your logo. You could draw a box around this letterhead. You could rotate the whole thing 90 degrees. You could make all kinds of insane diagonal stripes across it.

 You could also choose, from the File menu, Show Clippings — and then, by clicking one of the tabs (Animals, Food, Household, and so on) at the bottom of the Clippings window, select any of the ready-to-use graphics worthy of dragging into your drawing as an aid to the artistically challenged.

For control freaks only: The View buttons

Before you leave the drawing window, cast your eyes upon the lower-left corner of the screen. There you'll find this odd-looking array of controls.

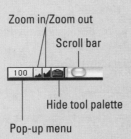

As you can tell, AppleWorks makes blowing up your work extremely easy. (I mean *magnifying* it; *destroying* it is up to you.) A quick click on either of those little mountain buttons makes the artwork smaller or larger. Or jump directly to a more convenient degree of magnification by using the percentage pop-up menu (where it says 100). You're not changing the actual printed size — only how it's displayed on the screen.

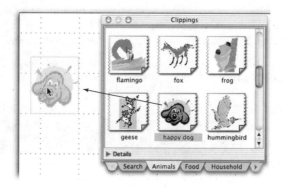

Keep those creative possibilities in mind when it comes time to design your real letterhead.

The return of Copy and Paste

All that remains is for you to slap this letterhead into your mail-merge letter:

1. **Using the Arrow tool, click your letterhead; from the Edit menu, choose Copy.**

   Now you need to return to your word-processing document. Fortunately, AppleWorks always keeps track of the last few files you've worked on.

2. **Open the File menu, and roll your cursor to the Open Recent command at the bottom. From the Open Recent submenu, choose "Thank-You Letter.cwk" in "Documents" on "Macintosh HD."**

   (This command is telling you not only what the file was called, but what folder and hard drive it's on.)

   Your letter springs to the fore.

3. **From the Format menu, choose Insert Header.**

   A *header* is an area at the top of every page, above whatever text you've typed. In this case, it looks like an empty text area.

4. **From the Edit menu, choose Paste.**

   Et voilà . . . your graphic pops neatly into the header.

You've actually done it: combined a database, a word processor, and a drawing program in a single project!

The urge to merge

Now comes the payoff; this is where the real fun begins.

Once again, open the File menu and choose Mail Merge. The Mail Merge palette reappears, listing the fields in your database.

Now click the Merge button on that palette. You see this box:

AppleWorks is offering to *merge* the information from the database (names, gift items, etc.) with the form letter. It can do so either by printing out the whole batch, by creating a new master document (where each page is a different letter), or by spitting out individual documents, one letter apiece.

For now, choose the middle option — "Save in a new document" — and then click Continue. In a flash, AppleWorks actually substitutes actual names for the <<*placeholders*>> on the screen, creating masterful letters like this one.

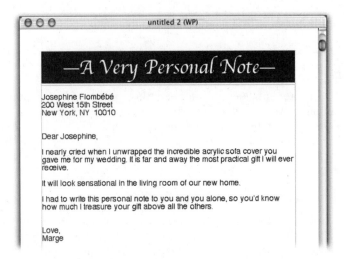

Save or print this document, as you see fit.

AppleWorks: The Other Spreadsheet

When most people talk about spreadsheet programs, they usually refer to Microsoft Excel, the $300 program that's universally adored by accountants (especially those who work at Microsoft). Fortunately, AppleWorks comes with a handy spreadsheet program that does most of what Excel can do, requires much less learning, and doesn't add a nickel to the personal fortune of Bill Gates.

A spreadsheet program is for doing math, tracking finances, figuring out which of two mortgage plans is more favorable in the long run, charting the growth of your basement gambling operation, and other number-crunchy stuff.

The not-so-grand total

Suppose, for example, that you're still recovering from the wedding for which you've just sent out handsome thank-you form letters. After enjoying a delightful honeymoon in sunny Tampa, you return home to find a stack of bills reaching to the moon and back six times: from the wedding caterer, from the wedding band, from the wedding photographer, and so on. Before long, the question that has occupied your attention for ten months now — "Is this the person with whom I want to spend eternity?" — has been replaced by a new one: "Is eternity long enough to pay off all these bills?"

As is so often the case in life, software can provide the answer. Start by launching AppleWorks, as you did at the beginning of this chapter. If you see the word AppleWorks next to your menu, then you're already running AppleWorks. In that case, open the File menu and choose Starting Points.

Either way, the Starting Points dialog box now takes center stage on your screen. This time, click Spreadsheet.

A blank spreadsheet now appears on your screen. It's a bunch of rows and columns, like a ledger book. The columns are lettered, and the rows are numbered. Each little rectangular cell is called, well, a *cell*. It's referred to by its letter and number: A1, for example, exactly as in a game of Battleship. Here, for example, is how you might calculate your potential for solvency after paying for the wedding:

1. **Click in cell A3. Type *EXPENSES:* and then press Return.**

    Notice that as you type, no letters actually appear in the cell. Instead, all the action takes place in the strip above the top row. Only when you press Return or Enter does your typing jump into place in the spreadsheet itself.

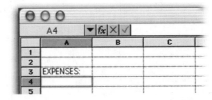

You should now see that the next cell down, A4, shows a faint colored border, indicating that your next typing will appear there.

2. **Type each of the expenses shown in the illustration below (Caterer, Photographer, and so on). After typing each, press the Return key to jump down into the next cell. In the last cell, type** *TOTAL:* **and then press Return.**

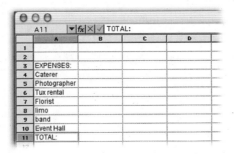

Having written down everyone to whom you owe money, you should be feeling better already.

3. **Click in cell B4, to the right of the Caterer item. Type dollar amounts for each wedding-money recipient, as shown in the next illustration, again pressing the Return key after each amount.**

AppleWorks can do far more than just display a bunch of numbers — it can also add them up.

4. **Carefully drag your cursor straight down the column of numbers, beginning in cell B4 (where the first number appears) and ending in the empty cell at the bottom of the column (to the right of the word TOTAL:).**

You've just told AppleWorks which numbers you want added up. By including a blank cell at the end of your drag, you also told AppleWorks where you wanted the grand total to appear.

5. **Click the Σ button on the toolbar at the top of the screen, as highlighted here:**

(On the freak chance that you don't see the toolbar, choose Show Button Bar from the Window menu.)

When you do finally click the Σ button, an amazing thing happens: AppleWorks adds the correct total of the highlighted numbers in the empty cell at the bottom of the column.

Even more amazing, this number is *live* — that is, it checks its own addition thousands of times per second. If you change one of the numbers in the column, the total updates instantaneously. Try it yourself:

The bold accountant

Your spreadsheets aren't limited to the bland and tiny typeface you've been looking at so far. You're welcome to spice up your numbers by formatting them with boldface, italic, different sizes, colors, and so on.

For example, in the wedding-cost example in this chapter, you might decide to show the grand total you owe in boldface red type. To do that, click the cell where the total number appears. Now use the commands in the Format menu, such as Style (to apply boldface) or Text Color

(to apply red). You can also make AppleWorks add the dollar signs and decimal points automatically to highlighted cells, too: From the Format menu, choose Number, and then choose Currency from the Number pop-up menu.

All the automatic-adding features still work, but now whatever number appears in that total cell will always be red and bold — a cheerful reminder of just how desperate your financial situation is.

6. **Click the cell that shows the Photographer fee. Type a different number, and then press Return.**

In the blink of an iMac, the Total cell changes to show the new sum.

The good news

So you owe a few thousand dollars. But life doesn't have to end. Surely you have a few assets you could sell to cover the cost of your recent nuptial festivities. Let's see if you could get out of hock by selling, for example, your wedding gifts.

1. **Click in column D3. Type *ASSETS:* and then press Return.**

You're about to begin typing a new column of information.

2. **Type *acrylic sofa cover*, and then press Return; *Harley*, and press Return again; *Ming vase*, and Return. Finally, type *TOTAL:*, and press Return one last time.**

You might have noticed that "acrylic sofa cover" is too long to fit in the column without spilling over into the next cell. No problem — just make the column wider. Do so by *double-clicking* the dividing line between the D and E column headings. AppleWorks makes the D column exactly as wide as necessary to contain the longest name in it.

Now you need to specify the approximate value of each of your gifts.

3. **Click the cell to the right of *acrylic sofa cover*. Type a dollar amount for each item, remembering to press Return after each one. The result should look like this:**

	A	B	C	D	E
1					
2					
3	EXPENSES:			ASSETS:	
4	Caterer	15232		Acrylic sofa cover	1.79
5	Photographer	423.22		harley	5000
6	Tux rental	150		ming vase	12039.44
7	Florist	235		TOTAL:	
8	limo	75			
9	band	269			
10	Event Hall	644.23			
11	TOTAL:	$17028.45			

(Cell reference box: F21)

4. **Drag through the column of numbers you've just typed, taking care to include one blank cell at the bottom of the column. Click the ∑ button on the toolbar.**

   As you could have predicted, AppleWorks adds up the newly typed numbers, showing your total assets at the moment. Once again, this total is "live" and continually updated. If you change one of the numbers above it, the total changes, too.

The final analysis

The automatic addition you've established is fine when you're stranded on a desert island without a pocket calculator. True spreadsheet nerds, however, don't content themselves with simple totals. In the real world, people use spreadsheets to create totals *of* totals, like this:

1. **In a blank cell beneath all the other numbers — cell C15, for example — type *GRAND TOTAL*, and then press Tab.**

   The Tab key works just like the Return key, except that it jumps to the next cell to the *right,* instead of the next cell *down.*

   The idea here is that you want AppleWorks to combine your two subtotals — to subtract the total amount you owe from the total value of your assets — so that you can see whether or not you'll break even from this wedding deal. To create this elaborate calculation, you'll build a *formula,* which is basically an equation exactly like the ones you used to build in junior high school. Formulas in a spreadsheet always begin with an equal sign.

2. **Type an equal sign (=). Click the cell that represents your total assets (cell E7 in the preceding illustration).**

   Up in the formula bar, AppleWorks automatically writes in the name of the cell you clicked.

3. **Type a minus sign or hyphen (-), and then click the total amount you owe (cell B11 in the preceding illustration). Finally, press Return.**

AppleWorks subtracts the second cell from the first, displaying the grand total. This time, you lucked out: Selling your gifts will earn you just enough money to cover the costs of the wedding — with enough left over for a bottle of sunscreen.

	A	B	C	D	E
1					
2					
3	EXPENSES:			ASSETS:	
4	Caterer	15232		Acrylic sofa cover	1.79
5	Photographer	423.22		harley	5000
6	Tux rental	150		ming vase	12039.44
7	Florist	235		TOTAL:	17041.23
8	limo	75			
9	band	269			
10	Event Hall	644.23			
11	TOTAL:	$17028.45			
12					
13					
14					
15			GRAND TOTAL:	12.78	

Amazingly enough, this grand total is also interactively linked to all the other numbers in your spreadsheet. If you change the price of the Ming vase, for example, both your assets total *and* your grand total cells change automatically.

If you study this example, you'll see that the best way to build formulas in a spreadsheet is say what you're doing out loud. "The number in this cell . . ." (you click the cell where you want the grand total to appear) "equals" (type an = symbol) "this number" (click the assets total) "minus" (type the – sign) "this number" (click the debts total). Muttering softly to yourself as you work may not be the best way to pass yourself off as a financial genius, but you will get your formulas straight.

The AppleWorks Slide Show

Technology has marched on since the days when teachers used overhead projectors to show transparencies, elderly relatives filled your evening with travelogues on the old slide screen, and you snorted yourself awake in the middle of deadly-dull board meetings. Yes, technology has marched on — but not much.

People still present information, one screen at a time — but now they can do it on the computer screen. (In fact, thanks to the iMac's *video mirroring* feature described at the end of Chapter 19, you can even route the presentation through an external TV or computer projection system.)

Designing the show

You *can* create and design a slide show from scratch. But when you have more desperation than time, use a presentation *template*. For example, suppose you're trying to persuade your new spouse that it would be in your best interests to sell off all your wedding gifts to pay for the wedding. You might start out like this:

1. **At the Starting Points window (choose Show Starting Points from the File menu), click the Templates tab, shown here.**

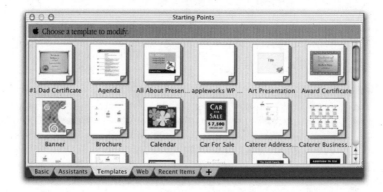

AppleWorks shows you all of its templates. Scroll or make the window big enough so that you can see the handful of templates whose names contain the word "Presentation."

2. **Click the presentation template you want.**

   For this important spouse-persuasion project, you'd best use something attention-getting — like the one called Hip Presentation.

   The presentation design you selected appears on the screen, filled with dummy text that has nothing to do with the case you're trying to make.

3. **Double-click the text ("Using Color in Art & Design," in this example) to activate the text box. Delete the dummy text and replace it with the words you actually want to appear in your slide show.**

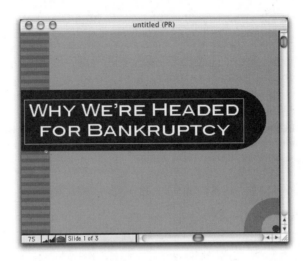

If there were other text boxes on this first slide, you could repeat this process.

4. **Advance to the next slide by clicking its icon in the Controls palette.**

   The Controls palette contains a scrolling list of slides, the second one of which is generally a *bulleted list* — a standard element of corporate presentations. You can think of this bulleted list as an outline to help both you and your audience focus on the points you intended to make here.

5. **Replace these bullets just the way you replaced the title.**

   In other words, double-click to activate the text box, delete the dummy text (such as "Bullet 1"), and replace it with your own text.

Now it's time to add another slide. But before you can do that, you have to tell AppleWorks which *master slide* design you want to use for it. Most slide show templates include two or three different underlying Master slides — design templates that contain pre-designed text boxes and graphic elements. Usually there's one that presents the title only, another style for bullet lists, and a third that's designed to accommodate a picture, chart, or movie.

6. **Click the Master Slides tab (marked by a star) in the Controls palette, and then click the Master slide whose design you want for the next slide.**

Master slides
Slides   Show

In this example, suppose you want another bullet slide.

7. **Return to the Slides tab in the Controls palette (click the second tab beneath it) and click the + button.**

AppleWorks creates another slide, represented by another miniature icon in this Controls palette. Edit the dummy text just as you did in Step 3.

Continue this way — creating new slides, and editing the text on them — until your slide show is complete. Along the way, you can paste in, or draw, other AppleWorks elements onto any slide: clippings, spreadsheet frames, text frames, tables, lines, arrows, and anything else you need to make your point.

Presenting the show

When your show looks good, save it (choose Save from the File menu and give it a name). Then click the Show tab on the Controls palette. Here's where you specify, for example, how you want to advance from one slide to the next — by clicking the mouse, by waiting a pre-determined interval, and so on.

For now, though, leave the settings as they are. Click the big triangular Play button on the Show tab.

Now AppleWorks goes into a special trance. All the familiar landmarks of the screen disappear, and the screen is flooded with the magnified image of your first slide. Each time you click the mouse, the next slide appears. You can also control the show like this:

- **Next slide.** Press the right-arrow key, down-arrow key, Page Down, Return, Tab, or space bar.

- **Previous slide.** Press the left-arrow key, up-arrow key, Page Up, Shift-Return, Shift-Tab, or Shift-space bar.

- **Last slide.** Press the End key.

- **First slide.** Press the Home key.

- **Stop the slide show.** Press the letter Q key, Esc, or ⌘-period.

In general, you'll find the AppleWorks presentation module to be great fun for all kinds of things: school reports, actual slide shows, product pitches, story-telling, and even presenting how-to tutorials for computer lessons.

Other cool stuff AppleWorks does

The little post-wedding mop-up example was only one example of AppleWorks' power. It left plenty of features unexplored, however. For example . . .

A little paint

If you've been following along, you haven't yet tried the Painting window. By this time, I trust that you know how to get there: From the File menu, choose Starting Points, and then click Painting. (Or just choose Painting from the *submenu* of the New command.)

Suddenly, you're in a pixel-blitzing wonderland, where you can create all kinds of "painted" artwork. This kind of artwork has pros and cons. The pro is that you can change the color of *every single dot* on the screen (instead of just making circles, lines, rectangles, and text, which is all that you can do in the Drawing window). The con is that you can't move or resize something in a painting after you've laid down the "paint" (which you *can* do in the Drawing window).

In a pinch, you could use this window to touch up a digital photo — giving Uncle Morty a third eye, for example.

Mailing labels

AppleWorks is great at mailing labels; the program even walks you through the process.

You start by creating a database, as described at the beginning of this chapter, to hold your addresses. *The hard way:* Create fields called Name, Address, City, State, and Zip, for example. *The easy way:* On the Starting Points screen, click the Assistants tab. Then click the button called Address List. The program walks you through a simple interview process for creating an address book. After you've put in a few names (choose New Record from the Edit menu after each one), be sure to save this file.

Then, from the Layout menu, choose New Label Layout. A special interview screen appears to walk you through the creation of a mailing-label design. It will ask you to specify what kind of Avery mailing labels you've bought (you buy these at office-supply stores), for example, and how many lines you want on a label.

The tricky part is this screen. Each row of controls governs one line of the mailing label. Most of the time, you'll want to set up the pop-up menus so that they look like this:

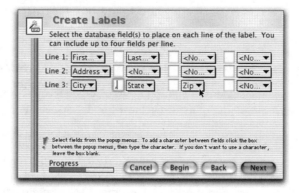

Don't forget to type a comma into the box between City and State.

At the end of the process, you'll see your addresses in a mailing label *layout,* ready to print. (To return to your original layout, open the Layout menu and choose "For the Screen.")

Chapter 10

iPhoto, iTunes — iLove It!

. . . .

In This Chapter

▶ Putting your photos in the digital shoebox

▶ Making hay with your photos: slide shows, Web pages, hardbound books

▶ iTunes: the digital jukebox

▶ iTunes: burning your own music CDs

. . . .

For decades, life as a Mac user was fraught with social hazards. You'd be at some party, and somebody would say, "Oh, I got this cool new program — but it only works on Windows." You'd have no choice but to avert your gaze in embarrassment, often by burying your face in the onion dip.

These days, Apple's fighting back. Your iMac came with an assortment of amazing software programs that run only on the Mac. These new programs, called things like iPhoto, iTunes, and iMovie, are designed to make you the ringmaster in control of pictures, music, and movies.

Nobody has ever seen anything quite like the "i-programs," as some people call them: They're beautiful to look at, extremely easy to use, and capable of feats that simply can't be duplicated on other computers. It's time to see a little onion dip on the cheeks of Windows fans for change.

This chapter describes iPhoto and iTunes. Chapter 11 goes into digital moviemaking with iMovie.

iPhoto: the Digital Shoebox

Digital cameras are amazing inventions. For one thing, they're incredibly economical: You never pay for film, and you never pay for developing. For another, the little built-in screen on a digital camera lets you see the picture before you actually take it — and after you press the shutter button, lets you see the picture *after* you've taken it, the better to delete it on the spot if it didn't come out well.

When you get the camera home, you can connect the camera to a computer and transfer the pictures to it. There they show up as graphics files, which you can e-mail to other people, turn into a slide show, or even edit. More than one person has erased an ex-spouse out of a favorite family picture using exactly these tools. (You think I'm kidding?)

But for years, that business of getting the pictures off the camera and onto your computer has been the hard part. Every camera came with its own software, which did very little with your pictures once the transfer was over. Sometimes you couldn't even find them on your hard drive after the transfer.

Fortunately, Apple has finally put an end to that chain of pain. The iPhoto program gives you a sweet, simple way to transfer your pictures from the camera, organize them, show them off, and send them on to other people.

Where to get iPhoto

Depending on when you bought your iMac, your iPhoto situation might fall in one of these two categories:

- ✔ iPhoto is already on your hard drive, in the Applications folder.
- ✔ iPhoto came on a separate CD in the box. To install the program, insert the iPhoto CD into your machine, double-click the CD icon to open its window, and then double-click the iPhoto.mpkg icon to start the installer program. (As with many installations, you can perform this one only if you have an *Administrator* account, which is described in Chapter 13. You'll be asked to click a little padlock icon and then to type in the name and password of an Administrator.)

In either case, what you really want is iPhoto version 1.1 or later; that's the version described in this chapter.

If it turns out that you have only version 1.0, visit the Apple Web site at *www.apple.com/iPhoto* for details on downloading and installing the latest version. And if you have something even later, congratulations! The basic discussion in this chapter still applies, but you have additional features at your command.

iPhoto meets camera

Once you've installed iPhoto, you can, of course, start up the program by finding it in your Applications folder and double-clicking it. But the whole point of the program is its magical synergy with your digital camera. And that relationship begins the moment you plug the camera's USB cable from the Mac into the camera. That simple act of plugging in generally opens iPhoto automatically.

Once iPhoto is open and the camera is turned on and connected, click the Import button shown in the following figure. If the camera picture at the left side of the screen correctly identifies your camera model, you're ready to transfer the pictures. (If you don't see the camera picture there, try waiting to turn the camera on until after iPhoto has opened.)

First, however, you have an important decision to make: Do you want iPhoto to *erase the camera* after retrieving its pictures? There's no downside to doing so — in fact, that's probably what you'll want most of the time, considering how few pictures fit on the average camera memory card. You don't have to worry about losing pictures, because the erasing process doesn't begin until *after* all of the pictures are safely transferred to the hard drive.

If you want to erase the card after the transfer, turn on "Erase camera contents after transfer." Either way, click the Import button. The program swings into action, grabbing your pictures from the camera and displaying them in miniature on the iPhoto screen, like in the following figure:

---

iPhoto-compatible cameras

The great thing about iPhoto is that it automatically recognizes dozens of camera models from Canon, Fuji, Hewlett-Packard, Kodak, Nikon, Sony, Minolta, and Olympus. It can communicate with all the cameras listed at *www.apple. com/iPhoto/Compatibility* — and, in fact, even a lot of cameras that aren't actually on that list.

iPhoto doesn't recognize every camera on earth, however. Some cameras are too old to trigger the automatic-iPhoto-opening process when you hook up the cable.

Fortunately, there are ways around these situations. In fact, it's perfectly possible to use iPhoto without a digital camera at all. It makes an excellent digital shoebox even for photos that you scan, download from the Web, or collect via e-mail sent from your friends.

If you have a camera that iPhoto doesn't seem to recognize, you might consider buying a memory-card reader (about $80), like the ones listed at *www.apple.com/iPhoto/Compatibility* — and then get the pictures into iPhoto by inserting your camera's memory card into this reader.

Otherwise, you can always get the photos onto the iMac using whatever software came with the camera. Then get the resulting folder of pictures into iPhoto just by dragging the folder itself into the iPhoto window. (That's also how you get scanned or downloaded pictures into iPhoto, by the way.)

Album list

New Album   Rotate   "Erase camera contents" option   Import/Stop button

Picture-size slider

Fun with pictures

Over time, you'll take more and more pictures, and download each set to iPhoto. The main iPhoto display area will fill with more and more pictures. The great thing is that all of your pictures are always available in this one massive, scrolling display. You'll never again be forced to sit in the sweltering attic, opening crumbling envelopes of ancient, disorganized photos, flipping through them in a hunt for one particular shot.

Nor are you forced to just sit and *look* at your pictures. This is the electronic age, dude! Time for interactivity! Let us count the ways.

Magnify or shrink them

The first time you see this little trick, you'll think it justifies the price of the iMac all by itself. Just drag the little slider at the lower-right corner of the window, like this —

— and watch in amazement as all of the photos grow larger or smaller. You can drag the slider so far to the right that each picture fills the screen — or so far to the left that they become the size of molecules.

Rotate a picture

If you're like most photographers, not all of your photos are taken in *landscape* mode, where the camera is held horizontally. Every now and then, you may have to turn the camera 90 degrees to take a picture — of, say, a giraffe, a skyscraper, or Michael Jordan.

Unfortunately, the camera doesn't know that you turned it sideways. When you import the photos to your iMac, those vertical photos wind up displayed horizontally, which is just wrong.

To fix the problem in iPhoto, just click the photo and then click the Rotate button, which is identified in the first illustration of this chapter. The photo crisply turns 90 degrees for your entertainment pleasure. (It always turns counterclockwise — unless you press the Option key while clicking, which makes it turn the other way.)

Crop a picture

Just taking the picture doesn't represent the end of the job for a real photographer. Part of the artistry in becoming a shutterbug is learning how to *crop* a picture — to trim away excess background. Sometimes, of course, you *want* the subject to look tiny and insignificant — when set against the backdrop of a building or the Grand Canyon, for example. Most of the time, though, a picture is more effective when it's a tight shot around the subject.

To trim out excess background in iPhoto, double-click the picture. It opens into a special mode called Edit (see the button beneath the picture?). At this point, grab your mouse. Start above and to the left of the subject, and drag diagonally so that the unwanted background turns faded, like this:

1. Drag diagonally

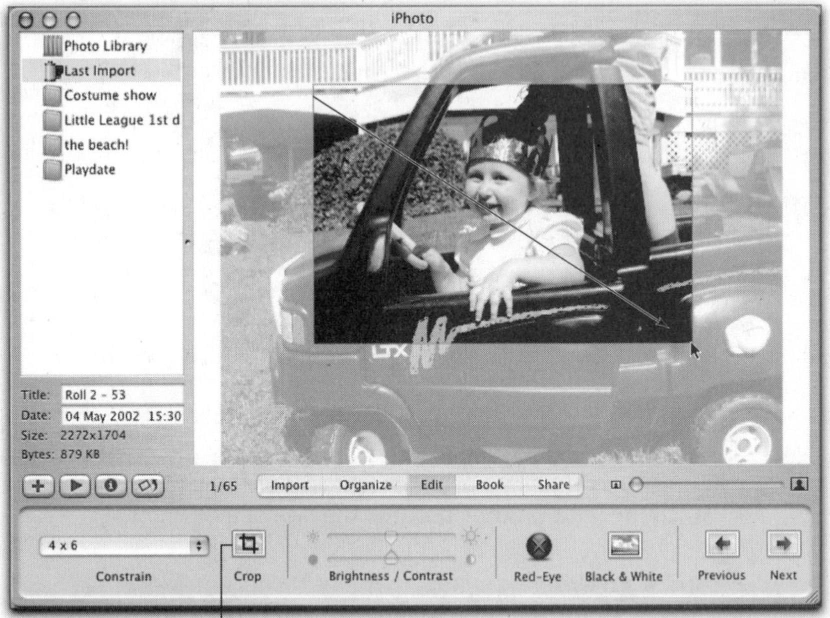

2. Click here

If you want to be sure that the photo remains photo-like in its proportions — ruling out the possibility that you'll wind up with a tall, skinny slice of the picture — use the Constrain pop-up menu at the lower-left corner of the window. Choose one of the standard photo sizes listed there, such as 4 by 6, before you drag across the picture.

Once you've highlighted the portion of the picture that you actually want to keep, click the Crop button on the bottom edge of the window. Savor the way iPhoto automatically enlarges your newly cropped image to fill the window. Then click the Organize button to return to your "slides."

You'll sleep well at night, by the way, knowing that *nothing you do in iPhoto ever changes the original photo.* Even if you crop a picture, for example, you can return to it, months or years later, click it in the iPhoto window, open the File menu, and then choose Revert to Original. iPhoto promptly brings back the picture as it looked the day you first imported it from the camera. Safety is a beautiful thing.

Adjust brightness, contrast, and redeye

When you double-click the picture, you may also have noticed the Brightness/Contrast sliders on the bottom edge of the window. These, as you can probably figure out, help you improve a photo by making it brighter or bringing out the difference between light and dark.

This is also your opportunity, by the way, to correct *redeye* — the occasional problem where somebody in a flash photo shows up with reddish pupils. Magnify the picture by dragging the slider at the lower-right corner of the window, drag diagonally across the affected area with your cursor, and then click the Redeye button.

If one particular person shows up with redeye in *all* your photos, on the other hand, call an exorcist.

Organize into "albums"

It's nice of iPhoto to keep all of your pictures on one massive, scrolling screen. On the other hand, that's not always the most efficient arrangement. Fortunately, it's a snap to create little folders — *albums,* as they're called in iPhoto — that contain subsets of these pictures.

The trick is to click the little + button at the lower-left side of the screen. iPhoto asks you to type in a name for the album you're about to create; do so and then click OK.

Now look in the list at the left side of the window: A new little book icon appears there. Above it in the list, click Photo Library (to see every photo you've ever taken) or Last Import (to see only the pictures you grabbed from the camera during your last importing session). Your challenge now is to select the pictures that you'll want to put into the newly created album. The routine goes like this:

✔ Click one picture to select it.

✔ ⌘-click additional pictures to select them, as well. (That is, click while pressing the ⌘ key.)

✔ To select several pictures in a row, ⌘-click the first one, and then *Shift*-click the last one. You've just highlighted all of the pictures in between, as well.

✔ Drag diagonally across a group of folders to select all of them at once.

✔ Drag diagonally while pressing the Shift key to select a separate group of pictures, without losing the ones you've already selected.

I realize that that's a lot of permutations to remember, but hey — that's why you have them written down on this page.

In any case, once you've highlighted the pictures, drag any *one* of them on top of the album book icon. A little red circle lets you know how many photos you're dragging, like this:

Are you ready to have your mind blown? Here we go: Dragging pictures into an album like this doesn't remove them from the main photo library. The main photo library (click Photo Library at the top of the list) *always* contains every photo you've ever taken.

No, when you drag pictures into an album, you're neither moving them nor even copying them. You're just creating imaginary duplicates that are *linked* back to the original pictures. Thanks to this quirk, you can put a single photo into as many different albums as you like. A picture of Harold, proudly displaying the trout that he caught on your joint vacation to Mississippi, winds up in several different albums that you've created: one called Relatives, one called Fishing, and one called Vacations, for example.

Showing off on the screen

iPhoto provides a number of different features for showing off your pictures on the screen. Set up some folding chairs, make lemonade, and then gather the family around the iMac. Then click the Share button beneath the pictures, and get ready for some spectacular visual fireworks.

- **Slide Show.** Click the album icon whose pictures you want to see in the slide show, and then click the Slide Show icon at the bottom of the screen. iPhoto asks how many seconds you want to see each picture on the screen — 2 is usually just about right — and lets you choose a piece of background music from the Music pop-up menu. Click OK to begin the show.

  As you see, it's quite spectacular, with pictures cross-fading into each other. At any time, you can press the space bar to freeze the show on a particular picture for audience scrutiny; press space again to continue the show. Press the right or left arrow keys to move forward or backward through the show at your own speed. (To re-enter automatic-advance mode, press the space bar again.)

  To stop the show, click the mouse.

- **Mail.** Start by selecting one picture, or a few. Then click the Mail button at the bottom edge of the screen. iPhoto asks you what size you want the photo to be — an extremely friendly gesture, because sending a *full-size* digital camera picture does your recipient absolutely no good. Thanks to a quirk of computer graphics, the *resolution* (number of dots) in a photo designed for printing is grossly overblown for the number of dots needed for viewing on the screen. That's why iPhoto offers to scale the picture down to a reasonable size, such as 640 by 480 dots.

Click Compose. After a moment, you'll find yourself facing an empty piece of e-mail (Chapter 8), with the file already attached, ready for you to type in the address and any comments you'd like to include. One click on the Send command sends your picture on its merry way.

✔ **Order Prints.** Click this button if you'd like your electronic photos turned into regular old glossy prints, exactly as though they came from the drugstore. The difference, of course, is that they get transmitted to the "drugstore" (actually Kodak) via the Internet, and you have print-size options from 4 by 6 all the way up to poster size. You'll be offered a complete price list when you click the Order Prints button — and the thrilling opportunity to type in your credit-card information.

✔ **Order Book.** More on this amazing feature in a moment.

✔ **HomePage.** Highlight some photos, and then click this button to turn them into a bona fide Web page, which iPhoto can actually post on the Internet for billions of people to see. This feature requires that you've signed up for an iTools account, as described in Chapter 6. You'll be offered a choice of designs for your online gallery, plus the opportunity to type in some captions for them.

Finally, click the Publish button and sit back with a magazine while your computer hangs your photos on the great refrigerator door of cyberspace. (Make careful note of the Web address you'll be shown on the screen. This is the address you need to give your friends and family — anybody who would like to actually see your photo gallery.)

✔ **Desktop.** Click one photo — a really, really good one — and then click this button at the bottom edge of the screen. iPhoto instantly fills your desktop background with that photo — an intoxicating and joyous feature that you'll soon wish had a physical counterpart in the world of wallpaper and house paint.

✔ **Screen Saver.** As noted in Chapter 3, Mac OS X offers a spectacular screensaver feature that fills your screen with animated, gently flowing photographs when your iMac isn't in use. (After all, you have to eat and take showers *sometime*.)

The iMac comes with some stunning, but canned, photos for this purpose (nature shots, space shots). But if you highlight the name of an album in iPhoto and then click the Screen Saver button at the bottom of the screen, you turn that album's contents into a screensaver. Of course, you may have to wait for half an hour or so to see the effect — that's when the screensaver finally kicks in — but you're sure to be amazed and impressed.

Professional bookmaking for the amateur

Screen saver, schmeen saver! If you really want to see what your computer can do, turn your pictures into a *book*. We're talking about a hardback, linen-covered, acid-free, full-color, professionally-published gift book that arrives in a beautiful slipcover in about seven days from an actual printing plant. It costs about $30 — more if you go beyond 10 pages — and creates an impact on the lucky recipients that neither you nor they will ever, ever forget.

Here's how you go about designing your book.

1. **Put the pictures you'll want to include into an album of their own, as described earlier in this chapter.**

   Feel free to drag them around on the screen so that they're in the right order for the book, like this:

   Remember that you can have 1, 2, 3, or 4 pictures on each page of the book.

2. **Click the Book button beneath the picture viewing area (in between the Edit and Share buttons).**

   Now you find yourself in a miniature book-design program.

Type captions here

Theme pop-up menu

Page Design pop-up menu

Drag pages to rearrange them

3. Choose an underlying design for your book, using the Theme pop-up menu.

For example, the theme called Classic leaves plenty of margin around your pictures, but Picture Book blows up your photos so that they fill the page edge to edge. Story Book goes for a more interesting, less square look by placing the photos at slight angles, and overlapping on each page.

4. Click each page of the book and design it, using the Page Design pop-up menu to specify how many photos should appear on that page.

As you change the number of pictures on a certain page, note that the pictures on the pages *following* it slide left or right to take up the slack. For that reason, consider turning on the Lock Page checkbox as soon as a certain page is exactly the way you like it, so that this slip-sliding won't ruin your design.

You can also designate special pages as the cover, introduction, and final pages. You can also rearrange the pages just by dragging them horizontally. Some of the page designs feature text boxes, too, where you can type in captions and descriptions. (To choose the font and size for the type, open the Edit menu, choose Font, and choose Show Fonts from the submenu.)

5. **When the whole book looks good, click the Share button, and then click the Order Book button.**

   The program now offers you the chance to choose the color you want for the cover. It may also warn you that some of the photos' resolution (quality) is too low to look good in your book. If you proceed without making the photos smaller, they'll look a little bit blotchy in the resulting published book — generally something you'll want to avoid, except perhaps in photo essays about skin-disease clinics.

How you wrap up your book-publishing process depends on whether or not you've created a "1-click account," a means of ordering stuff from Apple without having to type in your name and address over and over again. And to do *that,* you'll need an *Apple ID* — a name and password that you make up. The software guides you through both of these steps.

Finally, your book design is sent to the Internet, and the finished book — about 9 by 11 inches, with the photos printed directly onto the glossy, acid-free pages — arrives at the address you specify in about a week. Both the book and, by extension, you, look absolutely spectacular.

iTunes 2: The CD and MP3 Jukebox

iTunes is the ultimate digital jukebox. It plays music CDs, brings you Internet radio stations, creates and plays *MP3 files* (remarkably compact sound files that store CD-quality music), and even lets you burn new music CDs of your own, composed of your favorite tracks from *other* CDs. This, ladies and gentlemen, is power: You can actually create modified versions of your favorite CDs, in which all of the songs you can't stand have been eliminated.

You'll find iTunes in your Applications folder. The first time you run it, you encounter something called the iTunes Setup Assistant: a series of interview screens that lets you specify (a) whether or not you want iTunes to be the program your Mac uses for playing MP3 files from the Internet, (b) whether or not you want it to ask your permission every time it connects to the Internet, and (c) if you want the program to scan your hard drive for all MP3 files already on it. In general, you want to accept all of these proposals.

At last you arrive at the main iTunes screen, thoughtfully pre-stocked with a few songs. To play one, click its name and then click the big Play triangle at the upper-left corner of the screen (or press the space bar). Click the same button (or press the space bar again) to stop the music.

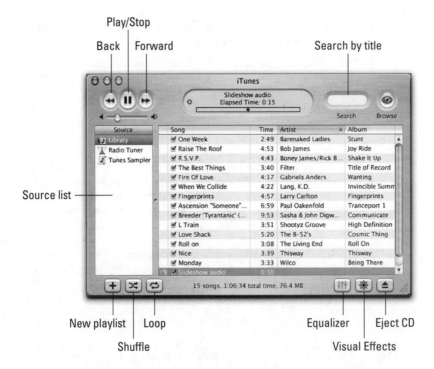

Here's some of the other fun you can have with your little database of music:

✔ **Back, Forward:** Hold down these buttons with your mouse to fast-forward or rewind through a particular song. Click *without* holding down the button to jump to the next or previous song. (The little speaker icon to the left of the song names lets you know which song is playing.)

✔ **Volume:** Drag the slider to make the music louder or softer. (Pressing ⌘-up arrow or ⌘-down arrow does the same thing.)

✔ **Shuffle, Loop:** These buttons work just as they do on a CD player. The Shuffle button plays the songs in a random order, so that you don't have to listen to them in the same sequence every time. When you've clicked the Loop button, your songs will play to the end and then repeat. If you see a tiny digit 1 superimposed on this button, your playlist will loop only once.

- ✔ **Visual Effects:** When you click this button, iTunes presents an onscreen laser-light show that pulses, beats, and dances in perfect sync to the music. The effect is hypnotic and wild. (For real party fun, invite some people who grew up in the '60s to watch.)

  Once the show begins, by the way, don't miss the Full Screen command in the Visuals menu. It makes the laser-light show fill your entire screen. No, you won't get a lot of work done, but staring at this psychedelic display may well expand your mind by several sizes.

- ✔ **Graphic Equalizer:** If you click this button, iTunes displays a handsome, brushed-aluminum control console that lets you adjust the strength of each musical frequency independently. Drag the sliders (bass on the left, treble on the right) to accommodate the strengths and weaknesses of your speakers or headphones. Or just use the pop-up menu above the sliders to choose a canned set of slider positions for Classical, Dance, Jazz, Latin, and so on.

Audio CDs

If you're a college student or a teenager, the main thing you may hope to accomplish with iTunes (or, indeed, the iMac itself) is to collect MP3 files of your favorite pop music.

But if that's not your particular passion, you may want to fill up the main list in iTunes just by inserting a music CD. The songs on it immediately show up in the list.

The iPod

The iPod is a beautiful, tiny, white-and-chrome Apple MP3 player that contains enough storage space to hold 1,200 or 2,400 songs, depending on which model you buy. Make a note to yourself: If you ever become a contestant on *Survivor,* choose one of these babies as your luxury item.

In any case, iTunes 2 is designed to be the loading dock for the iPod. All you have to do is connect the iPod to the Mac via its included white cable. You'll see the iPod's icon show up on your desktop as though it's a hard drive (which it is). You'll also see an iPod icon show up in the iTunes "folder list." Click its icon to see what's on it.

The beauty of this arrangement is that the icon automatically updates itself to reflect the music in your iTunes library. Every time you add or delete songs in iTunes, the contents of the icon are updated automatically to match.

At first, they may show up with the exciting names "Track 01," "Track 02," and so on. Fortunately, provided you have an Internet connection, iTunes thoughtfully goes online and consults cddb.com, a global database of music CDs and their contents. If it finds a match among the thousands of CDs there, it copies the album and song names right into iTunes, where they reappear every time you use this particular music CD.

Copying CD songs to your hard drive

You're entitled to be puzzled by the heading above this paragraph. You already have your music on CDs — what possible good does it do you to copy their songs to your hard drive?

Good question, and here's a good answer: Once you've copied your songs onto the iMac itself, you can play them whenever you like, without requiring the original CD. Once you've collected the music from *several* CDs in this way, furthermore, you can mix and match the songs on them in ways you'd never be able to do with a single CD player.

To *rip* a CD in this way (that is, to copy its songs onto your hard drive), insert the disc, and then make sure that only the songs you want to capture have checkmarks in the main list, like this:

Then click the Import button at the upper-right corner of the window. Watch the display at the top of the window to see how long the conversion is going to take, and which song iTunes is working on; iTunes plays the music as it works. (You can click the tiny X in this display window to cancel the importing.) As iTunes finishes processing each song, you see a small, circled checkmark next to its name in the main list to help you remember that you've got it on board and no longer need the CD in your machine.

When it's all over, you'll find the imported songs listed in your Library (click the Library icon in the left-side Source list). From there, you can drag them into any other *playlist,* as described next.

Playlists

When you click Library in the left-side Source list, you see, in the main part of the screen, every MP3 file iTunes knows about. Here's the best part: To find a particular song, just type a few letters into the Search blank above the list. iTunes hides all but the ones that match, instantly, even if there are thousands of songs there. (Backspace over what you've typed to see your full list again.)

But you may not want to listen to *all* your songs every time you need a little musical diversion. That's why iTunes lets you create *playlists* — folders in the Source list that contain only certain songs, like albums of your own devising. You might create one called Party Tunes, another called Blind Date Music, and so on. (If you've read the first part of this chapter, this concept should sound distinctly familiar: It's exactly the same idea as the little albums you can create in iPhoto.)

To create a new playlist, click the + button in the lower-left corner of the window. A new playlist shows up in the list above it. You can rename a playlist by clicking its name. Then all you have left to do is to add songs to it, just by dragging them out of the main Library list and onto the new playlist icon.

Exactly as in iPhoto, you're not actually copying songs; you're simply putting imaginary duplicates of them — pointers, really — in the playlist folders. It's perfectly OK to put the same songs into as many different playlists as you like.

Burning music CDs

This is a great time to be alive, isn't it? Only a few years ago, creating your own music CDs required a $50 million fabrication plant, an airtight "clean suit," and a knack for working with lasers. Now here you are with your little iMac, all set to become your own private record label — with little more talent than the ability to click a button.

When it's all over, you'll be able to play the resulting CDs on any standard CD player, just like the ones from Tower Records — but containing only the songs you like, in the order you like, with the annoying ones subtracted away.

Start by creating a playlist, as described in the previous section, filled with the songs you want, and dragged into the order you want. Keep an eye on the readout at the bottom of the list, which tells you how much time the songs will take (74 minutes is the limit for a CD).

Internet radio

Audio CDs and MP3 files aren't the only sources of sound you can listen to as you work. iTunes also lets you tune in to any of hundreds of Internet-based radio stations, which may turn out to be the most convenient music source of all. They're free, they play 24 hours a day, and their music collections make yours look like a drop in the bucket.

When you click Radio Tuner in the left-side Source list, you'll see, in the main list, categories like Blues, Classic Rock, Classical, and so on. Click the little triangle beside a name to see a list of radio stations in that category.

When you see one that looks interesting, click it and then click the Play button. Wait a moment for your Mac to connect to the appropriate Internet site, and then let the music begin!

Unfortunately, there's no easy way to capture Internet broadcasts or save them onto your hard drive. You can, however, drag the name of one into another "folder" in the Source List to make it easier to get to later on.

When everything is set up, click the Burn CD button in the playlist window. Insert a blank CD into the Mac and then click Burn CD again. (Use CD-R discs, the kind that you can record only once. CD-RW discs — the ones that you can erase and re-record — are not only more expensive, but may not work in standard CD players.)

The burning process takes some time — you can always cancel by clicking the tiny X button in the progress bar — but you can switch into other programs to get some work done while iTunes chugs away. When the process is over, the freshly burned CD pops out of the iMac. Label the top of it with a magic marker, and enjoy the head rush that comes from being a master of your own music.

Chapter 11

iSpielberg: Digital Movies and DVDs

In This Chapter

▶ Grabbing video shots from a digital camera

▶ Trimming and re-ordering footage in iMovie

▶ Adding music, sounds, and effects

▶ What to do with your finished movie

M aking digital movies on a computer isn't a new thing. For years, high-tech companies sold the $5,000 add-on circuit boards and $800 software programs you needed to do so. But the results weren't anything like what you'd see on TV. The finished movies played on your screen in a window the size of a Triscuit. And they were jerky. If you wanted full-screen, smooth video, you'd have had to assemble $100,000 worth of equipment. Not many people bothered.

But oh, what a difference a decade makes. You lucky, lucky soul: You're alive to see the dawn of a new era, in which ordinary mortals like you can make astonishingly high-quality movies with nothing more than a camcorder and your iMac. Everything you need — the circuitry and the software — is already built in. As you transfer your footage back and forth between the iMac and the camcorder, the film retains 100 percent of its quality, always playing full-screen, smooth, bright, and vibrant.

Got What It Takes?

This kind of moviemaking doesn't require the mountains of gear it once did, but it does require a *digital* camcorder.

Camcorders that accept only VHS, VHS-C, 8 millimeter, or Hi-8 tapes are *not* digital. If you bought your camcorder before 1997, it's not digital, either. True digital camcorders, which start at around $600, are very compact. Sony, Canon, JVC, and Panasonic make them. These cameras accept one-hour tapes called *Mini DV* cassettes, shown below, which record CD-quality sound and video of absolutely breathtaking quality.

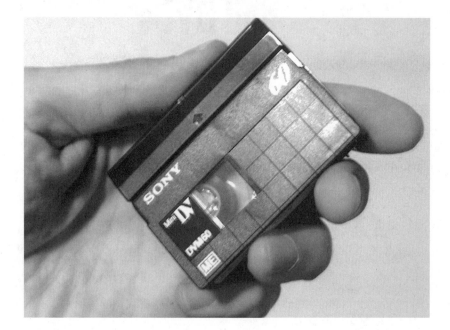

I realize that $600 is a lot to pay for your next iMac accessory. Before you take the plunge, test the waters by (a) reading this chapter and (b) taking the iMovie tutorial. To do that, launch iMovie. From the Help menu, choose Tutorial; you'll be led through the construction of a short Kids Washing the Dog movie using film clips that are already on your hard drive.

If you do decide to buy a camcorder, do your shopping on the Internet. At Web sites like *www.amazon.com*, you can survey long lists of digital camcorders and buy one at a discount — with no sales tax.

The last item you need is a "4-pin-to-6-pin" FireWire cable, which you'll have to buy from a computer store (or, to save money, from a Web site like *www.buy.com.*) *FireWire* is one of the built-in iMac technologies that makes all this possible. It's a high-speed cable that plugs into the FireWire jacks on the back of your computer. (See Chapter 19 for a picture.) Hook the tiny end up to the corresponding jack on your camcorder (this jack may be concealed by a plastic cover), and the other end to your iMac's FireWire jack.

Kinds of digital camcorders

A digital camcorder makes a pretty heady addition to your iMac. Using it and iMovie, you can edit your own home movies — a simple act that's sure to be appreciated by your fellow humans — or even produce professional-quality independent films.

You can plug either of two kinds of camcorders into the back of your iMac:

MiniDV camcorders. These are some of the smallest camcorders you can buy; Sony, Canon, Panasonic, and JVC make them, for example. The prices start at $600, but run up into the thousands. These camcorders take tiny, matchbox-sized cassettes that hold one hour each and cost about $8 per tape (from *www. bhphoto.com,* for example).

Digital8 camcorders. This fascinating hybrid, only from Sony, accepts 8mm or Hi-8 tapes,

which are much less expensive than MiniDV tapes. These camcorders are bulkier than MiniDV ones, but also less expensive.

Onto these cassettes, Digital8 camcorders record the same digital signal found on mini-DV camcorders, so the quality is just as good. But they can play back *either* digital video *or* traditional, analog video. This kind of camcorder, in other words, is a good solution if you have a library of old 8mm tapes that you'd like to edit in iMovie; your Mac can't tell which kind of tape the Digital8 camcorder is playing.

Either way, a FireWire cable connects the camcorder to your Mac. Beware, though: Editing video can put your brain into a dreamy trance. You'll look up and it'll be next week, with a pile of unread newspapers on your doorstep.

Filming Your Life

Not many people actually make *films* with their digital camcorders — writing a script, getting actors together, and all that jazz. Most people wind up just editing their home-movie footage, and that's a very good thing. If you've ever spent time at a friend's house watching six consecutive hours of little Goober spitting up, you know that a *good* home movie is an *edited* home movie.

The first step in making movies on your iMac is capturing life with your camcorder. There's not a lot to it, actually: Press the red button to start filming, press it again to stop. Oh, and take off the lens cap.

But the quality of your equipment is so good, and the results are so exciting, that it's worth learning a few tricks to make your stuff look more professional:

> ✔ **Go easy on the zooming.** Yes, I know, your camcorder has a zoom in/zoom out button that's really fun to use. It's also really nauseating to watch later. Try to limit yourself to a single zoom — or none — per

shot. Use the zoom mostly when it creates a visual punch line: There's little Timmy with a kite string in his hands, but your zoom-out reveals that the other end is, in fact, tied to the collar of a goat that's pulling him down the street on rollerblades.

✔ **Try a tripod.** For sure, turn on your camcorder's "image stabilization" feature, if it has one. But the biggest difference between home footage and pro TV footage is the tripod. These things are cheap — I found one for $30 at *www.amazon.com* — and the resulting stability makes an enormous difference to the quality of the finished movie.

✔ **For dialog, use a clip-on microphone.** The other hallmark of amateur work is the sound. The camcorder's built-in mike not only picks up its own machinery, but sounds lousy if you're more than six feet from the speaker. A tie-clip mike is about $20 at Radio Shack; pick up a couple of extension cords for it, too, plug them into your camcorder's microphone jack, and you won't believe how much better your flicks sound.

✔ **For iMovie movies, shoot too much.** MiniDV cassettes are expensive — maybe $6 per one-hour tape. If you didn't have an iMac, I'd suggest that you be very selective in what you film. But the beauty of iMovie is that it lets you *edit down* your video, and then *put it back* onto the videotape! You don't lose any quality in the process. For that reason, you may want to keep the camcorder running more liberally than you would otherwise. Doing so improves the chances that you'll catch really good stuff (especially if you're filming children, animals, or hurricanes). You can always cut the boring stuff and re-use the original tape later.

Step 1: Dump the Footage into iMovie

Once you've filmed and gotten some good scenes, you're ready for the fun to begin. Connect your camcorder to one of the FireWire jacks on the back of your iMac. Put the camcorder into what's usually called VTR mode (also known as VCR or Playback mode). Launch iMovie — its icon looks like a Hollywood clapper board, and it's on the Dock unless you removed it. (It's also in your Applications folder.) Then click the Camera icon, which you can see in this big-picture view of iMovie:

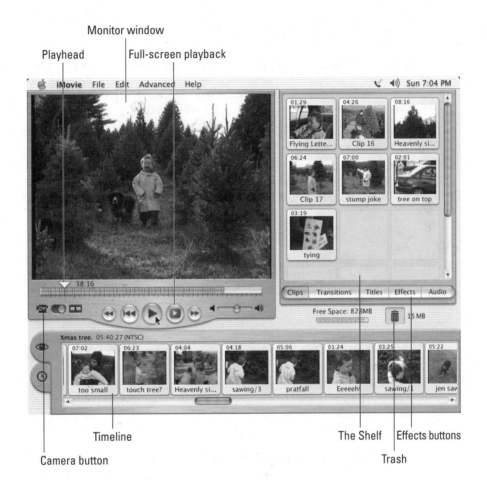

Monitor window

Playhead   Full-screen playback

Timeline   The Shelf   Effects buttons

Camera button   Trash

If all is well, you'll see a big blue screen at the upper-left with the words "Camera Connected" prominently displayed. You're ready to begin grabbing choice scenes from the camcorder for storage on the iMac.

Unless you have some weirdo off-brand camcorder, you can actually control the play, stop, rewind, and fast-forward functions of the camcorder using the buttons on the screen of your iMac — an impressive and tingly feature. You do so by clicking the buttons below the big monitor screen.

Capturing clips

Here's the deal: As you watch the tape, whenever you see a piece of footage worth including in your movie, capture it! You do that by clicking the Import button once to start, and again to stop, the capturing, while your camcorder plays. Or press the space bar, which is often easier and more accurate: Press once to start, once to stop.

Each time you grab a scene from your tape, it appears on the Shelf (see the figure at the beginning of Step 1), where it's represented by what looks like a 35mm slide. Congratulations: You've just created a *clip*. The whole business of movie editing, both on your iMac and in Hollywood, boils down to rearranging clips.

The Shelf is a waiting room, a place to store clips temporarily before you start plunking them into the *timeline* at the bottom of the screen. (The time-line can hold as many clips as your hard drive can hold.) Once you've cap-tured enough clips to start assembling your movie, drag them down into the timeline window.

How much footage can your iMac hold?

Considering that this entire book's manuscript consumes less than 2 megabytes of the 40,000 or 60,000 on your hard drive, you may have wondered why these models came with such enormous hard drives. You're about to find out.

Turns out that digital video, once transferred from your camcorder to your iMac, consumes a *huge* amount of hard-drive space — 210 megs of your hard drive *per minute* of video! Do the math, and you find out that a typical iMac can hold only a couple hours' worth of footage at a time.

Speed versus quality

Despite the awe-inspiring power and speed of an iMac DV, it's not quite potent enough to play video, while you're working on it, at full speed *and* with full clarity. You may notice some slight blotchiness in the picture as you build your movie.

It's important to note that this problem exists *only* on the iMac screen! Once you send your finished movie back to videotape, or save it as a finished QuickTime movie file, you'll get both stunning picture quality and full smoothness of playback.

This isn't such a big deal, however; the whole object is to edit the stuff on your iMac and then put it *back* onto your videocassettes, where you can play them for friends, family, and backers. Think of your iMac as a temporary operating table, where you work on a little bit of the patient at a time. You can transfer video between your camcorder and your iMac thousands of times; the footage will never deteriorate in quality, as it would with, for example, an audiocassette.

As you work in iMovie, watch the Free Space indicator above the timeline. The graph is blue when you've got plenty of space left, yellow when things are getting tight, and red when your hard drive is nearly full. At that point, it's time to dump your movie back out to a tape, as described later in this chapter, and then delete the retired clips from your hard drive. (Each file you save from iMovie appears in a folder of its own, which contains a Media folder. To delete video files you're *certain* you won't need again, throw away this Media folder.)

Naming, playing, and trimming clips

Once your clips are on the Shelf, you can do three things with them: rename them, play them, and trim them.

Renaming clips

As your clips show up on the Shelf, they take on such exciting names as Clip 01, Clip 02, and so on. Making a movie out of them is much easier if they're renamed Goober Smiles, Goober Falls Over, and so on. To do so, just click once on a clip's name, type the new name, and press the Return key.

Playing clips

To play a clip that's on the Shelf, click it once. You'll see the first frame show up in the Monitor. At this point, you can use any of the VCR-type buttons to play this clip, just as you used them to control your camcorder earlier in this lesson. You can use the same keyboard shortcuts, too.

Note, by the way, that pressing the Rewind or Fast-Forward buttons (or keystrokes) *repeatedly* makes iMovie play back faster and faster in the corresponding direction.

You can also drag the tiny box called the *playhead,* shown in the previous illustration, to view earlier or later parts of the clip.

Trimming clips

Even more important is *trimming* your clips. Like pro video editors, you'll quickly learn that it's always safest to capture, from your camcorder, more footage than you need — a few seconds before and after the main action, for example. Then, later, it's a snap to trim out the dead wood.

To trim a clip, click its picture in the Shelf (or in the timeline, if you've put it there). In the Monitor window, click just beneath the Monitor scroll bar, as shown here at left:

Two triangular handles appear. Drag these handles apart, as shown above at right. The scheme is simple: Everything between them remains in the final clip; everything outside of them will be lost forever. If you find using the mouse too clunky for making fine, frame-by-frame movements of these handles, click one and then press the arrow keys on your keyboard to move it one frame at a time. (Add the Shift key to move one of these handles in *ten*-frame jumps.)

As you choose parts of a scene to crop out, keep this tip in mind: If you plan to use iMovie's cross-fades from one scene into another, leave a second or two of extra footage on the clip you're trimming. The iMovie program will do its cross-fading during this extra stuff, leaving the *really* important action un-faded.

Finally, when you've got just the good part isolated, choose Crop from the Edit menu. Everything outside your triangle handles gets chopped out. (See the little Trash can icon on the screen? Its megabyte count increases to hint at the stuff you've cropped out. You can't double-click this Trash icon to pull stuff out of it, as you can the real Trash icon on your desktop. But using the Edit menu's Undo command, you *can* undo the last ten steps you took in iMovie — including cropping, deleting clips, and otherwise adding stuff to the iMovie Trash can.)

Step 2: Build the Movie

To assemble your clips into a movie, drag them out of the Shelf and into the timeline at the bottom of the screen. Once there, each clip is an individual tile that you can drag left or right to make it play before or after the other clips.

As you work with your movie, what happens when you click the Play button (or press the space bar) depends on what's highlighted:

✔ If a clip is highlighted with a bright yellow border in the timeline, pressing the space bar plays only that clip. To un-highlight all clips, choose None from the Edit menu, or just click above the timeline window.

✔ To highlight a stretch of just three or four clips for playback, click the first one, and then Shift-click the second one (that is, click it while pressing your Shift key).

> ✔ If nothing is highlighted, the whole movie you've built plays, starting at
> the location of the playhead under the Monitor. Press the Home key to
> start from the beginning.

When no clip is highlighted in the timeline, moreover, you can drag the playhead under the Monitor window to jump around in the whole movie under
construction. As you do so (and while you play back a clip), you'll see the
tiny cursor crawl across that clip's picture in the timeline. Once again, you
can use the arrow keys to more precisely position the playhead.

Adding a crossfade

Those slick-looking crossfades between scenes, as seen every night on TV
news and in movies, are called *transitions*. iMovie offers several styles; click
the Transitions button on the Effects palette to make the list pop up.

Click the name of the transition you want. Use the slider above the
Transitions palette to specify how many seconds long you want the cross-
fade to last. (One second is fairly standard.) Once you've done so, drag the
name of the transition into the timeline window, between the two clips you
want joined in this way. They'll scoot apart to make room for the new transition icon that appears.

The instant you do so, a tiny red progress line starts to crawl across the
transition icon. Your iMac is now processing the crossfade — as the pros
would say, *rendering it* — by melding the end of one clip and the beginning
of the next. This rendering business is par for the course in video-editing
programs; in most programs, however, you're supposed to sit there, staring
dully at the progress indicator, until it's over. In iMovie, you can go right on
building your movie; that little red line will keep quietly crunching its way
across the transition icon in the background. When it's finished, click in your
timeline just before the transition, press the space bar to play, and marvel in
your new ability to make home movies look pro.

To delete a transition, click its icon in the timeline and then press Delete; to
edit it (by changing its length, for example), double-click its icon, which
returns you to the Transitions palette.

Adding titles

iMovie even lets you add rolling credits and opening titles to your little home
flicks. It's not quite sophisticated enough to let you create "Long, long ago, in
a galaxy far, far away"–type openings, but it beats block lettering on shirt
cardboards.

Start by clicking the Titles button. A list of title-animation styles pops up. In the tiny text box underneath the list, type the text you'll want for the credits. Note that some of the effects, such as Rolling Credits, let you type in *pairs* of text blobs, as shown in the following figure at left. After you've typed in a couple of pairs, click the + button to tack on yet another pair to your credits. The program automatically adds the dots and lines up to the names, as shown here at right:

Click the Preview button to see what this effect will look like. Adjust the timing slider above the list, exactly as with transitions, and then drag the name of the title into the timeline.

If you want to insert this title *in front of* a clip, so that the text appears on a black background, turn on the Over Black checkbox. If you'd rather have the text appear *on top of* your video, leave that box unchecked. You'll soon discover that superimposing a title on a clip usually breaks the clip in half — the part with the title superimposed is now one clip, and the unaffected part is separate.

Editing a title works exactly as it does with transitions: To eliminate one, double-click the title's icon in the timeline and then press Delete; to edit, double-click its icon. You jump back to the Effects palette, where you can tweak the text, the amount of time it will stay on the screen, and so on.

Color Effects

On the Effects palette, click Effects. The various effects here (Adjust Colors, Black and White, Brightness/Contrast, and so on) change the look of whatever footage you drag them onto.

You won't be able to make, say, *Star Wars Episode 10: Jabba's Clubhouse* using these simple "special effects." And don't expect to use, say, the Brightness effect to rescue some footage that was too dark; it can't do magic. Still, every now and then, you may find them handy.

Point just beneath the scrubber bar to make the selection triangles appear, as described earlier in this chapter, and use them to select the region of the movie to which you want the effect applied.

Now click the effect's name, and then fool around with its sliders. The Effect In and Effect Out sliders let you ease into, or out of, an effect over the course of a clip. When it looks good, click the Apply button.

You may be surprised to discover that iMovie chops up some of the clips when you apply an effect; that's because technically speaking, you can apply these footage-changing effects only to an entire clip at a time.

What's nice about these effects, by the way, is that they're removable. At any time — even after your debut at the Cannes festival — you can restore a clip to its original, un-effected form. Just click the clip in the timeline and then, on the Effects palette, click Restore Clip.

On the other hand, if you're confident you'll never want to do so, you can reclaim some disk space by clicking the button on the Effects palette called Commit. (Great name for a button, by the way. Too bad relationships don't have a Commit button.)

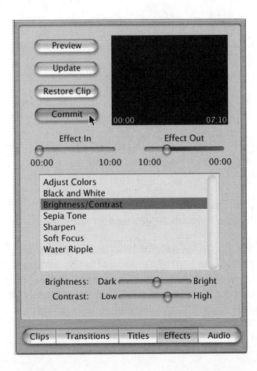

Grabbing music from a CD

As though a movie with crossfades and credits weren't pro enough, you can also add a music soundtrack. If you're a technically savvy musician (you know who you are), great; save your work as an AIFF file (you know what that is — its name *must* end with *.aif,* not *.aiff*) and import it into iMovie (you know how to do it).

If you're anyone else, you can rely on the kindness of your existing music CD collection, as long as nobody from the record company catches you. Insert a music CD into your iMac. In iMovie, click the Audio button on the Effects palette. A list of tracks from the CD appears. Click one, and then use the Play button on the Effects palette to find an appropriate snippet.

See the little clock tab on your timeline? Click it to view the audio tracks. Now every clip in your movie appears as a horizontal bar, whose length represents its playback length. All kinds of special editing options are available to you in this view, as you can see here:

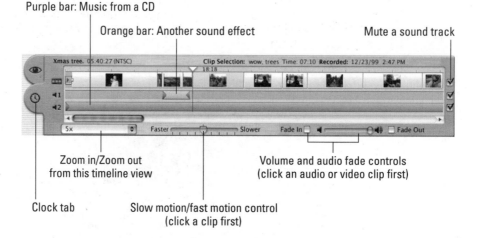

Purple bar: Music from a CD

Orange bar: Another sound effect

Mute a sound track

Zoom in/Zoom out from this timeline view

Volume and audio fade controls (click an audio or video clip first)

Clock tab

Slow motion/fast motion control (click a clip first)

Drag a song from the Music list down onto the bottom audio track. There it shows up as a colored stripe, as shown above.

Or, if you want to include only a part of the music, let the CD play; click the Record Music button once to start recording, and again to stop. The recorded music appears as a colored bar at the playhead point in the audio track, but you're welcome to drag it horizontally to make it start playing earlier or later.

You can, by the way, superimpose pieces of sound. Because there are only two tracks for sounds, including narration, music, and sound effects, telling the overlapping colored stripes apart can be a challenge. But on that occasion when you want your background music to be a simultaneous playing of Carly Simon and Scott Joplin, you'll be ready.

Narration and sound FX

If you click the Audio button on the Effects palette, you'll see that iMovie comes with a bunch of pre-recorded sound effects. Drag one onto an audio track to incorporate it into your film.

You can also record new sounds directly into your movie, thanks to the iMac's built-in microphone. Just click the clock tab of the timeline, so that you can see your audio tracks. Click above the tracks to set the playhead where you want to begin your narration. On the Effects palette, click Audio.

Finally, click Record Voice, lean close to the iMac microphone, and say what you've got to say. (The iMac microphone, if you were wondering, is the tiny pinhole at the lower-left corner of the screen.) You actually get to watch the movie play while you narrate, which makes it ideal for "Oh, here comes my favorite part"-type narrations. Click the Stop button (formerly the Record Voice button) to stop recording.

Your newly recorded sound appears as a colored bar in the sound track.

Editing sound in the timeline

Once you've laid a sound into the timeline, you can slide its colored ribbon right or left to align it better with the video. Drag a sound's triangular ending handle to make it end sooner; click a sound, then drag the volume slider to change its loudness; or click one of the checkboxes, Fade In or Fade Out, to add a professional-sounding fade when the music begins or ends. And, of course, you can delete the sound completely by clicking it and then pressing the Delete key.

Step 3: Find an Audience

After you're happy with your movie, and you've waited for all the little red rendering lines to fulfill their destinies, check your movie. Press the Home key (to rewind to the beginning) and then the space bar (to play it one last time). For a delightful taste treat, click the Full Screen button (the button just to the right of the big triangular Play button) to play the movie so that it fills your entire screen.

If everything looks good, you're ready to show your filmless film to people. You can do so in one of three ways: by sending it back to the videotape, by creating a QuickTime movie that other computers can play, or by preserving it forever on a real, live DVD.

Sending your movie back to the camcorder

There's a lot to be said for sending your finished video back to the camcorder's tape. By connecting the camcorder to a TV, you'll be able to play your masterpiece for anyone. And by connecting the camcorder to a regular VCR, you can make and distribute VHS copies to anyone who's interested.

Begin by putting a cassette into your camcorder. *Don't record over something important!* Consider keeping a separate cassette just for your finished projects, for example, so you never risk recording over some important original footage.

Now, from the File menu, choose Export Movie. The Export dialog box appears, as shown here. Choose To Camera from the Export pop-up menu, and then click Export.

If your camcorder is correctly connected to the iMac's FireWire jack, turned on, and in VTR (VCR) mode, it now records your movie. When the recording is complete, you can prove that the transfer was successful; click the Camera button in iMovie, and then use iMovie's usual Play and Rewind buttons to control the camcorder, making it show your work one last time in its final form.

Saving your movie as a QuickTime file

A *QuickTime movie* is a single file on your hard drive that you can double-click to watch, mail to other people, put on the World Wide Web, save onto another disk, and so on. The one big QuickTime bummer, though, is that these movies take up enormous amounts of disk space. A standard, 600-megabyte CD-ROM disc, for example, holds less than two minutes of full-screen video. Obviously, that kind of movie would be lousy for e-mailing to somebody or posting on the Web; it would take 56 *hours* to transfer by modem.

The object of creating a QuickTime movie, therefore, is to reduce the size of the file. You can do that in three ways:

✔ **Make the "screen" smaller.** Instead of filling your screen, most QuickTime movies play in a small, three-inch-square window.

✔ **Make the color fidelity worse.** Using a conversion process called *compression,* you can make the iMac describe the color of each dot of the movie using less information. The result is a smaller (but grainier) file.

✔ **Make the frame rate lower.** A QuickTime movie, like a movie-theatre movie, simulates motion by flashing dozens of individual still photos in sequence. The more of these *frames* appear per second, the smoother the motion — and the bigger the QuickTime file. By telling your iMac to save the QuickTime movie with only, say, 12 frames per second instead of the usual 24, you create a file that's only half as big (but doesn't play back as smoothly).

After wrapping up your iMovie movie, then, here's how you save it: From the File menu, choose Export. When the dialog box appears, choose To QuickTime from the "Export:" pop-up menu.

Now you have to decide how you want to compress your movie file. The Formats pop-up menu in the dialog box offers you several canned settings:

✔ **Web Movie, Small:** Shrinks the movie to a three-inch window, shows 12 frames per second.

✔ **E-mail, Small:** Shrinks your movie to a postage-stamp-sized "movie screen," showing only 10 frames per second — a file small enough to send someone by e-mail.

✔ **Streaming Web Movie, Small:** Same idea as "Web Movie, Small," except that it's designed for techies who know how to put movies online for playback right from their Web pages.

✔ **CD-ROM Movie, Medium:** Now we're talkin'. This option creates a movie that takes up nearly a quarter of the screen, playing a smooth 15 frames per second — with CD-quality sound. Don't try e-mailing *this* baby; it's too big to send. Play it off a hard drive, or save it onto a blank CD, as described in Chapter 4.

✔ **Full Quality, Large:** Creates a QuickTime movie that's almost like TV. Plays in a huge window that nearly fills the screen, showing 30 frames per second (TV quality), with CD-quality sound. This kind of movie format takes up gigantic amounts of disk space, and probably won't even play back smoothly. Think of it as a storage (archive) format, not a playback format.

✔ **Expert:** This command brings up a dialog box where Settings buttons let you specify *exactly* how your movie is compressed: how many frames per second you'd like, what size window it plays in, how much the colors should be compressed, and so on. *Hint:* Most of the time, you'll get the best results by choosing Sorenson Video, Sorenson Video 3, or H.263 from the Compressor pop-up menu. These compression methods create movies that take up a lot less disk space, without rendering the colors too grainy. Try each one to see which one produces the best size/quality tradeoff for your particular movie.

When you're finished setting up the size and quality of your finished movie, click Export. In the resulting dialog box, type a name for the finished movie (for best results, leave *.mov* at the end of its name), and then click the Save button. iMovie begins the massive task of converting your movie into the compressed version.

This conversion can take a *long* time. Do not attempt to sit and watch it happen; let it run overnight. Find something useful to do — like watching a movie.

When it's all over, you'll find the finished movie in your Home folder, inside the Movies folder. Double-click it to open it into a program called QuickTime Player; press the space bar to begin playback.

Burning your movie onto a real DVD

All flat-screen iMacs can burn CDs. But the more expensive models go one step beyond. Thanks to an option called the SuperDrive, they can actually "burn" real, live DVD discs, which play back in any standard DVD player. (You youngsters may think this is no big deal — but until the SuperDrive came along, burning a DVD required a $5,000 burning machine and a $2,500 piece of software to run it. You, on the other hand, made out like a bandit.)

There's no better way to screen your finished movies, even for technically backward friends and family who wouldn't know a computer if it fell on their heads. Chances are good that even they own a TV, though. And both you and they will be blown away by the picture and sound quality.

Not sure if your iMac can burn DVDs? Check your Applications folder for the presence of a program called iDVD 2. If you've got it, then your machine has everything you need to make DVDs of your very own.

Everything, that is, except the DVD itself. You can buy five-packs of blank DVD discs from the Apple Web site *(www.apple.com)* for $25 or less (the prices keep dropping).

Exporting your iMovie

When you're finished editing your project in iMovie, choose Export Movie from the File menu. In the Export dialog box, choose the "For iDVD" option. Click Export, type a name for the movie, and then click Save.

iMovie takes some time to prepare the DVD-ready file, which it puts into the Movies folder of your Home folder. This movie file will occupy a relatively enormous amount of space.

Setting up the DVD

As you probably know, a DVD is slightly more complicated than a videotape. When you pop a DVD into its player, you get a *menu screen* — a bunch of buttons that let you jump to any scene in the movie.

To design that screen, you need the delightfully simple program called iDVD 2, which you'll find in your Applications folder. Open the iDVD 2 folder to find the actual iDVD *program* icon, which you should double-click to get started.

The first screen you encounter looks like the box shown here at top:

Click New Project, type a name for your DVD (previous illustration, bottom), and then click Save. After a moment, you arrive at a thrillingly animated screen, accompanied by some tribal-sounding music, as shown in the following illustration.

This is, as they say, only an artist's conception of how your finished DVD menu screen will look. You're about to change it beyond all recognition.

Designing the menu screen

To design the background for your menu screen, start by clicking the Theme button in the lower-left corner of the screen. A tidy little drawer pops out of the left side of the screen, like this:

Running man = Animated backdrop with music

Main menu screen for your DVD

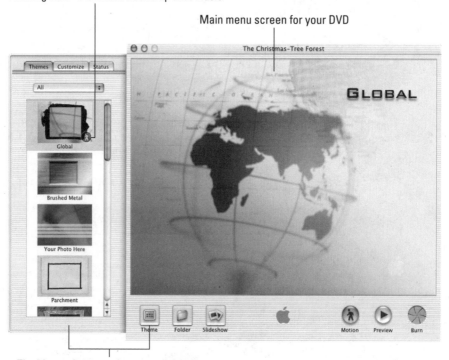

The "drawer" opens when you click here

Try clicking each of the sample backdrops in turn, considering how each might look as your main menu screen. You'll notice that some of them (those marked by a walking-man icon) have actual motion to them, which you may consider either astonishingly professional-looking or cloyingly annoying.

In any case, keep exploring these canned options until you find a look that you like for your main menu screen — a sandy background for vacation movies, a pink or blue ribbony one for baby videos, and so on. Nor should you feel limited to the ones Apple provides; you can use any image you like as a backdrop. Just drag a graphics file from your desktop (or the Pictures folder in your Home folder) into the iDVD window, like this:

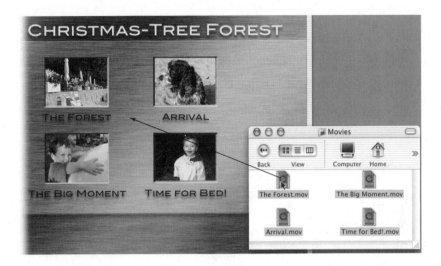

Creating movie buttons

Next, drag your exported movie from your Movies folder into the iDVD window, as shown in the preceding illustration. In fact, you may want to drag several — each menu screen holds up to six movies, as long as their length doesn't exceed 90 minutes. Drag them around into a sequence you like; click their names to retitle them.

More than six movies

All right, you prolific bigwig. So you've got more than six movies, eh?

The main menu on a DVD can contain only six buttons, take it or leave it. If you've prepared more than six iMovie movies, you'll have to spill them over onto a second menu page.

To do that, delete the sixth movie from the main screen, if you've added one (click it and then press the Delete key). Then click the Folder button at the bottom of the window. iDVD creates a new button for you, which you should feel free to rename or even dress up with a graphic of your own (by dragging a photo or graphics file onto it from, for example, the Pictures folder in your Home folder).

Then double-click the "folder" button you've just created. iDVD now gives you a second empty page, which you can fill with movie buttons just as you did the first.

Well, six of them, anyway.

By branching out to secondary menu screens in this way, you can effectively fill your DVD with dozens of individual movies. Pity your viewer as you do so, however — remember that somebody's actually going to have to *navigate* your menu screens with their remote controls.

Dressing up those buttons

You can even specify which individual *frame* of each movie will appear as its button. To do so, click the movie button and then drag the tiny slider until you find a nice frame to represent that movie in this "table of contents" view, like this:

1. Click a "movie button" to see these controls.

2. Drag the slider to find just the right frame to serve as your button.

3. Turn off this checkbox if you don't want the movie button to play continuously.

While you're at it, consider the Movie checkbox (also shown in the previous picture). If it's turned on, then this movie button, when selected by remote control, will actually *play* about 30 seconds of the movie hiding behind that button. If you'd rather your buttons not do anything fancy when they're highlighted, turn off the Movie checkbox.

By the way, you're not limited to the fonts, colors, and button shapes that iDVD proposes, although they do look awfully nice as Apple has prepared them. If you click the Customize tab on the Themes panel shown two illustrations ago, you'll see that you can override all of these design elements. Use taste, though. The last thing the world needs is a bunch of cheesy-looking DVDs.

Previewing the work

When you've arranged the menu screen the way you like it, click the Preview button in the lower-right corner to summon a virtual remote control to the screen. You can use it to try out your simulated DVD. Click one of the miniature movie buttons, for example, to play that movie.

When the menu screens look just the way you like them, click the Burn button at the lower-right corner of the screen. Insert a blank DVD; the SuperDrive does the rest.

It takes about two hours to burn one hour of video in iDVD; if you've opted for the long-play, 90-minute mode, burning takes *dramatically* longer, and the picture quality is not as good.

When the burning is complete, the DVD pops out of your iMac. Label it, using magic marker on the top surface, and handle it only by the edges as you pop it into any standard DVD player. Your audience will at last get to savor your digital video in its full glory.

The iMac's Built-In DVD Player

The iMac can't just dish out DVDs — it can also take them. It can play back standard DVD discs you've rented from Blockbuster, rented from online DVD clubs like *www.netflix.com* and *www.DVDovernight.com,* or made yourself using iMovie and iDVD.

To play a DVD movie, open your CD tray by holding down the ⏏ key at the upper-right key on your keyboard. Put the DVD into the tray, and then tap the same key again to make the tray close itself.

The very first time you insert a DVD, you wait about a minute, and then you get a strange dialog box that says: "Since this is the first use of a DVD disc, the drive region must be initialized before playing. New Drive Setting: Region Code 1. You can only change the drive region 5 more times."

As an anti-illegal-copying system, your iMac requires that you tell it where you are in the world — and you can only change your mind about that five more times. If you're not especially interested in becoming a software pirate, this shouldn't be much of a limitation; just click Set Drive Region and get on with your life. (You have to do this using an administrator account, or with an administrator supervising you, as described in Chapter 13.) Click OK in the confirmation box, too.

Now you're in a program called Apple DVD Player, and the DVD movie starts playing automatically. Put the popcorn in the microwave; it's showtime.

You might have wondered, by the way, how, in the absence of a remote control, you're supposed to pause a flick when nature calls. Simple: Just move the mouse. Doing so makes the iMac's virtual remote appear, which looks like this:

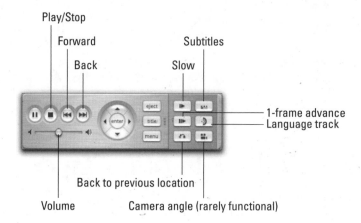

Now you can control the iMac like a VCR, using a combination of buttons on the remote and keys on your keyboard. For example:

- Click the square to stop, the triangle to play. You can also press the space bar to play and stop.

- Hold down the Forward or Backward button to fast-forward or rewind through the movie, watching in fast motion. You go at 4 times regular speed using this method (or whatever speed you've selected in the Scan Rate submenu of the Controls menu).

  You have much greater control, though, if you learn the ⌘-right arrow and ⌘-left arrow keystrokes. They let you switch between 2x, 4x, and 8x speeds (press repeatedly to cycle through these speeds) — and don't even require the remote control.

- *Click* the Forward or Backward button (without holding down the button) to jump to the next "chapter" of the movie.

- Adjust the volume by pressing ⌘-up arrow and ⌘-down arrow, or by dragging the volume slider on the remote.

- Full-screen mode is by far the most satisfying one (choose Enter Full Screen from the Video menu). But when you're trying to show off, choose Half Size or Normal Size from the Video menu. Now you've got the movie playing in a window of its own, which continues to play away even as you use other programs to surf the Web, reply to e-mail, or whatever.

Once your DVD disc is playing, the Menu button brings up the disc's special features. They may include foreign-language sound tracks, director's narration, subtitles for the hearing impaired, and a list of "chapters" (scenes) in the movie.

If you click the Advanced Drawer button shown in the previous illustration, you open a pull-out panel of advanced controls, including ones that let you play the movie in slow motion.

In Apple DVD Player, choose Apple DVD Player Help from the Help menu to read about even more fancy stuff you can do with DVDs. After a certain point, though, you'll probably decide that just *watching* Hollywood movies on your computer is fancy enough.

Part IV

Toward a New, Nerdier You

The 5th Wave   By Rich Tennant

JERRY AND LYLE ATTEMPT TO LOAD THE NEWEST VERSION OF "TOAST," CD BURNING SOFTWARE

OK, I got the Sunbeam fire wired to the iMac. Try putting the CD in the slot again.

In this part . . .

*E*nough about turning the computer off, e-mailing tribal members halfway around the world, and typing up mundane little bestsellers. Now it's time to get technical.

Not all of computer mastery is about fiddling with digital photos and listening to Internet radio stations. Sooner or later, you're going to have to confront some of the iMac's ickier, computerish aspects: How to switch it back to Mac OS 9 for compatibility's sake, how to set up a small network, how to set up security and privacy, and what to do when things go horribly wrong.

These are the topics of the next five chapters.

Chapter 12

Back to Mac OS 9

In This Chapter

▶ Why your iMac has two operating systems

▶ How to switch back to Mac OS 9 — and why

▶ Making old programs and old equipment work with your spanking-new iMac

*T*his chapter is about *operating systems* — the software that actually controls your iMac and is responsible for its look and its behavior. No, this reading isn't going to be quite as fluffy as *People* magazine, but look at the bright side: you'll emerge from the other end a better person for it, and you'll finally understand a few of your iMac's most bizarre personality quirks.

A Tale of Two Systems

All the way through this book so far, you've been enjoying descriptions and pictures of the operating system called Mac OS X (that's a Roman numeral ten, and you should pronounce it that way). Mac OS X has a lot to recommend it, including the fact that it virtually never crashes, it looks awesome, and it's generally extremely easy to figure out.

Unfortunately, it's only one of *two* operating systems that the modern-day iMac fan winds up having to learn about.

From the very first day you turned on the iMac, you might have noticed something peculiar about the main Macintosh HD window: It contains *two* System folders. One is just called System, and it bears a big X to tell you that this is the Mac OS X operating system. The other is called System Folder, and the 9 on its icon tells you that this is a copy of Mac OS 9, which is an older operating system.

Max OS 9   Max OS X

Mac OS 9 isn't anywhere near as stable or as beautiful as Mac OS X. It does, however, have about 15,000 things going for it: all the software programs that were written in the decades before Mac OS X came along. Sooner or later, you may run across — or download — a program that looks interesting, but hasn't been adapted to be Mac OS X-compatible.

Fortunately, your iMac can run Mac OS 9 just as well as it runs Mac OS X. In fact, it can run Mac OS 9 in either of two ways, both of which are described in this chapter.

The only downside to all of this is that now you've got *two different* operating systems to learn. The look, features, and locations of favorite commands are different in each one.

Two Mac OS 9 Methods

You can return to Mac OS 9 in either of two ways. Here's a quick rundown, so that you'll know what you're getting into:

✔ **Run Classic.** Your iMac came with a very special program called Classic, which you can think of as a Mac OS 9 *simulator*. It runs automatically whenever you try to open a pre-Mac OS X program.

At that point, the Classic (Mac OS 9) world takes over your screen, looking exactly like a Mac OS 9 computer. The 🍎 menu now has stripes, the menu bar is light gray instead of striped, and the name of the program you're using now appears on the right side of the screen instead of the left.

At this point, you are, in effect, running two computers at once: a Mac OS 9 computer running inside your Mac OS X one. At this point, you can run your older Mac OS 9 programs without a hitch.

I'm aware that this sounds hideously technical. Remain calm, however. The upcoming discussion will make it a lot less frightening. Furthermore, five years from now, none of this will be necessary, because every good piece of software will be available in a Mac OS X version.

✔ **Restart the Mac in Mac OS 9.** You can also return to Mac OS 9 by restarting your computer with the Mac OS 9 operating system in control. In this scenario, no trace of Mac OS X remains. (This isn't the same as running the Classic program, which still leaves Mac OS X in control.)

You should think of this trick as only a workaround — and an inconvenient one at that, because it involves turning your computer off and on again as you switch between Mac OS 9 and Mac OS X. There's only one time when you'd want to do it: When you want to use some scanner, printer, or drawing tablet that requires Mac OS 9 (and doesn't work in the Classic simulator).

You'll find instructions for setting up both of these configurations in the following pages.

Classic: The Mac OS 9 Simulator

The way you're most likely to encounter Mac OS 9 is in the form of the Classic simulator. It starts up automatically whenever you double-click the icon of a pre-Mac OS X program. At that point, the iMac says to itself: "Well, this program won't run in Mac OS X, so I'll just go ahead and launch my Mac OS 9 impersonator."

If you want to try this for yourself, double-click the Macintosh HD icon on your desktop, double-click the System Folder (the one bearing the 9 logo), open the Apple Menu Items folder inside it, and finally, double-click Calculator. (This isn't the beautiful Mac OS X Calculator you experimented with earlier in this book; it's the old, black and white, Mac OS 9 version.)

The first sign you have that something funny is going on is the appearance of a progress bar like this:

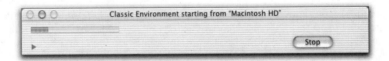

This bar is designed to entertain you while Classic starts up, which takes a couple of minutes. During the startup process, you'll also see a little Classic (numeral 9) icon bouncing up and down in your Dock, bursting with enthusiasm.

If you'd like even more entertainment, click the tiny triangle to the left of the progress bar. The screen expands to show you the full-size Mac OS 9 startup screen, as shown here:

Start up Classic automatically

If you find yourself doing a lot of waiting for Classic to start up, you might prefer to instruct your iMac to start up Classic *automatically* when the computer turns on. The iMac will take that extra minute or two to start up each day, as it loads first one operating system (Mac OS X) and then another (Mac OS 9).

But you won't care. You'll be going through the mail and doing bills, rather than sitting there staring at the progress bar.

Best of all, when you do need to run a Mac OS 9 program, you won't have to wait while Classic

starts up. The simulator will already be turned on and waiting for you.

If all of this sounds good, open your System Preferences program (click its icon on the Dock), and then click the Classic icon. Turn on the checkbox called "Start up Classic on login to this computer," and then close the window. From now on, your little Classic world will be turned on and waiting for you when you finally sit down to work.

When all the bouncing stops, you'll see a number of changes on your screen. Your menu is now rainbow-striped, and the commands in it are very different. The menu bar is light gray, the fonts are smaller, and the menus and commands are different. In short, you've now gone back in time to Mac OS 9.

Once Classic is running, you're free to use the Mac OS 9 program you originally double-clicked (the Calculator, for example) — or almost any other Mac OS 9 program, for that matter.

Understanding the Classic world

The icons of open Mac OS 9 programs appear on the Dock, just like Mac OS X programs. (Well, maybe not *just* like them: pre-Mac OS X programs often show up with blotchy, ragged icons on the Dock. They haven't been redesigned for the graphic elegance of the newer system.)

Remember, you're now running two operating systems simultaneously. Whenever you click the icon of a Mac OS X program on the Dock, you bring forward that program *and* you switch into Mac OS X. Your menu turns shiny blue. But when you double-click the icon of a Mac OS 9 program on the Dock, you bring forward that program and you switch into Mac OS 9. The menu is now striped.

You can even copy and paste information between the programs you have running in these two worlds.

It's important to note, however, that Mac OS 9 doesn't offer any of the fancy technologies that make Mac OS X so stable. In Mac OS X, a program might crash or lock up — but all of your other programs soldier on, unaffected. In Mac OS 9, however, one buggy program can still freeze or crash the entire Classic bubble. At that point, you may have to exit the entire Mac OS 9 portion of your machine, losing unsaved changes in any of your Mac OS 9 programs.

Even then, though, you won't have to restart the actual computer. All your Mac OS X programs remain safe, open, and running.

Getting out of Classic

There's no good reason to quit the Classic simulator, ever. Once you've waited for it to open, you may as well leave it running quietly in the background, so that you won't have to wait for that long Classic startup process the *next* time you want to use an older program.

On the other hand, if some program in the Classic half of your iMac should crash or bomb, you might wish you had a way to exit Classic, if only to restart it afresh.

To do so, open the System Preferences program (the light-switch icon on your Dock). Click the Classic icon to reveal this dialog box:

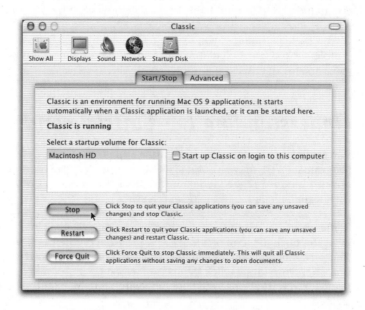

Just click the Stop button to shut down the Classic program. (Or, if it has crashed so badly that the Stop button doesn't work, click the Force Quit button instead.)

Restarting in Mac OS 9

If you're lucky, the Classic program is the only trace of Mac OS 9 you'll ever see.

Unfortunately, it only goes so far. It does a very good job at tricking your older programs into thinking that they're running on a Mac OS 9 computer — but your Mac is still not *actually* running Mac OS 9. Certain older pieces of add-on equipment, notably printers, expansion cards, and scanners, don't work except on a true Mac OS 9 computer. The Classic simulation just isn't good enough.

If you want them to work properly, you have only one option: restart the iMac *in* Mac OS 9. When you're finished using that scanner (or whatever), you can restart the Mac again, this time with Mac OS X "in charge."

Switching to Mac OS 9

Suppose you're running Mac OS X, and you need to duck back into Mac OS 9 to use, say, your scanner. The routine goes like this.

1. **Open System Preferences.**

   You can choose System Preferences from the menu, or you can click the light-switch icon on the Dock. The System Preferences screen appears.

2. **Click Startup Disk.**

   You now see controls that look like this:

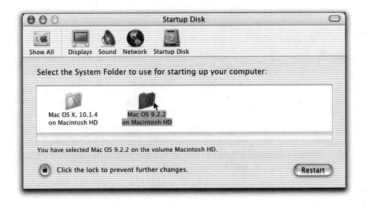

   The icons here represent the various System folders that your iMac has found. If you're like most people, you'll find only two icons here: the Mac OS 9 one and the Mac OS X one.

3. **Click the icon of the Mac OS 9 System folder, and then click Restart.**

   (If the little padlock icon in the lower-left corner looks locked, you must first click it and then seek the assistance of someone with an *Administrator* account on this Mac, as described in the next chapter, for the purpose of typing in his or her name and password. You're about to make the kind of change that's off limits to ordinary underling accounts.)

   The Mac asks you if you're sure you know what you're doing.

4. **Click "Save and Restart" (or press Enter).**

Your Mac restarts. When the screen lights up again after a moment, you see the startup display that was once adored — or at least endured — by millions of Mac fans before the invention of Mac OS X.

For example, you'll see a parade of little icons across the bottom of the screen. (These are little pieces of software called *extensions,* each of which adds one feature or another to the iMac. They offered a handy way to give your Mac new features — until there were so many of them that they began to fight with each other, triggering system freezes and other kinds of instability. No wonder Apple eliminated them in Mac OS X.)

You're now fully back in Mac OS 9, ready to use all your old add-on equipment and software — just without the benefit of Mac OS X's stability, good looks, and other features.

You'll find that things work quite a bit differently in Mac OS 9. For example:

- The Trash is now a separate icon sitting in the lower-right corner of the screen.

- You don't open your programs from within the Applications folder. Instead, the Mac OS 9-compatible programs are generally in a folder called "Applications (Mac OS 9)."

- There's no Dock anymore, either. When you want to open a program or document, just double-click its icon.

- The name of the program you're using appears in the upper-*right* corner of the screen, not the upper-left. Furthermore, that upper-right corner of the screen is a *menu* that lists all the programs that are currently running, just like the little triangles underneath the icons in the Mac OS X Dock. Use this menu to switch from one program to another, if you like.

Switching to Mac OS X (long way)

Once you've finished your work in Mac OS 9, the process of returning to Mac OS X is very similar.

1. **From the menu, choose Control Panels.**

   The Control Panels window opens. This is the Mac OS 9 equivalent of System Preferences.

2. **Double-click the icon called Startup Disk.**

   The Startup Disk control panel appears, as shown here. After a moment, you'll see the names of both of your system folders.

3. **Click the icon of your Mac OS X System folder, and then click Restart.**

   Mac OS X starts up. After a moment, you'll be in familiar territory.

Switching to Mac OS X (short way)

The ritual of using the Startup Disk icon in the Control Panels window to switch back to Mac OS X is all well and good — if you bill by the hour.

But if your time is your own, you may prefer this sneaky shortcut. After you're finished with your Mac OS 9 work, choose Restart from the Special menu. Just as the screen lights up again, hold down the letter X key. Hold it down, in fact, until you see the smiling Macintosh icon and your cursor turns into a colorful spinning beach ball. Then you can let go of the key, confident that your computer is now starting up in Mac OS X.

(Note to techies: This trick works only if the Mac OS 9 and Mac OS X System folders are installed on the same hard drive.)

Chapter 13

Mono-Mac, Multi-People

● ●

In This Chapter

▶ Privacy and security come to the iMac

▶ Password-protecting your stuff

▶ The inter-account wormhole

▶ Setting up accounts, logging in, and logging off

● ●

*I*f you're the only one who uses your iMac, you're hereby excused from this chapter. Go out and play.

If you're not the only person who uses your Mac, though, read on.

All About Accounts

Pity the hapless Mac in a school, office, or family situation. Through the course of the day or the week, different people sit down to do their work. Each one may "bookmark" a few Web sites, create a few files, and perhaps change the desktop background.

This, if you stop to think about it, is a recipe for disaster. What's to stop one person from accidentally, or deliberately, throwing away the files of another person? How will you feel if you carefully download and install a fabulous digital photo as your desktop background — and then return to the Mac the next day to find that some idiot has replaced it with a full-screen shot of SpongeBob SquarePants? And as the Favorites menu in Internet Explorer gets longer and less manageable, because it now lists everybody's favorite Web sites all in one menu, how will you and your coworkers/schoolmates/family members keep from resorting to fisticuffs?

Mac OS X has a cool, collected response to all this: "No problem. I'll keep your worlds separate."

In other words, Mac OS X was intended, from the first instant of its conception, to be a *multiple-user* system. One person, the *administrator,* is designated as the machine's owner and technical overlord; the administrator can set up individual *accounts* for each person who'll ever use the machine. Each person will have a name and, if the administrator wishes, a password.

Thereafter, each time you turn on the machine, you see a list of everyone who uses it, like this:

Using the mouse, you click your own name. (If you were given a password, you must enter it correctly before proceeding.)

And now the iMac's ready to use — except that only *your* folders, programs, and documents show up on the screen. The stuff that belongs to the other students/children/workers is hidden from your eyes.

This arrangement has two benefits: convenience (because you don't have to stare at everyone else's junk and poor taste in desktop pictures) and security (because nobody can open anyone else's files or folders).

Setting Up Accounts

As noted above, in every multiple-user setup, one person is the administrator, or the iMac master — for example, the teacher, parent, or monsignor.

This is the only person who's allowed to create and delete other accounts, as befits his or her exalted status. In the following discussion, let's pretend that the master is *you*.

Suppose, for example, that you work in a monastery, where you must share the iMac with three other people: the easily overwhelmed Brother Brian; Harold, the seven-year-old altar boy; and Giuseppe, the cybermonk who manages the group's Web site. Suppose you want to set up the iMac so that each person gets a perfect setup. Here's how you'd do it:

1. **Open System Preferences.**

   As usual, that entails clicking the light-switch icon on the Dock. The System Preferences window opens.

2. **Click User Accounts.**

   Now a special dialog box appears, bearing a list of people who already have accounts on this iMac. If it's a new iMac, there's probably only one name here.

3. **Click New Account. In the resulting dialog box, type *Harold the Altar Boy*, as shown here.**

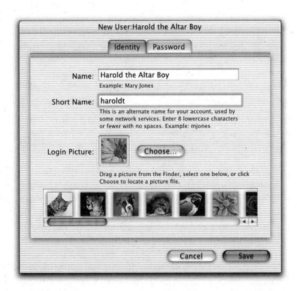

In a family situation, the name could be Chris or Robin. If it's a corporation or school, you'll probably want to use both first and last names.

Unless you intervene, the iMac automatically makes up a *short name,* too. This is an abbreviation of the person's actual name, which can save time when people log in to the Mac or connect to it from across the network. The short name has to be fewer than eight characters and all lowercase letters.

Here, too, is where you can choose a little picture to represent this account holder. You'll see this picture next to your name each time you turn on the iMac to log in.

If you like the choice of pictures that Apple has provided along the bottom of the window, just click one to select it. If there's some other graphics file on the hard drive that you'd rather use instead — a digital photo of your own head, for example — click the Choose button. You'll be shown a list of what's on your hard drive so that you can select it.

4. **Click the Password tab. If you like, make up a password.**

   If security is an issue, you can require that each person type in a password before using the Mac each time. In fact, you're supposed to type it twice, to make sure you didn't make a typo the first time. (You see only dots as you type, so that nobody can discover a password by peeking over your shoulder.) The password can't be longer than eight characters, and capitalization counts.

   Once you've created a password, you can also create a password *hint* in this box (like "street address, junior year in college"). Later, if you ever forget your password, the Mac will show you this cue to jog your memory.

5. **Turn on "Allow user to administer this computer," if you wish.**

   This is a biggie. Only an administrator is allowed to install new programs into the iMac's Applications folder, add fonts to the Library folder for everybody's use, make changes to the most important System Preferences panels (including Network, Date & Time, Energy Saver, Login, and Startup Disk), and decide who gets accounts on the Mac.

   You may want to make Brother Giuseppe, the expert, an administrator just like you. In the event you're off on a pilgrimage when one of your underlings needs to change some important iMac setting, Giuseppe will be able to fill in in your absence. (Administrators *must* have passwords, by the way.)

   For Brother Brian and little Harold, you might prefer to leave this checkbox turned off. They probably won't notice much difference between their worlds and the administrator world that you see — except that they'll find their access blocked to a number of settings in System Preferences, as indicated by the padlock at lower left in the following picture.

   These are settings, such as the iMac's date and time clock, that only you (or another wise administrator) are trusted to change correctly.

If little Harold really wants to change, say, the clock or the phone number your iMac dials to get online, you don't necessarily have to push him off the machine so that you can sign on with your special powers. Instead, you can just click the little padlock icon, type in *your* name and password when asked, like this:

Then stand and supervise Harold as he makes the changes he wants to make.

6. Click Save.

You return to the Users list. To create a similar setup for Brother Brian, click New User, and then start over from Step 3.

If you ever want to modify the settings you've created, just double-click somebody's name in the Users list. You return to the Identity dialog box, where you can change a person's name, password, or administrator status. (You can't change a user's short name once the account has been created.)

Logging On

At last, you're ready to roll. From now on, whenever you turn on the iMac, you'll see the list of people for whom you've created accounts, as shown at the beginning of this chapter.

Help! I forgot my password!

If you're an ordinary, peon mortal account holder, forgetting your password isn't a big deal. Your administrator can simply open up System Preferences, click Users, click your name, and then click Edit to re-establish the password.

But if you *are* the administrator, things are a bit stickier. Still, you can get out of this scrape easily enough.

Find the Mac OS X Install CD that came with your iMac. Insert it into the machine. Then, from the menu, choose Restart. As the Mac starts

up again, press down the letter C key, which starts up the Mac from the CD and launches the Mac OS X installer.

On the first installer screen, choose Reset Password from the Installer menu. When the Reset Password screen appears, click the hard drive that contains Mac OS X. From the first pop-up menu, choose the name of your account. Now make up a new password and type it into both of the boxes. Click Save, close the window, click the installer, and restart. You're saved.

Start by clicking your own name — or, if you're a keyboard speed freak, type the first letter or two (or press the up or down arrow keys) until your name is highlighted, and then press Return or Enter.

Now type in your password, if you set one up. You can try as many times as you want to type the password in; with each incorrect guess, the entire dialog box shudders violently from side to side, as though shaking its head "No." After three wrong guesses, your hint will appear, if you set one up.

If you get the password right, you're in. Enjoy your V.I.P. entrance to your private, pre-established world.

Non-administrator users will find that their worlds are somewhat limited. For example, they may occasionally encounter a message about not having enough *access privileges*. For example, Brother Brian will get that whenever he tries to open a folder belonging to Harold (in Harold's Home folder). And little Harold will find that he can't save new documents he creates anywhere except in his own Home folder or on the desktop.

Shared Folders

Ever notice the Users folder in the main hard drive window? It contains the individual Home folders of everybody with an account on this machine.

If you try to open anybody else's Home folder, you'll see a tiny red "no go here" icon on most of the folders inside, telling you: "look, but don't touch."

There are, however, exceptions. For example, two of the folders in each Home folder are designed to be distribution points for files your co-workers want you to see: Public and Sites.

These folders contain files that you're welcome to open, read, and copy to your own folders — stuff that other people have wanted to "publish" for the benefit of their co-workers. You have Public and Sites folders in your own Home folder, too, of course; here's where you should put files that you want other people to have copies of.

Within the Public folder is something called Drop Box, which serves the opposite purpose: It lets anyone *else* hand in files to *you* when you're not around. They can't open this folder, but they *can* put things into it.

Finally, sitting in the Users folder is one folder that doesn't correspond to any particular person: Shared. This is the one and only folder that everybody can access, freely putting in and taking out files. It's the common ground among all the account holders. It's Central Park, the farmer's market, and the grocery-store bulletin board.

Logging Off

In this remarkable, time-share universe, nobody should shut the machine down at the end of a work session. Instead, learn to choose Log Off from the menu. The iMac automatically closes your programs (offering you the opportunity to save any open documents first), and then presents the list of iMac-sharers. The cycle begins anew.

Deleting Accounts

Sooner or later, one of your iMac's happy users may graduate, get fired, or get divorced. In short, there may come a time when you need to delete a person's account.

To delete an account, open System Preferences, click Users, click the appropriate name in the Users list, and then click Delete User. Mac OS X now offers a list of people who have administrator accounts on your machine, and asks you which one should assume control of the deleted person's folders. Click the appropriate administrator account and then click Delete.

In other words, deleting somebody's account doesn't delete all of the corresponding documents, settings, and so on. All of the dearly departed's folders remain on the Mac — but under the control of an administrator.

Once you, the administrator, have deleted somebody's account, you'll discover the word Deleted tacked onto that person's Home folder (such as "Harold Deleted"). If, upon deleting the account, you designate yourself as the lucky recipient of that person's stuff, you can see and access these "Deleted" files.

Bizarrely enough, though, you still can't *delete* the Deleted folder — at least not in Mac OS X. If you try, you'll be told, "The operation could not be completed because this item is owned by root." You can, however, restart the computer in Mac OS 9 (see Chapter 12) and deleted them *then*.

Chapter 14

Networks for Nitwits

· ·

In This Chapter

▶ Connecting your iMac to one other computer using Ethernet

▶ Sharing files, sharing printers, sharing your cable modem or DSL

▶ Connecting your iMac to other Macs using a wireless AirPort Card

· ·

*T*his chapter certainly won't appeal to everybody. If you're a *Survivor* contestant, for example, sitting there with an iMac as your luxury item and eating rice on some island somewhere thousands of miles from the nearest other computer, you're excused from reading this chapter. Go warm up for the reward challenge; learning how to connect two computers into a network is the last thing on your mind right about now.

But if there's more than one computer at your place, you might be gratified to learn that the iMac is one of the world's most networkable machines. Once you've wired it to your other computers, all kinds of joys await you:

✔ You can copy files from one machine to another just as you'd drag files between folders on your own Mac.

✔ You can send little messages to each other's screens.

✔ Everyone on the network can consult the same database (such as FileMaker Pro) or calendar (such as Now Up-to-Date).

✔ You can play games with each other over the network.

✔ You can share a single laser printer, cable modem, or fax modem among all the Macs in the office.

✔ You can even connect to Windows machines without having to buy any additional software.

That's a lot of payoff for just one Saturday afternoon of fiddling around, trying to get your net to work.

Two Ways to Build the Network

The first step in creating a small network is connecting your Macs. (Technically, they don't even have to be Macs — more on this later — but let's start simple.) You can string them together using either of two connection systems: Ethernet or AirPort.

Ethernet made eathy

Ethernet, a special kind of computer-to-computer connection, is fast, easy, and fun to pronounce.

It's very easy to connect your iMac directly to *one* other computer using Ethernet. It's more complicated to set up an entire *network* of Macs in an office.

Nonetheless, you paid good money for this book (or visited a good library). I won't let you down. I'll lead you by the brain, step by step, through both scenarios.

The two-Mac scenario

To connect your iMac to one other Mac, you need an *Ethernet crossover* cable. (It's not the same as a regular Ethernet cable.) You can get one for $10 or less at computer stores like CompUSA or from a mail-order joint like *www.buy.com.*

Plug your Ethernet crossover cable into each computer's Ethernet jack, which is identified in Chapter 19. It looks like an overweight telephone jack (the Ethernet jack, not Chapter 19).

That's as difficult as the wiring gets. Skip ahead to "Sharing Files."

The more-Macs scenario

Suppose you have an iMac, an iBook, a Power Macintosh, and a laser printer — not to mention an office in which you'd like to wire all of this equipment together. Visit your local computer store, or a computer-stuff Web site like *www.buy.com.* Buy an *Ethernet hub,* which will set you back about $40, depending on the number of jacks it offers. Ethernet hubs usually offer between 4 and 24 jacks, or *ports.* You need one port for every gadget you hope to connect. This one, for example, can accommodate five computers or printers:

(If you have a cable modem or DSL — two kinds of expensive, high-speed Internet connections — you might want to shop for a hub that doubles as a *router*. It connects to your cable modem or DSL box and distributes its services to four to eight computers, depending on how many empty Ethernet jacks it comes with.)

Also buy enough Ethernet *cables* (also called Cat 5, 10BaseT, or 100BaseT), in long enough lengths, to connect all your computers and printers to the hub. The idea is that every computer and laser printer should be plugged directly into your hub. In short, the hub is the octopus body; the wires are its arms; your computers are its fingertips. (Don't plug any computer directly into any other machine.)

Most people try to hide the hub and its ugly mass of wires by stashing it in a closet. Some even hire an electrician to snake the Ethernet cables through the walls, attempting to save themselves from the techno-ugliness of exposed wires.

Once that's set up, you're ready to set up the software. Skip ahead to "Sharing Files."

Your ride to the AirPort

You young kids today — you don't know how lucky you are! Why, when I was your age, I used to have to connect my Macs by *plugging in wires!*

iMacs are considerably less restricted. Embedded in the screen is a built-in *radio transmitter antenna* that gives these iMacs wireless smarts. These antennas communicate through the air to an AirPort base station ($300), which is what's actually connected to the Internet. It's exactly the same idea as cordless phones, which similarly connect with a base station.

An AirPort setup lets you perform any of these stunts:

✔ Surf the Internet without any wires attached to your computer. You can position the iMac even in a room with no telephone jack — as long the base station, up to 150 away, *is* connected to a phone jack.

✔ Up to 50 computers can share the same cable modem or DSL connection, if you have one — once again, from up to 150 feet away.

✔ Play multiplayer Macintosh games with other AirPort-equipped Mac owners — without having to physically connect them.

✔ Copy files between your iMac and other Macs — again, without any wires.

Setting all of this up may require some patience. Once it's set up, however, wirelessness shall be yours.

Installing an AirPort card

Your iMac can't do any of those wireless stunts without an AirPort card ($100), which looks like a Visa card made of sheet metal. You can buy it from an Apple store or from the Apple Web site (*www.apple.com*).

Once you have the card in hand, you have to install it. This is not a five-minute procedure; you're well advised to open the Help menu before you begin, search for *airport,* and print out the step-by-step, illustrated instructions:

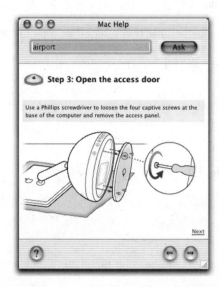

The process entails leaning the machine gently onto its face, unscrewing the screws on its base plate (admiring the way they remain fastened to the plate so you don't lose them), and slipping the AirPort card into the slot you'll find there.

Next, install the software that came on the AirPort CD-ROM — and get ready for the fun.

Going online with a base station

Your iMac is now ready to communicate wirelessly with the AirPort Base Station, which looks exactly like a shiny, chrome, six-inch flying saucer:

If you have a cable modem or DSL connection, plug it into the base station's Ethernet jack. If you connect to the Internet via standard phone lines, connect the modem jack on the base station to a telephone jack on the wall, using a piece of phone wire. Either way, your iMac can now get online via the base station, even through walls and floors.

Suppose your iMac is in the TV room, for example, and you launch your Web browser. Your base station, upstairs in your office, silently begins to dial. Now your iMac is on the Internet, fully connected at full speed, without actually being connected by wires to anything.

Note to teachers and small businesses: A single base station can accommodate up to *50* AirPort-equipped Macs (laptops, for example), all surfing the Web simultaneously. Just keep in mind that the more Macs are online simultaneously, the more slowdown you'll begin to notice.

Setting up your base station

The key to preparing a base station is the program called AirPort Setup Assistant. It's in your Applications folder, in the Utilities folder. Run this program. One screen at a time, it will ask you for the answers it needs for the setup; for example, you'll be asked to give your base station a name and password. Note, too, that you should undertake this phase of the setup only if your iMac can *already* get onto the Internet on its own.

Going online with AirPort

Once you've installed your AirPort hardware and software, there's not much involved to getting onto the Internet with it.

Haul your iMac over to some table from which you've never before surfed the Internet. Then notice the radiating-lines icon on your menu bar, which looks like this:

From this symbolic menu, choose the name of the base station with which you'd like to connect. Most people have only one base station, so you'll see only one listed. (In this example, it's ingeniously named "AirPort Network." If it says "No AirPort Networks in Range," well, you pretty much know what the problem is.) Fill in the password, if you're asked for it.

Now try using an e-mail or Web-browsing program. As soon as you try to connect, your base station dials the number. (The base station has no speaker, so you're spared the usual screeching, hissing, and so on. Lights on the base station blink instead.) Once the connection is complete, you should notice no difference between Web surfing wirelessly and surfing . . . wirefully.

While you're connected, you can check the strength of your radio signal to the base station by glancing again at the menu-bar symbol. The four radiating lines show you your signal strength. The farther away you go from your base station, the weaker the signal, and the slower your Internet surfing speed gets.

As advertised, the radio signal sent between the base station and your laptop isn't fazed by walls — much. Glass, paper, and wood are invisible to the signal, but concrete walls slow it down substantially. Solid metal is almost impenetrable, much to the disappointment of iMac fans on elevators, subway trains, and meat lockers.

(If you have trouble, call Apple's help line, 800 275-2273. You'll probably be advised to open the Network pane of System Preferences. There, if you choose AirPort from the Show pop-up menu, you'll find four tabs that let you configure your AirPort apparatus to within an inch of its life.)

Most people name the base station for its location: "Upstairs Base Station," or "Mr. Mullen's Math Class." You can leave the password blank, unless you worry about the guy next door surfing the Web via your base station. (This scenario assumes that you live in a *very* tightly packed neighborhood, that your neighbor owns a Mac with an AirPort card, and that he's smart enough to try logging onto your base station without a password.)

When it's all over, you'll have successfully configured your base station — and wired your network (or unwired it, depending on how you look at it).

Sharing Files

In File Sharing, you can summon the icon for a folder or disk attached to another computer on the network. It shows up on your own screen; at this point, you can drag files back and forth, exactly as though the other Mac's folder or disk is a gigantic CD you've slipped into your iMac.

Yes, it's a miracle, but you'll have to work for it.

Phase 1: Setting up the computers

These instructions assume that you've already networked your Macs, whether with wires or without (using AirPort), as described earlier.

The instructions differ depending on what operating system your Macs are running: Mac OS X or Mac OS 9. (See the previous chapter for more on the differences between the two.)

Setting up a Mac OS X machine

Use these instructions for your iMac or other Mac OS X computers.

1. **Open System Preferences.**

   As always, you can click its icon on the Dock or choose its name from the menu. Either way, the System Preferences program opens.

2. **Click the Sharing icon.**

   The Sharing panel appears, like this:

Note that only administrators (see Chapter 13) are allowed to change the kinds of settings you're about to fiddle with. If the little padlock icon in the lower-left corner of the dialog box looks locked, call an administrator over, click the lock, and prove that you have permission to do what you're doing by asking the administrator to enter the administrator's name and password.

3. **In the Computer Name blank, type a name for the computer.**

   It may already say "Pee-Wee Herman's Computer," or whatever, but you might want to change this to a nice and descriptive name like Front Desk iMac.

4. **Click the Start button near the top of the dialog box.**

   The feature takes a moment to warm up. When the button finally says Stop, you can quit System Preferences.

5. **In the Users panel of System Preferences, create an account for each person who'll be accessing this Mac from across the network.**

   The previous chapter contains step-by-step instructions.

Repeat this complete process on each Mac OS X machine in your office, giving each one a different computer name.

Now you're set up. Rent a video; you've earned it.

Setting up a Mac OS 9 machine

Setting up a Mac that's running Mac OS 9-point-whatever, if there is one on your network, follows almost exactly the same steps as outlined above — but the locations of the controls are different. For example:

- **Setting up user accounts.** As with Mac OS X, nobody can connect to a Mac OS 9 machine unless they have an *account* on that machine. To set up these accounts, choose Control Panels from the menu. Open the File Sharing control panel. Click the Users tab. Then click New User to set up an account for someone.

- **Naming the computer.** Use the File Sharing control panel. (Choose Control Panels from the menu.)

- **Clicking Start.** You do this, too, in the File Sharing control panel. But there's one important additional step: Turn on the checkbox called "Enable File Sharing clients to connect over TCP/IP," as shown here.

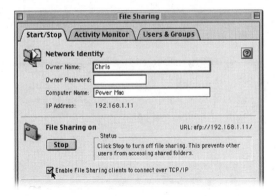

Phase 2: Connecting from your iMac

You've just turned on the File Sharing feature on every Mac. Now it's time to *use* your network.

Suppose you're seated at your iMac, and you need a file that's on the Power Mac down the hall. Why expend the energy necessary to get out of your chair and walk over there, when you can let your network do the work?

You'll have to follow a pretty lengthy sequence of steps — but, mercifully, you have to go through it only once for each Mac you "visit."

1. **From the Go menu, choose Connect to Server.**

    You get a dialog box like the one shown in the next illustration.

2. **Click Local Network.**

In the second column, you should, eventually, see a list of every Mac that you prepared as described in Phase 1. (If not, then something's wrong with your network wiring, or you haven't prepared those Macs as described in the previous pages.)

3. **Double-click the name of the Mac you want to access.**

Now the "Connect to the file server" box appears, where you're supposed to input your name and password.

4. **Type your short user name, press Tab, and type your password.**

For details on your *short user name,* see the previous chapter. This is the name you (or your administrator) typed in when creating your account on that Mac. If you're not sure what it is, visit the Mac that you're trying to visit from across the network. Open System Preferences, click Users, click your name, and then click Edit to find out what it is.

If nobody has set up an account for you on that machine, on the other hand, click the Guest button; you'll have only limited access to what's on the other Mac. (If the Guest button is dimmed, then someone has turned off Guest access altogether. You're completely out of luck.)

5. **Click Connect, or press the Return or Enter key.**

   Now a list of disks and folders appears. These are the folders on the other Mac that you're allowed to open. (The nature of this list depends on what kind of account you have on that Mac, as noted in the following section.)

6. **Double-click the name of the disk or folder you want to open.**

   At last, the disk or folder you've connected to appears on the right side of your screen, illustrated with what looks like a tiny hard drive with a globe balanced on it. It usually appears just below your Macintosh HD icon.

   You can open this icon to open, copy, move, rename, or delete the files on it, exactly as though the files were on your own computer — with certain limitations, described next.

7. **If you think you might someday want to get at the other Mac's files again, drag its hard drive's icon onto the right side of your Dock.**

The next time you want to connect to it, you'll be able to skip almost all of the preceding six steps. Instead, you'll just click its Dock icon (which may eventually change to a question-mark icon), type in your password, and enjoy instant access to the disk or folder as it pops open instantly.

Phase 3: What you can do once you're in

When you tap into a *Mac OS 9* computer from across the network, you're allowed complete freedom. Once you've brought its hard drive onto your screen, you can trash, rename, move around, or otherwise wreak havoc with the files and folders you find there.

But Mac OS X is an extremely secure operating system that fiercely protects its System folder and the Home folders of everybody who uses it. That's why you generally can't visit another Mac OS X computer across the network unless an administrator has first set up an account for you on that Mac.

Even then, you'll be able to see only what's in certain designated folders. Precisely which folders are available depends on whether you're a *guest,* a *normal user,* or an *administrator* (see the previous chapter).

If you're a guest

If you're just a guest — somebody for whom an account hasn't already been set up — you'll be able to:

✔ **Put things into** anyone's Drop Box folder. Take a look here at left:

This is what you see when you connect to a Mac OS X machine as Guest — a list of everyone who has an account on it. When you double-click someone's name, you'll discover that there's nothing inside that folder except a Drop Box folder (and sometimes a Public folder, described next), as shown above at right.

You can copy files into a Drop Box, but can't open it. If you're a guest, you can give, but you can't take.

✔ **Open** anything that people have put into their Public folders. (If no Public folders show up, then there's nothing in them for you to see.)

The rest of the Mac is invisible and off-limits to you.

If you're a normal account holder

If you have a normal Mac OS X account, you'll enjoy Drop Box access, Public folder access, *and* the freedom to see and manipulate what's inside your own Home folder on that other Mac. You can do anything you like with the files and folders you find there, just as though you're actually seated in front of that Mac.

All other disks and folders on the Mac, including the System and Application folders, are invisible to you. Mac OS X machines on a network, as you're by now starting to figure out, have been sanitized for your protection.

If you're an administrator

When you connect to a Mac OS X machine with a guest or normal account, you never even see the name of the hard drive on that machine. Instead, you see only the names of the *people* who have accounts on that machine. (Double-click one to get to its Drop Box and Public folders.)

But if you've been designated an *administrator,* you get to see both those user folders *and* the rest of the hard drive to which you're connecting. You're free to see and manipulate the contents of the Applications, Desktop, Library, and Users folders, too.

Disconnecting yourself

When you're finished using a shared disk or folder, drag its icon to the Trash (whose icon changes to a big Eject symbol as you drag). Or highlight its icon and then, from the File menu, choose Eject. Shutting down your Mac also breaks the connection, of course.

That's it — you've made it through alive! If you had hired a consultant to set up your network, you'd have paid several hundred dollars.

Networking with Windows

The Mac may be the greatest computer on earth. But in the hallways of Corporate America, PCs running Microsoft Windows rule the earth.

Fortunately, you can connect to those machines nearly as easily as you can to other Macs (provided they're on the same network as you, of course). You'll find complete instructions in Chapter 17.

Chapter 15

When Bad Things Happen to Good iMacs

In This Chapter

▶ The top ten problems that beginners encounter and how to solve them

▶ The next ten after that

▶ The next ten after that

Introduction to Computer Hell

Let's face it: Computers are appliances. As such, they have minds of their own. And like other expensive appliances (cars, homes, pacemakers), they tend to get cranky at the worst possible times.

Now, when that happens, most beginners immediately suspect the circuitry. I understand the instinct. I mean, when VCRs, lawnmowers, or electric razors go on the fritz, you're right — you need a repair shop. But a computer's different; it has *software*. When your iMac starts behaving oddly, it's probably a software problem, not a mechanical one. That means that you can fix it yourself, for free. Almost always.

This chapter reveals the steps you can take to restore your iMac's software to health.

Frozen Programs

The old Chinese curse used to be, "May you live in interesting times."

The modern curse should be, "May you be visited by the Spinning Beachball of Death." That's a reference to the colorful, spinning cursor that appears whenever the Mac decides to lock up, becoming utterly unresponsive to your clicks or keystrokes.

First resort: Force quit

Usually, you can escape the SBOD by *force quitting* the program you're in, which has somehow gotten stuck.

To do that, open the menu and choose Force Quit. (If you can't even open the menu, there's an alternative way: hold down the Option and ⌘ keys. While they're down, press the Esc key at the upper-left corner of the keyboard.)

Either way, this box appears:

Click the name of the program you've been using, click Force Quit, and click Force Quit in the confirmation box. That program immediately departs the scene, without even giving you a chance to save any unsaved work. You should feel free to keep using your other programs, or even to re-open the program you just quit. Having had its little time-out, it should be ready for action.

Last resort: Restart the Mac

Very, very rarely, even force-quitting all your programs doesn't help the Mac out of its funk. If the machine is truly locked up, and even the force-quit method does nothing for it, you can always force-*restart* the Mac.

To do that, find the Power button on the left side of the white domed base. Press it in firmly for at least six seconds, or until the screen blinks off. Now you can turn on the iMac again normally.

Things Are Too Slow

If your iMac starts seeming to run more slowly than it once did, the #1 favor you can do for it is *installing more memory*. You can get it from any mail-order company, such as *www.chipmerchant.com*. When you call, tell them that you have an iMac; they'll tell you what kind of memory chips you need and in what quantities they're available.

Installing memory isn't especially difficult, but it does entail removing the base plate of your iMac. For instructions, choose Mac Help from your Help menu. Look up "installing memory." If it looks too hard, get an Apple dealer to do it for you.

Having lots of memory to kick around in is a joy. Your iMac runs faster and generally acts like a new machine. It's a situation I heartily recommend.

Startup Problems

Problems that you encounter when you turn on the iMac are especially disheartening when you're a new Mac user. It does wonders for your self-esteem to think that you can't even turn the thing *on* without problems.

No chime, no picture

First resort: Chances are very, very, very good that your iMac simply isn't getting electricity. It's probably not plugged in. Or it's plugged into a power strip whose On/Off switch is currently set to Off.

Last resort: If that doesn't solve the problem, your iMac is as dead as Elvis. Get it in for repair. But that's virtually never the actual problem.

Picture, no ding

Every iMac makes a sound when you turn it on. The speaker-volume slider (in the Sound panel of System Preferences) controls the sound of the startup chime.

First resort: Press the Louder button on your keyboard a couple of times (see Chapter 3) to make sure that you haven't muted your speaker.

Last resort: When headphones are plugged into the iMac, no sound can come out of the iMac speaker. Unplug the headphones, in that case.

Some crazy program launches itself every time you start up

In the words of programmers everywhere, "It's a feature, not a bug."

As you can read in Chapter 18, you can set up a certain program or document to open automatically every time you log in or turn on the iMac. This feature is supposed to be a time-saver for people who work on the same documents every day.

If you'd rather stifle this gesture, open System Preferences (click its Dock icon). Click Login. On the Login Items tab, click each program or document listed there and click Remove, as shown here.

Kernel panic

When random text gibberish starts superimposing itself on your startup screen, you've got yourself a *kernel panic* — the computer version of a nervous breakdown. No wonder a kernel panic quickly leads to an *owner panic.*

Kernel panics are rarer than Bigfoot sightings in New York City. But if you actually get one, it's probably the result of a hardware glitch: some memory board, accelerator card, graphics card, SCSI gear, or USB hub that Mac OS X doesn't like, for example.

Simply restarting the computer usually solves the problem. If it doesn't, detach any gear that didn't come from Apple. If you're able to pinpoint the culprit, seek its manufacturer (or its Web site) on a hunt for updated drivers, or at least try to find out for sure whether the add-on is compatible with Mac OS X.

Freezes during startup

If the Mac locks up during the startup process, you need to run Mac OS X's disk-repair program, as described at the end of this chapter.

Blue screen during startup

Most of the troubleshooting steps for this problem (which is usually accompanied by the Spinning Beachball of Death cursor) are the same as those described under "Kernel panic," above. But there's one other cause to examine: a corrupted font file in your *Mac OS 9* System Folder.

To test for this problem, restart the iMac in Mac OS 9 (see Chapter 12), open its System Folder (the one with the 9 on it), and drag the Fonts folder to the desktop. Restart the iMac in Mac OS X. If the startup proceeds smoothly, you know there's a damaged font file in that Fonts folder.

If three days of trial-and-error are your idea of fun, you can try to figure out *which* font is damaged. Otherwise, throw away that Fonts folder. Then use the Mac OS 9 installation CD that came with your iMac to reinstall Mac OS 9. (The installer won't disturb any of your files or settings; it will just replace the missing fonts.)

"I don't want to have to log in every day — it's my own iMac!"

The whole idea of the name-and-password system described in Chapter 13 is to keep everybody's files and settings separate.

But if you're the only person who uses your Mac, it might seem a bit silly that you have to log in each morning. And it *is* silly — and you can bypass it.

Open System Preferences. Click the Login icon. Click the Login Window tab. Turn on "Automatically log in," type your name and password, and click Save, like this:

From now on, the iMac won't display the usual list of account holders at startup. It will assume that you're you, and it will take you straight to the desktop. Of course, this means that anybody else in your house, office, or school has full access to your files, without having to know a password — but then, you're only reading this if there *isn't* anyone else who might use your iMac.

"I can't log in! I'm in an endless startup loop!"

If your Mac uses the user-accounts feature described in Chapter 13, you might one day find that the usual list of account holders doesn't appear when you turn on the machine, thus preventing you from getting access to your own stuff. Even if you shut down or restart the iMac, it keeps taking you into one particular person's account each time it turns back on.

The reason: Somebody has turned on the Automatic Login feature described in the previous paragraphs. The solution: Either turn off Automatic Login or choose Log Out from the menu.

Forgotten password

If you or one of the other people who use your Mac have forgotten the corresponding account password, no worries. Your Mac OS X Install CD offers you a handy Reset Password command. It's described in Chapter 13.

Viruses? What viruses?

You hear an awful lot about viruses these days — malevolent little programs written by malevolent little creeps who get kicks from gumming up people's computers. Fortunately, 99.9999% of all viruses are written for Windows PCs, not the Mac. In fact, at this writing, there isn't even *one* virus that works in Mac OS X.

A special kind of automated software robot called a *macro virus* may still affect you if you regularly download Microsoft Word and Excel files by e-mail. Even then, there's not much to worry about: When you open such a file, a big fat dialog box will warn you if it contains macros. Simply click the Disable Macros button, open the file, and get on with your life.

Sleep well!

Software Situations

The iMac is one beautiful piece of hardware, sure to wind up in quite a number of museums (including the little-known Museum of Products that Resemble Desk Lamps).

But what really makes the world go 'round is software. Programs are what make your time go by, make your checkbook balance, and make your pulse race as you visit the Web — and they're the most likely things to go wrong.

Minor eccentric behavior

When a single program is acting up, try the following steps, in this sequence:

First resort: Restart the program

If a program starts exhibiting one eccentric behavior or another, the first step to take is simply to quit the program and start it up again. Restarting the flaky program lets it load from scratch, having forgotten all about its previous problems.

Second resort: Toss the preference files

Take this simple test. Log in using a different *account* (see Chapter 13), maybe a dummy account that you've created just for testing purposes. Run the flaky program. Is the problem gone?

If so, then the glitch exists only when *you* are logged in — which means it's a problem with *your* copy of the program's preference files. These are tiny files in your Home folder, in your Library folder, that memorize the way you like to have each program: where you've parked its toolbars, your preferred font settings, and so on.

Return to your own account. Open your Home folder, open the Library folder inside it, and open the Preferences folder inside *it.* Here you'll find preference files for all of the programs you use. Each ends with the file name suffix *.plist.* Find the one that bears the name of the problem program, and throw it into the Trash.

Now try opening the program again. If the glitch has gone away, you're home free. (The program creates new, fresh, virginal preference files automatically.)

If that didn't work, it's worth noting that you actually have *three* Preferences folders. In addition to your own Home folder's stash, there's a second one in the Library folder in the hard drive window (which administrators are allowed to trash), and a third in the System folder's Library folder (which nobody is allowed to trash).

The only way to throw away the .plist files from inside the System folder is to restart the Mac in Mac OS 9, as described in Chapter 12.

Third resort: Log out

Sometimes you can give Mac OS X or its programs a swift kick in the software derrière by logging out (choose Log Out from the menu) and logging back in again. It's an inconvenient step, but not nearly as time-consuming as restarting the computer.

Last resort: Trash and reinstall the program

Sometimes reinstalling the problem program clears up whatever the glitch was.

First, you should throw away all traces of the program. Just open the Applications folder and drag the program's icon (or its folder) to the Trash. In most cases, the only remaining piece to discard is its .plist files (the preference files) described in the preceding paragraphs.

Then reinstall the program from its original CD or installer — after first checking the company's Web site to see if there's an updated version, of course.

Application won't open

If a program won't open (if its icon bounces merrily in the Dock for a few seconds, for instance, but then nothing happens), begin by trashing its preference file, as described in the previous paragraphs. If that doesn't solve it, reinstalling the program usually does.

You can't rename a file

The file is probably locked. Does its icon bear a tiny padlock symbol in the lower-left corner? If so, click it, choose Show Info from the File menu, and turn off the Locked check box. Or maybe the file is on a locked *disk,* such as a CD-ROM disc. You *can't* rename anything on a locked disk.

Finally, of course, you can't rename anything that doesn't belong to *you.* That goes for any of the Mac's own system files (in the System folder, for example) or any files that belong to other people's accounts (see Chapter 13).

System Preferences controls are dimmed

Many of Mac OS X's control panels are off-limits to people who have normal *accounts* (see Chapter 13). That is, only people with administrator accounts are allowed to make changes, as indicated by the padlock icon at the lower-left corner of such panels.

As described in Chapter 13, though, you don't actually have to have an administrator account *yourself* to make such changes. Just call an administrator over to your desk, click the padlock, and ask him or her to type in his or her password and supervise the change you're about to make.

"My hard drive is overrun with alien files!"

Mac OS X is actually based on an operating system called *Unix*. This is something that sends goose bumps of excitement down the spines of computer nerds, but feelings of dread in everyday mortals. It's an extremely technical operating system that requires years of study.

That's why Apple has *hidden* literally thousands of intimidatingly named files. That's why, if you open the System (X) folder on your hard drive, it appears to be practically empty. It's really seething with files, but you can't see them.

Unless you start up your Mac in Mac OS 9, or access it from across a network. In that case, you may see some of these files — *mach, mach.sym,* and *mach_kernel* may appear in the main hard-drive window, for example.

Don't touch them!

Moving, renaming, or deleting them can cripple your iMac so badly that you won't even be able to turn it on. At that point, a complete reinstallation of Mac OS X will be required.

Can't empty the Trash

It's enough to drive you buggy: There's something in the Trash that refuses to be deleted. One error message after another tells you that the Trash can't be emptied.

First resort: Bypass the lock

In general, a file that's been *locked* (as indicated by the tiny padlock on its icon) can't even be moved to the Trash. Still, locked files sometimes make their way Trashward; somebody who's had a few beers, for example, may have locked a file *after* putting it into the Trash, for example.

The solution is to press Option as you click and hold on *the Trash icon itself.* Now, when you choose Empty Trash from the pop-up menu shown here, Mac OS X empties the Trash without complaint, locked files and all.

Last resort: Check the permissions

If emptying the Trash gives you "Could not be completed because this item is owned by Arnold," you're trying to move or delete another Mac account holder's stuff. As you know by now, that's a big no-no in Mac OS X.

If the file or folder's original owner is no longer in your life, then you can blow past such permissions problems by restarting the Mac in Mac OS 9 (Chapter 12) and then deleting the files manually. You'll find them in the Users folder, in the person's own Home folder, in a folder called Trash.

Hardware Headaches

These glitches aren't as common as software problems, but they're just as frustrating.

Your mouse is jerky or sticky

The beauty of the iMac's mouse is that it's an *optical* mouse. Unlike old-fashioned mice, it doesn't have a little ball on the underside that rolls around collecting grit and crud like some kind of sticky toddler.

Instead, it has a tiny electronic eye that watches the ground beneath the mouse as you move it around, passing its movement information along to the cursor on the screen.

This ingenious system breaks down only when it's on *glass or mirrored* surfaces. If yours is, slip a piece of paper or a mouse pad underneath.

Until that trouble strikes, here are two fun facts about your mouse:

- ✔ You can turn the ring on the bottom of it to adjust the clicking "tension."
- ✔ If, in the middle of dragging something across the screen, you run out of desk surface, squeeze the sides of the mouse. While you're squeezing, you can pick up the mouse and set it back down without "letting go" of whatever you clicked.

Double-clicking doesn't work

You're probably double-clicking too slowly, or you're moving the mouse a little bit during the double-click process.

The CD drawer won't open

If the CD drawer is empty, it should open when you *hold down* (not just tap) the Eject button at the upper-right corner of your keyboard. If there's a CD in it, it should pop out when you simply *tap* the Eject key.

But if the drawer won't open when you press the button, something's jammed. The solution: Shut down the iMac (choose Shut Down from the menu). Turn it on again — but as it lights up, press the mouse button continuously until the CD pops out.

The screen is too dim

Tap the F15 key on the top row of your keyboard. That's the Brighter button. (F14 is the Dimmer button.)

The Wrong Program Opens

As noted in Chapter 4, the Mac generally does something very courteous when you double-click a document icon: It automatically opens the program that created it.

To figure out which is the proper program to open, though, your iMac relies on *two different* systems — basically tables of parent-and-child, program-and-document relationships — one old and one new.

It's possible to live a long and happy life without knowing anything about these code systems. Indeed, the vast majority of Mac fans may never even encounter them. But you may discover that understanding creator/type codes and file name suffixes can be useful in troubleshooting and appreciating how Mac OS X actually works.

And if you find the following discussion confusing, well, just think how the Mac must feel.

File name extensions

When you double-click a document icon, the iMac first inspects its three-letter *file name extension* — a suffix following a period in the file's name, as in *Madonna Hairstyles Master List.doc* or *family finances.cwk*.

"That's strange," you must be saying, glancing back and forth between this page and your iMac screen. "I don't *see* any of those extensions."

That's because the iMac comes set to *hide* most file name extensions, on the premise that they make the Mac look technical and threatening. If you'd like to see them, however, open the Finder menu, choose Preferences, and, in the resulting box, turn on "Always show file extensions." Now examine a few of the files in your Home folder's Documents folder. You'll see that their names now display the previously hidden suffixes.

Before (extensions hidden)   After

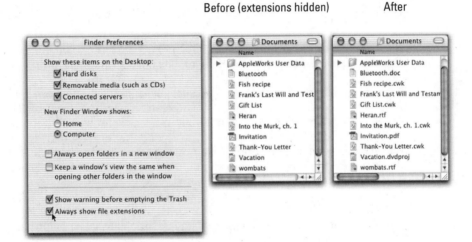

You can hide or show these suffixes on an icon-at-a-time basis, too. Just highlight the icon or icons you want to affect. From the File menu, choose Name & Extension from the pop-up menu, and then turn on "Hide extension," as shown here.

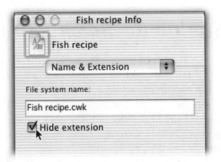

The point is that the Mac has memorized which suffix "belongs" to which parent program. Files ending ".doc" open in Microsoft Word. Files ending ".cwk" open in AppleWorks. And so on.

Type and creator codes

Before Mac OS X came along, Mac OS 9 relied on something similar yet different: invisible, four-letter *creator codes* and *type codes,* as they're called. Apple kept track of which software companies used which four-letter codes, so that no two codes were alike. These codes were always hidden.

The four-letter creator code of a Macintosh document identifies the program that will open it.

This is where things get hairy: Mac OS X, believe it or not, recognizes *both* creator codes (like Mac OS 9) *and* file name suffixes (like Windows).

The rule to remember is that *creator codes override file name extensions.* In other words, a file called Flank Steak Recipe.txt generally opens in the TextEdit program — *if* it doesn't have a four-letter creator code behind the scenes. If that file has the invisible creator code that corresponds to the old Mac OS 9 program called SimpleText, however, it opens in SimpleText (which also requires opening the Classic simulator described in Chapter 12) no matter what its file name is.

But if there's no Mac OS 9-style creator code, Mac OS X next looks for a file name suffix. If it finds that, it consults an invisible database of icons and suffixes, the master index that lists the correspondence between documents and the applications that generate them.

If the desktop file discovers a match — if, say, you double-clicked a document with suffix .cwk, which corresponds to the AppleWorks entry in your desktop database — then the corresponding program opens the document, which now appears on your screen.

Reassigning documents to programs

So how does all this geeky knowledge pay off in troubleshooting terms?

The problem with file name extensions — the Mac's preferred source of software genealogy information — is that they aren't always sure-fire in pinpointing which parent program should open a particular document. Suppose, for example, that you've downloaded a graphic called Barney.JPEG. Well, almost any program these days can open a JPEG graphic — AppleWorks, Word, Preview, Internet Explorer, and so on. How does your iMac X know which of these programs to open when you double-click the file? And what if it opens the *wrong* program?

Reassigning a single document

Double-clicking a downloaded graphics file generally opens it in Preview, the graphics viewer included with Mac OS X. Most of the time, that's a perfectly good arrangement. But Preview can only *display* graphics — it can't edit them. What if you decide you want to edit a graphics file? You'd want it to open, just this once, into a different program — AppleWorks, for example.

To do so, highlight the file's icon and then, from the File menu, choose Show Info. The Show Info window for that file appears.

From the pop-up menu, choose "Open with application." The pop-up menu just beneath it tells you what program *usually* opens this kind of document. From this pop-up menu, choose the name of the program you'd rather open this particular file, like this:

Reassigning all documents of this type

So much for the one-shot, one-document procedure. What if you're the editor of, say, a book called *Wallpaper For Dummies,* and the author has sent you 400 photographs to use in the book — all of them in the TIFF graphics format? Mac OS X comes set to open *every* TIFF file in its little Preview program, where you can only look at pictures, not edit them.

Sure, you could reassign all of these files, one at a time, to a different program, but you'd be 135 years old before you'd finished. What you really want, of course, is to tell the Mac: "For heaven's sake, make *all* TIFF files open in AppleWorks from now on!"

To make it so, highlight *one* of the TIFF files in question, open the File menu, and then choose Show Info. In the Show Info window, choose a new "parent" program from the pop-up menu, as shown in the previous illustration. But this time, follow up by clicking Change All at the bottom of the window. (This button is dimmed until you've actually selected a different program from the pop-up menu.) In the confirmation box, click Continue.

You've just taught Mac OS X to open *all* TIFF files from now on in AppleWorks. You can, and should, use the same technique to reassign other kinds of documents to your favorite programs — either because you *prefer* those other programs or because the iMac's been opening those kinds of documents in the *wrong* program from the beginning.

Error Messages

Ah, yes, those good old American error messages. Yes, kids, these are the new-millennium equivalents of "DOES NOT COMPUTE." These are messages, appearing in an *alert box* like the one shown here, that indicate that something's wrong.

"There is no application available"

First resort: Not everything on the iMac is meant to be a plaything for you; the iMac reserves a few files for its own use. Certain items, especially in your Library and System folders, give you the "Application not found" message if double-clicked because they're there for your iMac's use, not for yours.

Last resort: In Chapter 3, you can read about programs and the documents that they produce (like parents and children). Sometimes, the "No application available" message means that you're trying to open a document (child), but the iMac can't find its parent (the program used to create it).

So if you double-click an AppleWorks document, but the AppleWorks program itself isn't on your hard disk, the iMac shrugs and asks, in effect, "Yo — how am I s'posed to open this?" To remedy the situation, reinstall the missing program on the hard disk.

More often, though, you're double-clicking something you downloaded from the Internet or America Online — something created by *someone else,* using a program you don't have. For example, let's say I send you a word processor file, but you don't have the same word processor program I do.

To read such files, drag them onto the Dock icon of the program you'd rather use to open them. Here, for example, is a text file (originally created with Microsoft Word) being dragged onto the AppleWorks icon:

The same applies to generic *graphics* documents. These files, in technical-sounding formats like PICT, JPEG, and GIF, can be opened by almost any program. (America Online or Netscape Navigator, for example, can open all three.) Yet if you try to *double-click* a generic graphics file, you'll probably open them in the Preview program. But if you'd rather open them in one specific program — and don't feel like performing the surgery described in the following pages — you can always drag the graphics files onto the Dock icon of the program you'd rather use to open them. (Graphics files can be opened by *many* different programs: AppleWorks, TextEdit, Internet Explorer, America Online, and so on.)

"You do not have sufficient access privileges"

Mac OS X, the iMac's operating system, is an extremely stable and secure hunk of software. As you can read in Chapter 13, it hides or protects itself rather fiercely, so that no clueless or malevolent human winds up moving, deleting, or renaming important files, causing a computer meltdown as a result.

Therefore, you get this message whenever you try to mess with the files in, for example, the System folder.

But you also get this message when you try to open or move files that belong to *other account holders* on this machine. (See Chapter 13 for details on accounts.) What's yours is yours, and those are the only files and folders you're allowed to move, open, trash, rename, and so on.

People with *administrator* accounts (again, see Chapter 13) have slightly greater freedom. These blessed souls are at least allowed to add to, or remove icons from, the Applications folder, for example. Everybody else, though, gets the old "Not enough privileges" door slammed in their faces when they try to open *any files at all* that aren't in their Home folders, or that they didn't create themselves.

In short, Mac OS X is like a tough-love parent who says, "I'm grounding you because I love you."

"DNS Entry not found" or "Error 404"

You get these messages when using your Web browser (see Chapter 7). It says that the Web page you're trying to visit doesn't exist. Usually this means you've made a typo as you typed the Web address (sometimes called a *URL*), or the page's address has changed and you don't know it, or the computer the Web page is on has been taken off the Internet (for maintenance, for example).

Fixing the Disk

Mac OS X comes with a powerful disk-repair program called Disk Utility. It's a useful troubleshooting tool that can cure all kinds of strange ills, including problems like these:

- ✔ The iMac freezes during startup.

- ✔ The startup process interrupts itself with the appearance of the *command line* — a text-only, intimidating-looking screen where only programmers dare to tread.

- ✔ Your programs show up as *folders* instead of double-clickable icons.

Now, you have a copy of Disk Utility on your hard drive — but like a painter who can't paint the last corner of the floor because he's standing there, Disk Utility can't check the disk it's *on*. That's why you have to restart the computer from the Mac OS X Install CD that came with your iMac, and run Disk Utility from there. Proceed like this:

1. **Start up the Mac from the Mac OS X Install CD.**

   The best way to do that is to insert the CD and then restart the Mac while holding down the C key.

   After a minute or two, you wind up at the Mac OS X Installer screen. Don't be fooled — installing Mac OS X is *not* what you want to do here. Don't click Continue!

2. **From the Installer menu, choose Open Disk Utility.**

   After a moment, the Disk Utility screen appears.

3. **Click the First Aid tab.**

   Now you see something like this:

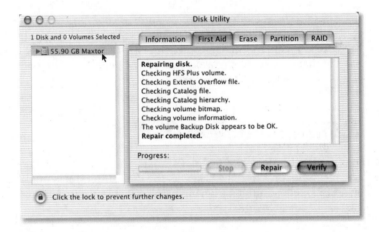

4. **Click the icon for your hard drive at the left side of the window, and then click Repair.**

   The Mac whirls into action, checking a list of very technical disk-formatting parameters.

   If you see a note that says, "The volume 'Macintosh HD' appears to be OK," that's good news. That's as upbeat and confident as Disk Utility gets. (The message's last line says "Repair completed" whether or not any repairing was done at all.)

   Disk Utility may also tell you that the disk is damaged, but that it can't help you. In that case, you'll have to call Apple's help line (see the next chapter) or buy a more heavy-duty disk-repair program like Drive 10 (*www.micromat.com*).

Reinstalling Mac OS X

If some troubleshooting effort has left you exhausted and panting on the beach of desperation, and Mac OS X continues to act up, you may have to make the ultimate sacrifice: reinstalling Mac OS X.

There are two ways to go about it:

- **Reinstall Mac OS X.** Just update your copy of Mac OS X (in your System folder). This process leaves all of your files and folders alone.

- **Wipe out everything.** Restore the iMac to the way it was the day you first turned it on, with all programs and folders exactly the way they were when they left Apple's factory.

  In short, this method *completely erases your hard drive.* You'll use it under only two circumstances: (a) when you've tried all other troubleshooting steps including calling Apple, and (b) when you're ready to sell your iMac. In that case, you may want to wipe it clean, free of any of your own stuff, and all ready for its next owner.

Reinstalling Mac OS X

Just insert the Mac OS X Install CD that came with your iMac and then restart the machine, pressing the C key as the computer starts up. When the CD window opens, double-click the Install Mac OS X icon. Proceed with the installer that presents itself.

Reinstalling Mac OS X this way *doesn't touch your files, folders, or settings.* It simply patches whatever holes have opened up in the undercarriage of your operating system. In certain cases, this process is just the ticket.

Unfortunately, Apple continues to hone Mac OS X with successive versions — 10.1.4, 10.1.5, whatever. If you've installed downloaded updates since you got your iMac, this method may be doomed; the original installer that came with the iMac will refuse to install Mac OS X if it detects a more recent version already on your hard drive.

Wiping out everything

If you're really having trouble, or you otherwise want to start your iMac fresh, one last, desperate option remains available to you: *erasing the hard drive completely* and starting over. That's the purpose of the six Software Restore CDs that came with your iMac.

The Restore process described here doesn't just give you a fresh, clean System folder — it gives you *all* of the programs that originally came with your iMac. In fact, it puts every single file and folder back the way it was the day you bought the iMac.

Don't even think about using them until you've first backed up your entire Home folder, as described in Chapter 4.

Once you've done that, insert the CD called "Software Restore 1 of 6." From the menu, choose Restart. Then, immediately after the screen goes black, hold down the letter C key until you see the smiling Mac. You've now started up the iMac from the CD.

After a moment, you'll see a small dialog box containing a Restore button. Think hard about what you're about to do — and then click it with the mouse. You'll be asked to insert the other CDs from time to time, until the software-restoration process is complete.

If you're planning to sell the iMac, that's all there is to it; it's clean and fresh. If you were trying to start fresh for your own sake, restart the Mac and then copy your backed-up Home folder stuff into your new Home folder. Welcome home!

Chapter 16

Beyond the iMac: Where to Go from Here

In This Chapter

▶ Moving up to Mac OS X: the next generation

▶ Where to turn when things go wrong

▶ Facing the future, credit card in hand

▶ Now get outside for some fresh air

The first 15 chapters of this book are the crash course. Now, Grasshoppa, it's time for you to venture forth into the world by yourself. Go for the gold. Do the right thing. Use the Force.

But first, a few parting words of wisdom.

Where to Turn in Times of Trouble

You own the world's most forgiving, self-explanatory computer. But things will go wrong. And not even this astoundingly complete book can anticipate the problems you may encounter while running BeeKeeper Pro or No Namo Scanner Doodad Plus. Fortunately, the world is crawling with help possibilities.

Your 15 minutes of free help

For example, during the first three months you've owned your iMac, you can call Apple's delightful toll-free hotline at (800) 500-7078 and ask your questions of the gurus there. (Hint for the budget-conscious: Apple doesn't know when you bought your iMac. They measure your 90 days, therefore, from your first *call*, not really from the day you bought your machine.)

Beyond those 90 days, Apple charges you nosebleed-inducing fees for your use of their experts (unless the computer actually turns out to need fixing, in which case the fee is waived). The number for this service is (888) 275-8258 (toll-free again), and you can choose to have your wallet milked in either of two quantities: one problem solved for $50; ten for $290.

The bottom line: Try to have all your problems in the first 90 days.

$150 for three years

If you anticipate needing phone help at least three times, you're far better off buying AppleCare. It's an extended-warranty program that covers all iMac troubles for three years, including mechanical problems. During that time, you can call Apple's help line all you want at no extra charge. Keep in mind, however, that you must sign up for this program during the first year you own your iMac.

Free help sources

If spending money isn't your way of problem solving, consider these all-expenses-paid avenues:

- ✔ **Apple Knowledge Base:** The mother of all troubleshooting resources. This is the collection of 50,000 individual technical articles, organized in a searchable database, that the Apple technicians themselves consult when you call for help.

  If you like, you can visit this library using your Web browser; the address is *www.apple.com/support.* You can search it either by typing in keywords or by using pop-up menus of question categories.

- ✔ **Apple's Web page:** Also at *apple.com/support,* you can find download-able manuals, software updates, frequently asked questions, and many other resources.

- ✔ **MacFixIt Web page:** You get hundreds of discussions of little tweaky specific iMac problems at *www.macfixit.com.*

- ✔ **Bulletin boards online:** The other great source of help is an electronic meeting place like America Online, where you may get your question answered instantly — and if not, you can post your question on a bulletin board for somebody to answer overnight. Try keyword **MOS**, for example. (See Chapter 6 for details on keywords.)

  If you're Internet savvy, you can visit a newsgroup called *comp.sys.mac* for similar assistance. (See Chapter 6 for information on newsgroups.) If you're polite and concise, you can post questions to the multitudes here and get more replies to them than you'll know what to do with.

Otherwise, your next resort should be a local user group, if you're lucky enough to live in a pseudometropolitan area. A user group, of course, doesn't exist to answer *your* personal questions; you still have to do some phoning and hobnobbing and research. But a user group *is* a source of sources. You can call up and find out who will know the answer to your question. (To find the nearest user group, call Apple's referral service at (800) 538-9696.)

As for your continuing education — after you spend a month's salary on a computer, I'll bet you can afford $30 more for a subscription to *Macworld*, *MacAddict*, or *MacHome Journal* magazine. Agreed, huge chunks of these rags may go right over your head. But in every single issue, you'll find at least one really useful item. You can learn all kinds of things just by reading the ads. And if you're not in touch with the computer nerd world at least by that tenuous thread — via magazine — then you might miss stuff like free offers, recall notices, warnings, and other consumer-oriented jazz.

Where to Get the Inside Dirt

The Web sites listed in the previous paragraphs are great for Mac troubleshooting. But when the computer is running *smoothly,* consider visiting these sites for news, rumors, and commentary:

- **MacSurfer** *(www.macsurfer.com):* A daily roundup of articles about the Mac from newspapers and magazines around the country. Click a listing to read that article.

- **MacCentral** *(www.maccentral.com):* News, updates, tricks, and product announcements — all about the Mac.

- **SiteLink** *(www.sitelink.net):* A Web page that links to other Web pages about the Mac (and the iMac). You'll be on the Web until you're 90.

- **Lots of Homegrown Web sites:** The Web is full of additional iMac-related Web sites. Generally, they're unproofread but entertaining, each run by one or two people. You might scope out, for example, iMac2day, iMacOnline, Daily iMac, Everything iMac, and so on. (The Web address is always the same: *www.___.com,* where the Web page name goes in the blank. No spaces allowed.)

Upgrading to Mac OS 10.2 — and Beyond

If you bought your iMac before the fall of 2002, it came with the version of Mac OS X called Mac OS X *10.1.* (It may be 10-point-1-*point*-something, like 10.1.4 or 10.1.5.) This is a splendid operating system, without a doubt.

But Apple never stops tinkering with its crown jewel, the Mac operating system. From time to time, you'll connect to the Internet and encounter a Software Update dialog box like the one shown in Chapter 3.

It's notifying you about a free upgrade to an even better version of Mac OS X. It's almost always a good idea to click Install. (It's also a good idea to go see a movie or two during the time it will take for the new software to download from the Internet.)

Apple has even bigger plans for Mac OS X, though. In subsequent versions, Apple plans to add a redesigned Sherlock program (see Chapter 4), an online chat-room program, even easier connections to Windows computers, and more. In fact, if you bought your iMac after the fall of 2002, it may already have this newer, juicier version of Mac OS X. (Open your menu and choose About This Mac to find out.) The advice in this book is still sound — but you have a few additional features designed to make the iMac faster, easier, and trouble-freer.

You'll also be offered the opportunity to download or buy this update for *original* iMac models. Whenever you upgrade your operating system in this way, however, you run the risk that any *add-on* programs — that is, software that didn't come from Apple — might develop quirks and tics. Your big, everyday, came-with-the-iMac programs like AppleWorks and Mail probably won't be affected. But stuff you've bought, or downloaded from the Internet, may occasionally behave oddly after a system-software upgrade.

In that event, you have two choices:

 Contact whoever made the software in question — or visit the corresponding Web page. Check to see if an upgrade is available. (It almost always is.)

 Do without the software.

Save Changes Before Closing?

If you decide to get more into this Macintosh thing, use the resource list at the beginning of this chapter as a starting point.

But wait a minute — the point of this book wasn't to convert you into a full-time iMac rabbit. It was to get you off the ground. To give you just enough background so you'll know why the computer's beeping at you. To show you the basics and help you figure out what the beanie heads are talking about.

Don't let them intimidate you. So *what* if you don't know the lingo or have the circuitry memorized? If you can turn the thing on, get something written up and printed, and get out in time to enjoy the sunshine, you qualify as a real iMac user.

Any dummy knows that.

Part V
The Part of Tens

The 5th Wave   By Rich Tennant

In this part . . .

Here's what we *For Dummies* book authors often refer to as "the chapters we can write in one day apiece" — a trio of top ten lists, for your infotainment pleasure.

Chapter 17

Ten Cool Things You Didn't Know Your iMac Could Do

• •

*1*t's fast, it's hip, and it complements any décor. But the iMac does more — much more. Try *these* some lazy Saturday afternoon.

Talk

It's been said that we spend the first year of a child's life trying to get it to talk, and the next 18 years trying to get it to shut up. Well, with the iMac, getting it to talk is fantastically easy.

Start by opening your System Preferences program (click the light-switch icon on the Dock). Then click the Speech icon; on the Speech control panel, click the Text-to-Speech tab, as shown here.

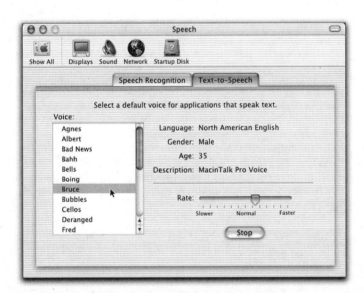

Now is your chance to choose a voice for your particular iMac. The voice menu lists about two dozen different voices. They're great: male, female, kids, deep voices, shaky voices, whispered voices. Click each one to hear it say a funny sentence in its own voice. And don't miss the Rate slider, which governs how fast each voice talks.

When you're happy with your Mac's voice, the next step is to give it something to say. Two built-in iMac programs can talk: AppleWorks and Mail.

In AppleWorks, you have to do a little setup to get at the speech controls. From the AppleWorks menu, choose Preferences, and choose Button Bar from the submenu. In the Customize Button Bar dialog box, scroll down to the Word Processing triangle; click it. Scroll down even more, until you see the Speak Text button. Drag it out of the dialog box and onto the button bar at the top of your screen. Click Done.

Now open an AppleWorks word-processing document and type up something you've always wanted to have said to you, such as, "You are *such* a god! Holy smokes — *everything* you do turns out fantastically! I'd give anything to be more like you."

Then move that mouse on up to the pair-of-lips icon that you added to your button bar. Click it. Aren't computers great?

In Apple Mail, you can have any piece of mail read aloud to you. With a piece of correspondence on the screen before you, hold down the Control key and click inside the text. From the contextual menu that appears, choose Speech, and choose Start Speaking from the submenu. (Repeat this ritual, but choose Stop Speaking, when you've heard enough.)

Of course, Apple didn't create a talking iMac just for you to fool around making up silly sentences. This technology has some actual, useful uses. For example, there's no better way to proofread something important than to listen to it being read to you.

Sing

Although it's a little humbling that your iMac may be more talented than you are, it does indeed sing. It has a somewhat limited repertoire — in fact, it knows only four songs — but it can use any lyrics you want, and it never even stops to take a breath.

To make your iMac sing, you simply need to get it talking, as described in the preceding section. Then choose one of these voices in the Speech panel of System Preferences:

- ✔ **Pipe Organ:** Sings to the tune of the Alfred Hitchcock theme.
- ✔ **Good News:** Sings to the tune of "Pomp & Circumstance," otherwise known as the graduation march.
- ✔ **Bad News:** Sings to the tune of the funeral march.
- ✔ **Cellos:** Sings to the tune of "In the Hall of the Mountain King," from *Peer Gynt*, by Edvard Grieg. Such culture!

Punctuation marks make the iMac start over from the beginning of the melody. Sample lyrics for the Good News graduation-march melody, for example, should look like this:

You just won the jackpot good luck and God bless

Too bad you owe half to good old IRS!

Listen

The Mac wouldn't be much of a conversation partner if all it did were talk to *you*. Believe it or not, your little machine can also *take spoken commands*. You can't exactly say, "Answer my e-mail, compose my report, and change the oil in the Subaru," but you can open programs by voice and even exchange knock-knock jokes with your machine.

Turning on speech recognition

Open System Preferences and then click the Speech icon. See where it says "Apple Speakable Items"? Click On.

The first time you do this, a small instructions window appears. Read it if you like, and then click Continue.

Now a weird, round, UFO-like floating window appears. The word *Esc* in its center indicates the "listen" key — the key you're supposed to hold down when you want the Mac to respond to your voice. (You wouldn't want the Mac listening all the time — even when you said, for example, "Hey, it's cold in here. *Close the window.*" Therefore, the Mac comes ready to listen to you only when you're pressing that key.)

What the iMac can understand

You can't exactly chat away in conversation with your iMac; it is, after all, only a hunk of plastic, glass, and metal. In fact, the only commands it understands are the utterances listed in the Speech Commands window (below, right). To see this list, click the bottom tip of the little round window (below, left) and choose Open Speech Commands Window:

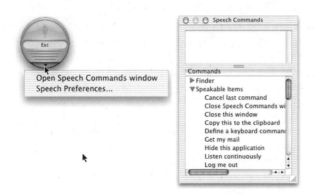

When you start talking, you'll also see the Mac's interpretation of what you said written out in a yellow balloon just over the Feedback window.

- **Open Sherlock.** Say this to open Sherlock, the file-finding program described in Chapter 4.

- **Go to my home directory.** That's a fancy way of saying, "Open my Home folder."

- **Make a new folder.** Just what it says.

- **Close this window.** Closes the frontmost window instantly.

- **Empty the trash.** This one works only when you're in the Finder and there is, in fact, something in the Trash.

- **Switch to AppleWorks.** Actually, you can say "switch to" and the name of *any* running or recently used program.

- **Quit all applications.** Saves you the trouble of switching into each program and choosing Quit.

- **Show me what to say.** This command opens the Speech Commands window that you're probably looking at right now.

- **What day is it?** Tells you the date.

- **Tell me a joke.** Begins a pathetic knock-knock joke. You've got to play along, providing the "who's there?" and "so-and-so *who?*" answers. (You don't necessarily have to say, "Who's there?" You can also say "Stop," "Go away," or even "Stop with the jokes!")

When you switch from one program to another, the list in the Speech Commands window may change, so that you see whatever special commands work in the new program.

Speaking to the Mac

When you're ready to try talking to your computer, keep in mind that the microphone is the little pinhole at the lower-left corner of the screen.

Now you're ready to begin. While pressing the Esc key, begin speaking normally. Try one of the commands in the Speakable Commands list, like "What time is it?"

If all goes well, a few things should happen. First, the lines in the little round Feedback window change color, indicating that the Mac is hearing you. Second, a balloon above the Feedback window tells you what the Mac *thinks* you said. Finally, the Mac *does* whatever you told it to do. In the case of the knock-knock jokes, you'll actually hear it converse with you using whatever voice you selected in the Speech panel of System Preferences.

Play Movies

Your iMac is quite handy with movies. It can make them, record them, and show them.

The cornerstone to all this is a technology bundle called *QuickTime,* which is built right into Mac OS X.

Getting movies to play on your screen is simple: Just double-click a movie file's icon to open it. It opens a program called Movie Player or QuickTime Player, as shown here.

Beginning   End

Play/Stop
(or just press the space bar)

To play the flick, click the little "play" triangle to make it play back. (Or press the space bar.) You'll quickly discover a few disappointing facts about digital movies: They often play in a small window, and they're generally short. That's because QuickTime movie files take up obscene amounts of hard drive space for each minute of footage.

The bigger challenge, therefore, is simply *getting* a movie you want to watch. Several sources spring to mind: You can download movies from the Internet or America Online (see Chapter 6), although these enormous files take enormous amounts of time to transfer to you by modem. The CD-ROM that comes with each issue of *MacAddict* magazine, and the newsstand issues of *Macworld* magazine, also contain QuickTime movies each month. Finally, of course, you can always make your *own* QuickTime movies, using a camcorder and the iMovie program described in Chapter 11.

Send Faxes

Because your iMac has a built-in fax modem, you're in for a delicious treat. Faxes sent by an iMac come out looking twice as crisp and clean when a real fax machine receives them. And sending faxes couldn't be more convenient for you — no printout to throw away, no paper involved at all. Your iMac sends the thing directly to another fax machine's brain.

Installing FAXstf

The first step toward achieving this heaven is installing the software, which is called, for some reason, FAXstf. Don't even ask me how it's pronounced.

The installation process is a long and winding road, but there's happy faxing at the other end. Now then:

Open your Applications folder, and then open the Installers folder inside it. Now you should see the icon called FAXstf Installer. (If not, it's possible that Apple stopped including this software with new iMacs since this book went to press. You can still buy FAXstf software, however, from *www.faxstf.com*.)

In any case, double-click the FAXstf Installer. At the welcome screen, click Continue, Accept, Install, and whatever other blue, pulsing buttons present themselves during the installation process.

When the installation is complete, click Exit (if you see that button) and then visit your Applications folder yet again. This time, open the Utilities folder you'll find there. Open the program called Print Center, which you may have visited once before, when setting up your printer.

Click the Add Printer button. In the resulting Printer List window, choose FAXstf from the pop-up menu, like this:

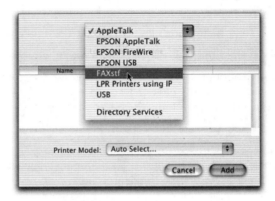

Then click the words Apple Internal Modem, click the Add button, and quit Print Center. You're ready to fax!

Sending a fax

Here's how the faxing process goes:

1. **Type up (or open) whatever it is you want to fax.**

   Usually, this means a letter you've written in, say, AppleWorks. Make sure it's in front of you on the screen.

2. **From the File menu, choose Print.**

   The Print dialog box appears. Make sure the Printer pop-up menu says Apple Internal Modem, like this:

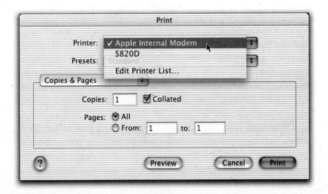

Note that the fax is, in effect, masquerading as a *printer*. That's important to remember! If you ever intend to use your *real* printer again, you'll want to choose *its* name from this pop-up menu instead.

3. **Click Print.**

You see a dialog box like the one in the following illustration.

4. **From the Copies & Pages pop-up menu, choose Addresses.**

You're about to enter — the Fax Number Zone. As you can see here, you're offered the chance to open your iMac's Address Book, the very same one that contains the names and addresses you use for e-mail.

5. **Click the Address Book icon.**

Now your Address Book opens, listing everyone who has a fax number. You can winnow down the list by typing a few letters of the lucky fax recipient's name into the Search box.

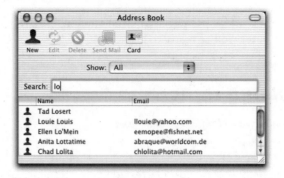

Of course, in many instances, the person you're faxing isn't yet *in* your Address Book. It's up to you to add that person's name by clicking the New icon and typing in the contact information. Be sure to open one of the phone-number pop-up menus to choose FAX from the list, like this:

Click Save when you're finished typing in the new person's name.

In any case, once you've found (or added) the correct name in your Address Book, proceed:

6. **Drag the person's name (or the little silhouette) directly into the names list of the Print dialog box in the background.**

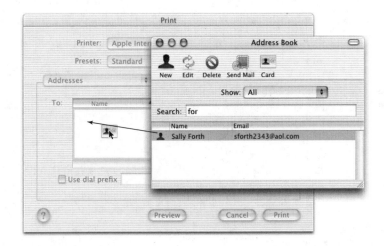

That person's name appears in the list of recipients. You can add other recipients as long as the Address Book window is still open.

7. **Close the Address Book window.**

If the fax is long-distance, be sure to turn on "Use dial prefix" and type in a 1. (If that gets to be a nuisance, you could always add the 1 to the appropriate fax numbers in your Address Book.)

8. **Click Print.**

After a moment, a Modem Center dialog box appears; its Status column keeps you posted on the progress of your outgoing fax. You'll hear the usual dialing sounds of a modem happily going about its work. Before long, all is quiet once again, and your fax is on its way.

Incidentally, before you get completely addicted to this electronic-faxing business, you should take a moment to fill in your *own* information for use on the cover page.

To do that, open your Applications folder. In the FAXstf folder, open the program called Fax Browser. From the Fax Browser menu, choose Preferences. In the Preferences dialog box, click the Address button to open your Address Book once again.

Your mission here is to create an Address Book entry for *yourself.* Click New, fill in the blanks (click the down-pointing black triangle button to see all of them), and then click Save. Now find yourself in the Address Book (type a few letters of your name in the Search box, if necessary). Then drag your own name, or the tiny silhouette next to it, up into the strip at the top of the Identity tab, like this:

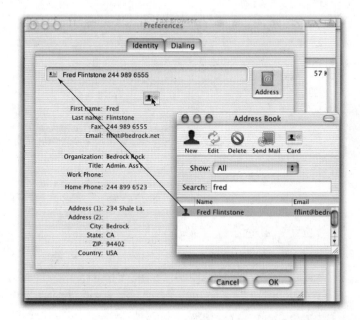

Then close the Address Book and click OK. From now on, your fax recipients will know how to get in touch with you — or to fax you back.

Receive Faxes

If you promise not to tell anyone, here's a little secret: Your iMac can *receive* faxes, too.

Of course, if you want to be able to get faxes, you must treat your iMac like a fax machine: that is, dedicate a second phone line to it — or live with having to plug it into your phone jack (thus blocking normal voice calls) every time you're expecting a fax.

Here's how to do it: First, open your Applications folder, open the FAXstf folder, and open the program called Modem Center.

On the Modem Center toolbar, click the Setup button. In the resulting dialog box, choose Receiving, like this:

You'll see a box that lets you specify how many rings have to go by before the fax/modem answers the phone. If it says 0, then yours won't answer the phone.

When the fax comes in, the Modem Center program opens automatically. When the Status line tells you that the fax is complete, there's nothing more to do but *look* at the fax — by opening Fax Browser. (If Modem Center is on the screen, the quickest way to get there is to click the Fax Browser icon on its toolbar.) In Fax Browser, click the name of the fax you want to see — and you can see it in the bottom part of the window. There you can read it and, if you like, print the fax.

There. I just saved you $200.

Fit in Your Pocket

It happens to the best of us: You've truly integrated your iMac into your life. It's got your calendar, your phone numbers, your to-do list — everything you need. And now you need to leave the house. What's an iMac fan to do?

Your options are:

- ✔ Stuff your iMac into your pocket before each trip. Shred your clothes and look like an imbecile as you walk into business meetings with unsightly bulges.
- ✔ Get a PalmPilot.

A PalmPilot is one of those amazing handheld computers, about the size of an audio cassette. You can buy various models from various companies like Palm and Handspring, from about $100 for a plastic, basic model to $400 or more for amazing color-screen models.

Each comes with a little stand that plugs into your iMac and sucks out a copy of all your critical information: your calendar, phone book, to-do list, memos, and even e-mail.

The really great part is that, when you return home from your trip, you plug the PalmPilot back into your iMac — and any changes you made while on the road are automatically sent *back* to the calendar and address book on the iMac.

You can't run iMac *programs* on a PalmPilot, but you *can* keep your life's critical information with you without buying a second computer or new wardrobe.

All of this presumes, however, that you keep your appointments and phone book in a free program called Palm Desktop. (It may have come with your Palm, or you can download it from the Palm Web site. Try *www.palm.com* or, more directly, *www.palm.com/support/palmdesktop.html.*)

Suppose you return from a meeting with several new phone numbers you've written into your PalmPilot. You just place it in the cradle, press the Sync button, and your PalmPilot and your copy of Palm Desktop (on the iMac) automatically update each other.

Take Pictures of the Screen

Not just anybody can be a computer-book author. If possible, the candidate should have years of technical training, a PhD in computer programming, and the ability to take apart a computer and put it back together blindfolded.

Of course, I don't have any of that. But I do know how to take *screenshots*.

Screenshots are printable illustrations of the Mac screen. They appear everywhere in this book. If you can make screenshots, you're halfway home to being able to write computer books of your own.

To capture your screen image, press Shift-⌘-3. You hear a satisfying camera-shutter sound, and a new graphics file appears on your desktop called *Picture 1*. Each time you press Shift-⌘-3, you get another file, called Picture 2, Picture 3, and so on. You can open these files in Preview, AppleWorks, or another graphics program, in readiness for editing or printing.

If you're interested in capturing only *part* of the screen, though, you press Shift-⌘-4. Your cursor becomes a tiny + symbol. Now drag diagonally across the screen to capture only a rectangular chunk of it. When you release the mouse, you hear the camera-click sound, and the Picture 1 file appears on your desktop as usual.

Run Windows Programs

It's true: Never again must you feel game-deprived. The iMac can run almost any Windows program alive. All you need is a program like VirtualPC for Mac OS X *(www.connectix.com)*. Your Windows programs won't run quite as fast as they would on the fastest actual Windows *computers* — but they'll run.

Talk to Windows Computers

If you've read Chapter 14, you're already aware that you can hook up several Macs in the same building into a network, which makes it very easy for everyone to be online simultaneously, or share a printer, or copy files back and forth. But what if there's a Windows PC in the house? Hey — it could happen.

In that case, one possibility is buying a program like Dave (no relation), which you can read about at *www.thursby.com*. But that entails paying $150 and performing some technical setup.

Another possibility is using the built-in Mac-to-Windows software in Mac OS X. It's not especially good looking, but it works.

The following instructions assume that both the Mac and the Windows PC are connected to an Ethernet hub:

1. **On your Windows PC, share a folder.**

   Lord knows, this isn't a book about Windows. But in Windows XP, for example, you'd start by clicking a folder with the *right* mouse button. Choose Properties from the shortcut menu, click the Sharing tab in the resulting dialog box, and turn on "Share this folder on the network," like this.

   In the "Share name" box, type a name for the folder as it will appear on the network (no spaces are allowed).

2. **On the Mac, open the Go menu and choose Connect to Server.**

   The Connect to Server dialog box appears.

3. **In the box at the bottom, type *smb://*, followed by the Windows machine's name. Add a slash (/) and then type the name of the shared folder.**

   For example, you might type this into the Connect box: *smb://DellPC/MyDocuments*. "DellPC" is the name of the Windows computer, and "My Documents" is the name of the shared folder (leave out any spaces from its name).

   To find out the correct name for your PC, open the Start menu, right-click the words My Computer, and choose Properties from the shortcut menu. In the resulting box, click Computer Name. (What you want is the "Full computer name," *not* the "Computer description." Capitalization doesn't matter.)

4. **Click Connect.**

   Now the Authentication dialog box appears, which looks like the box at left:

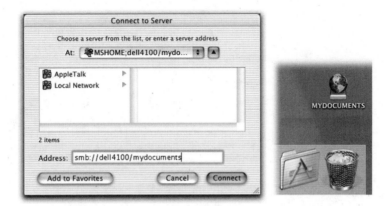

(If this box doesn't appear, it's possible that your Windows PC is on a *workgroup* — a kind of mini-network. You'll see the workgroup name on the same screen where you looked up the computer's name in Step 3. In that case, try inserting the workgroup name into your network code, like this: *smb://MSHOME;DellPC/MyDocuments*. Yes, that's a semicolon after the workgroup name. This stuff makes you appreciate the simplicity of Macintosh, doesn't it?)

5. Type your name and password, if necessary, and then click OK.

If you have an account on the Windows PC, great — use that name and password. If the PC isn't in a corporation where somebody administers access to each machine, you may be able to leave the password blank.

Now the shared folder from the Windows machine shows up as an icon on your iMac's screen, as shown at right in the previous illustration, just as though you've tapped into another Mac. Double-click it to open it, or drag files into or out of it exactly as described in Chapter 14.

Chapter 18

Ten Features that Didn't Quite Fit the Outline

· ·

*T*his chapter is filled with miniature iMac lessons. It reveals iMac features you'd be unlikely to discover on your own, unearths shortcuts and slick tricks, and shows you how to tailor your iMac so that it perfectly fits your personality.

In short, the following discussions are useful, surprising, delightful — but utterly random. They just didn't fit tidily into any other chapter. That's a syndrome we writers try to avoid, but greatly prefer to writer's block. May you find enlightenment even in randomness.

Closing All Windows at Once

Suppose you've opened a gaggle of folders. Their windows are lying open all over the screen. And suppose that the niggling neatness ethic instilled in you by your mother compels you to clean up a bit.

You could, of course, click the close button of each window, one at a time. But it's far faster to click only *one* window's close button while pressing the Option key. Bam, bam, bam — they all close automatically, one after another. (You can perform the same trick, by the way, on the yellow Minimize button. Option-click it in one window to send *all* open desktop windows scurrying down to the Dock, out of your way.)

Multitasking Methods #1

As you discovered early on, the iMac lets you run more than one program simultaneously. (Remember when you tried some tricks with both Stickies and the Calculator open on the screen at once?) You can switch from one program to another by clicking the program's icon in the Dock.

So how does the Option key play into all this? When you switch from one program to another, you can make the program you're *leaving* hide itself, and all of its windows, automatically. Just press Option while clicking the new program's icon on the Dock (or while clicking in its window). That way, you always keep nonessential programs hidden.

Multitasking Methods #2

Efficiency fans eschew the mouse, a little fact you've probably picked up on by this point in the book. Anything that's worth doing, goes the thinking, is worth doing with the keyboard alone.

To that end, Apple has equipped you with a handy keystroke that lets you switch among your various open programs without your having to click the Dock — or even use the mouse at all. It's ⌘-Tab.

That is, hold down the ⌘ key. While it's done, keep tapping the Tab key. With each tap, you highlight a different icon on the Dock. When you've highlighted the icon of the program you want to jump to, let go of all keys. The iMac responds by bringing that program to the front, ready for action.

Make an Alias of a File

The File menu has a command called Make Alias. Although you might expect this command to generate names like One-Eyed Jake or "Teeth" McGuire, the term *alias* in the Macintosh world represents something slightly different — a duplicate of a file's *icon* (but not a duplicate of the file itself). You can identify the alias icon because of the tiny, tiny arrow that appears on its icon. (The word *alias* sometimes appears, too.)

Spy Photos

Spy Photos alias

What's neat about aliases is that, when you double-click an alias icon, the iMac opens the *original* file. If the 1980's were your formative years, you might think of the alias as a beeper — when you call the *alias*, the *actual* file responds.

Trash, aliases, and a word of caution

If you trash an alias, you're deleting only the alias. The original file is still on your disk. If you delete the *original* file, however, the alias icons will remain uselessly on your disk, rebels without a cause, babies without a mother, days without sunshine. When you double-click an alias whose original file is gone, you'll just get an error message. (The error message offers you the chance to attach this orphaned alias to a *different* "real" file — but the original file is still gone forever.)

Likewise, if you burn your inauguration speech file's *alias* onto a CD, thinking that you'll just print it out when you get to Washington, think again. You've just copied the alias, but you *don't* actually have any text. That's all in the original file, still at home on your hard disk.

So who on earth would need a feature like this? Well, there's more to the story. An alias, for one thing, requires only a tiny amount of disk space (a couple of K) — so it's not the same as making an actual copy of the full-sized, original file. (And you can make as many aliases of a file as you want.) Therefore, making an alias of something you use frequently is an excellent time-saver — it keeps the alias icon readily accessible, even if the real file is buried somewhere four folders deep.

Here's the drill:

1. **Click the real icon once.**
2. **From the File menu, choose Make Alias.**

Or, as a shortcut, just drag any icon out of its window while pressing Option and ⌘.

You can put that alias anywhere you like, confident that it serves as a handy elevator button that takes you to the real file that spawned it. The *real* file can be anywhere on your hard disk, or even on a different disk. You can move the real file from folder to folder or even rename it, and the alias still opens it correctly.

Self-Launching Programs

If your daily routine begins with the same program each morning — your e-mail and word-processor programs, for example — you can tell your iMac to fire them up automatically, saving you a couple of manual mouse clicks.

To specify what you'd like to auto-open, open the System Preferences program (the light-switch icon on your Dock) and click the Login icon. As shown here, you can now build a list of programs or documents that will auto-launch each time you log in.

Click Add to summon the Open dialog box. Navigate to your Applications folder, find the icon of the program you want to self-open, select it, and then click Choose. Or, if you want to open a certain *document* each morning, navigate to your Documents folder and select the file there.

You can also specify the order in which your startup items auto-open just by dragging them up or down in the list. To remove an item, click it in the list and then click Remove.

The Secret Life of a Scroll Bar

You may remember from Chapter 1 that the little square box inside a scroll bar lets you view what's hidden in a window — what's above or below what you're seeing, for example. (Man, I sure *hope* you remember — otherwise, you've been using your iMac all this time without ever writing a memo taller than three inches.)

The trouble with scroll bars, though, is that you have to use them one at a time. If you want to move diagonally to see a different part of a window, you have to scroll first horizontally, then vertically.

But not if you know the secret trick: Press ⌘ and Option. Now drag *inside* the window, marveling that you can now scroll up, down, or diagonally in one smooth move. Notice how your cursor becomes a butler's white-gloved hand, as though to say: "Your wish is my command, master."

An Instant "You Are Here" Map

See the tiny folder icon in the title bar of any window? You may already realize that it's a *handle*. If you click it (and hold down the mouse button until the icon darkens), you can use it to drag the open window to another place, such as your backup disk or (in the case of perfectionist computer-book authors) directly to the trash.

But when you're lost in the sea of your hard drive, and you're examining the contents of some window and you've forgotten how you got here, a handy navigational trick awaits you. While pressing the ⌘ key, click the name of the window, like this:

A menu drops down, listing the disks and folders that this one is *inside* of. If you're looking at the Seattle window, for example, you can backtrack to its parent folder — called Washington, let's say — just by choosing it from this very secret menu.

Folder Burrowing in the Dock

As Chapter 3 makes clear, you should consider the Dock the primary nesting grounds for the programs, files, and folders you use often. Whenever you click something on Dock, you open that something.

But here's a trick worth putting into practice right this very minute. Try dragging a *folder* onto the right side of the Dock — your Applications folder or Home folder, for example.

Now you can open anything *inside* those folders without leaving a messy trail of windows behind you. The trick is to click the Dock folder *and hold* the button down for a moment. (Or, if you can't wait for that extra second, Control-click the Dock folder icon.)

Either way, a pop-up menu of the folder's contents sprouts at your cursor tip, like this:

Choose anything from this menu, or even choose something that's in one of the *folders* in this list, to open it.

It shouldn't take much of a leap for you to figure out how you might put your *entire hard drive* onto the Dock, thereby gaining quick access to anything on it, in any folder at all.

Adding folders to your Dock has another handy benefit, too: They still work as folders. That is, you can still drag files and other folders on top of them, even though they're in the Dock.

The Secret Programs' Dock Menu

Speaking of secret pop-up menus in the Dock, here's another one. If you click-and-hold the Dock icon of a *program* (or Control-click it), you get a handy pop-up menu of commands. The beauty of this menu is that it lists all of the documents that are currently open *in* that program — in this case, AppleWorks:

Choose the name of a document to jump right to it. You can also choose Quit (to quit the program without actually switching to it first), Show In Finder (to jump to the program's icon, in your Applications folder or wherever it happens to be), or Keep in Dock (to ensure that the program's icon will remain on the Dock even after you've quit out of it). That's a lot of power that most people never even discover!

Redesigning the Finder Toolbar

At the top of every Finder window is a row of navigation and function buttons called the *toolbar*. Just click any of these icons to trigger the corresponding function or open the corresponding disk or folder. Click Computer, Home, Favorites, or Applications, for example, to jump to those folders.

If you'd rather do without this toolbar, just click the little white-glob-of-toothpaste button in the upper-right corner. (That's a shortcut for choosing Hide Toolbar from the View menu.) The toolbar disappears. To bring it back, choose Show Toolbar from the View menu.

Different buttons, smaller buttons

But you don't have to do without the toolbar altogether. You might simply prefer that it take up less screen space.

To make it so, open the View menu and choose Customize Toolbar. The dialog box that appears, shown here at bottom, offers a Show pop-up menu at the bottom, which lets you choose picture-buttons only (Icon Only) or, for the greatest space conservation, Text Only, shown here at top:

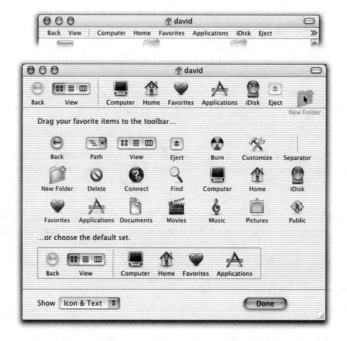

While this window is open, you might want to survey the optional, alternative buttons that Apple has provided for your toolbar enjoyment. There's an Eject button that makes the iMac spit out whatever disk is currently highlighted, a Burn icon that records a blank CD, a New folder button, and so on.

You can add these to the toolbar just by dragging them into place from the gallery before you. Remove icons from the toolbar by dragging them up or down off the toolbar, or rearrange them by dragging them horizontally.

Click Done to make your changes stick.

Adding your own stuff

As useful as some of Apple's toolbar-gallery icons may be, the toolbar really takes off only when you add your own icons. You can drag *any icons at all* onto the toolbar — files, folders, disks, programs, Web sites, or whatever — to turn them into one-click buttons. Just drag them right up there from any window or the desktop. (You can do this at any time, even when the Customize Toolbar window isn't open.)

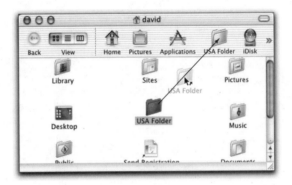

To drag toolbar icons around, rearranging them horizontally, just press ⌘ as you drag. And to take an icon off the toolbar, ⌘-drag it clear away from the toolbar. (Watch your Trash on the Dock turn into a pair of snipping scissors as you do it. Cute!)

Chapter 19

Ten Back-of-the-Mac Jacks

*T*he front of your iMac is bare as a baby's bottom, but the back is broken up by a bunch of boxy connectors. You may not need all of them today, or even tomorrow — but you'll certainly need some of them. Here's how to identify them, and what to plug into which.

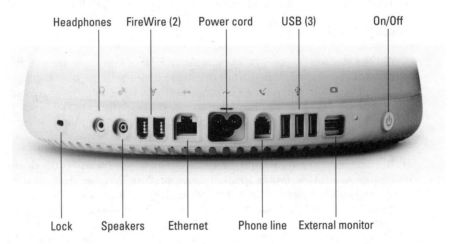

Headphones   FireWire (2)   Power cord   USB (3)   On/Off

Lock   Speakers   Ethernet   Phone line   External monitor

Lock

Just because bad guys are hardened and immoral doesn't mean they don't also have good taste in computers. The truth is, the iMac's sleek lines, high horsepower, and easy portability make it a prime target for theft, especially when the machine sits in public places like schools and businesses.

The little jack at the far left side of the back panel accommodates something called a Kensington Security cable *(www.kensington.com),* which provides a way for you to lock down the machine. Your iMac is then immune from theft — except perhaps by crooks who are also prepared to steal the desk it's attached to.

Headphones

Plug in your favorite Walkman-style headset when you need to listen to music or games without disturbing those around you — or without them disturbing you. (If you buy a headphone-jack Y splitter, two people can even listen simultaneously.)

Speakers

Oh, yes indeedy: The iMac is more than hi-tech — it's hi-*fi,* capable of churning out gorgeous stereo sound.

The monophonic speaker built into the half-soccer-ball base of the iMac is OK, I guess, although there's very little chance you'll mistake your living room for Carnegie Hall.

But the real fun begins when you attach a pair of miniature speakers, like the globule-shaped, transparent ones that come with the higher-priced iMac models. (If yours didn't come with them, you can buy them from *www.apple.com.*) If you play iMac games, particularly CD-ROM discs, you won't believe what you've been missing; the sounds are much richer and deeper.

Nor are you limited to Apple-branded speakers; the world is filled with even more powerful computer speakers. Just be sure that you buy speakers that are especially designed for computers. They must be *self-powered,* and they must be *shielded;* the magnets inside normal stereo speakers are enough to distort the image on your monitor like the Sunday comics on Silly Putty.

On the other hand, you'll get the same extremely rich sound by popping a pair of Walkman headphones into the headphone jack on the back of the iMac. (When you do so, the iMac's built-in speakers automatically shut up.)

FireWire

FireWire is an especially lovable jack. The three things most people plug here are:

- ✔ **A camcorder.** This is where you plug a digital camcorder when you want to edit your home movies (Chapter 11).

✔ **Another hard drive.** You can plug in external hard drives here, including little pocket drives — a convenient option if you're the kind of person who needs a little more space, or who'd like to haul around a lot of data from place to place.

✔ **The iPod.** Oh, the glory of this beauty! It's a portable music player — an MP3 player, to be precise — although it probably belongs in an art museum. It's mirror-finish stainless steel and part white acrylic, and it fits in your hand like a deck of cards whose edges have been laser-rounded for your comfort.

Unlike other players of its size, however, this one has enough capacity for the average person's entire music collection — the songs of 130 or 260 CDs can fit on this thing, depending on which model you buy. And the iPod runs for 12 hours per battery charge.

What's especially cool about the iPod is that it needs only a single cable — a white FireWire cable — to mate with your Mac. Over this cable, it draws both the power to recharge its battery and the music, which it copies automatically, and *quickly* (about 9 seconds per album) from your iTunes music library (see Chapter 10).

The FireWire cable also permits the iPod's hard drive to show up on your Mac's screen as, well, a hard drive icon, which is precisely what it is. At this point, you can drag data files and folders to or from the iPod, which is now a very fast, extremely chic-looking backup disk.

You may see the occasional scanner or digital camera that has a FireWire cable, too.

What's so nice about FireWire is that, first of all, it's extremely fast, which is why speed-intensive gadgets like camcorders and hard drives are such a natural for it. Second, FireWire is easy to plug and unplug. It's nothing like the balky jacks of the '90s that preceded it, which required that you shut down the Mac completely before attaching or disconnecting your add-on gear.

Ethernet

This is your networking jack. You'll be very happy to have it when a second or third Mac joins your household, because this is where you plug the Ethernet cable that will connect your iMac to the network. (Details in Chapter 14.)

One important caution: This jack looks and works almost exactly like a telephone jack. It's actually slightly larger — but it's still possible to snap a phone wire into this jack. In fact, many a hapless computer owner has done just that by accident, and then spent days trying to figure out why their machines couldn't dial up to the Internet. Don't plug anything in here except an Ethernet cable.

Power Cord

You gotta love Apple's attention to detail. The iMac's power cord connects here — and when it's in place, its little molded face plate blends in smoothly with the rest of the iMac surface, so that it looks like it's permanently attached.

Phone Line

This is where you plug the wire that goes to a phone jack, for faxing and dialing-the-Internet purposes. (An iMac-matching white one even came in your iMac box.)

USB

USB stands for *Universal Serial Bus* ("bus" meaning "connector"), which you'll never need to know.

You will, however, become intimately familiar with USB. Apart from camcorders and hard drives, almost everything worth connecting to the iMac plugs in here. For example:

✔ **Printers.** Most inkjet printers (see Chapter 5) connect to your USB port. Even some laser printers do.

✔ **Scanners.** If the point of a printer is to take something on the screen and reproduce it on *paper,* a scanner, then, is the opposite — its function is to scan an image on paper and throw it up on the iMac *screen.* After the image has been scanned and converted into bits and bytes that the iMac understands (meaning that it's been *digitized*), you can manipulate the image any way that you want. Erase unwanted parts, make the background darker, give Uncle Ed a mustache, shorten your brother's neck — whatever.

The more dignified use for a scanner is grabbing real-world images that you then paste into your own documents, particularly in the realm of page layout and graphic design. Got a potato-industry newsletter to crank out? Scan in a photo of some fine-lookin' spuds, and you've got yourself a graphic for page one.

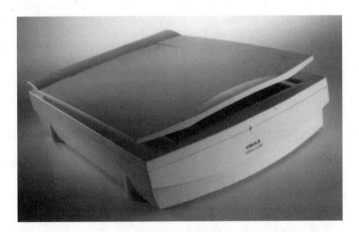

A middle-of-the-line color scanner costs around $100 — which sometimes even includes software that can do a decent job of converting scanned articles into typed-out, editable word-processor documents. (When shopping, be careful to buy a scanner that's *Mac OS X compatible.*)

✔ **Digital cameras.** Ordinarily, the concept of paying $500 for a camera that lacks any way to insert film would seem spectacularly brain-dead. Yet that's exactly the point of *digital cameras,* like those from Canon, Kodak, Casio, Olympus, Sony, and others. They store photos without film — actually, on a memory card that generally holds between 12 and 50 photos — and when you get home, you can dump the images into your iMac (after connecting a cable), thereby freeing your camera's RAM for another round of happy-go-lucky shooting.

If the camera you buy has a resolution of three or four *megapixels* (millions of dots per shot), the pictures are every bit as sharp as traditional photos, capable of nearly poster-size blowups without any deterioration in quality.

✔ **PalmPilots.** As noted in Chapter 17, a Palm organizer (also available as part of a cell phone) is a handy data bucket that lets you carry your address book, calendar, and other information around in your pocket. It comes with a USB *cradle* — a little stand that connects to your iMac and updates the little device with your latest information.

✔ **Zip drives, floppy drives.** As I'm sure you're aware by now, the iMac comes without a floppy-disk drive. In truth, that's no big deal; floppies are embarrassingly old, slow, and low-capacity. Your iMac came instead with a disc drive that can record and even re-record CD's — the same idea as floppy disks, except that a CD holds roughly 800 times as much as a floppy.

Every now and then, though, somebody hands you a floppy disk or a Zip disk, or maybe you need to transport a lot of files between two Macs. If that happens a lot, you can always buy an add-on disk drive for your iMac — one that plugs into the iMac's USB or FireWire jacks.

For about $60 or less, you can equip your iMac with the missing limb: a true-blue, bona fide floppy disk.

For $100 or $150, you can buy a *Zip drive,* whose disks look like floppy disks that have been hitting the Ben & Jerry's a bit too often. Each holds 100MB or 250MB and costs about $12. Zip disks are convenient, sturdy, and easy to work with; the advantage here is that hundreds of thousands of people already own Zip drives. You can carry your project around on a Zip disk in your pocket, for example, confident that your friendly neighborhood Kinko's, corporate office, or print shop is likely to have a Zip drive that can accept it (the disk, not your pocket).

✔ **Musical-keyboard adapters.** *MIDI,* pronounced like the short skirt, stands for Musical Instrument Digital Interface. What it *means* is "hookup to a synthesizer." What it *does* is let your iMac record and play back your musical performances using a synthesizer attached to it. When you record, the iMac makes a metronome sound — a steady click track — and you play to the beat. Then, when you play back the music, your keyboard plays *exactly* what you recorded, complete with feeling, expression, and fudged notes; you'd think that Elvis's ghost was playing the instrument, except that the keys don't move up and down. Then you can edit your fudged mistakes and wind up sounding like [insert your favorite musician here].

All you need is a little box called a MIDI interface (about $50) that connects your iMac's USB jack to the synthesizer. You also need a program that can record and play back the music, called a *sequencing program,* like EasyBeat and Cubase VST. And, of course, you need to get your hands on a synthesizer. Or, for making sheet music, investigate Nightingale, Sibelius, or Finale. Check out a music store, or read some reviews on the Web, and get jammin'.

✔ **Joysticks.** The iMac, with its high-speed G4 chip and superb graphics, makes a great game-playing machine. But how can you get the feeling of soaring over the fields of France in a fighter plane using a *mouse* to control the action? You can't. You need a joystick. It works just like a real airplane joystick, controlling your movement in flight simulation, driving simulators, shoot-'em-ups, and other games. They cost between $20 and $50, and you can find them on a Web site like *www.buy.com* by searching for "Mac joystick" or "Macintosh joystick."

✔ **The iSub.** Even with Apple's external speaker globules, you may not consider yourself a fully realized sound entity. You're still missing a third piece of the dream sound system: a *subwoofer*. The term may suggest an underwater dog, but it's actually a transparent, bubble-like, separate module that fills in the lower range of musical notes. It looks like this:

If you're much of a stereo or home theatre nut, you already know that a subwoofer adds subsonic thudding and power to any music. If you use your iMac's CD drive to listen to music CDs, or its DVD drive to watch movies on disc, this additional item (officially called the Harmon/Kardon iSub) makes the sound system second to none — on computers, anyway. You can get the iSub subwoofer from *www.apple.com,* among other places.

The USB port also accommodates your keyboard, your mouse, and many other kinds of doodads.

You might inspect these three jacks, each marked by a three-pronged tree symbol, and assume that you therefore have room to plug in three of the gadgets described above.

In fact, calculating the number of available USB connectors is a bit more complicated. One of these back-panel jacks gets used up by your keyboard, which brings the total down to two.

But check out the ends of your keyboard! There, as a convenience, Apple has installed two additional USB jacks, which brings the total up to four.

On the other hand, you'll probably want to plug your *mouse* into one of these keyboard jacks, leaving only three USB jacks free (two on the back, one at the end of the keyboard). So it *is* three after all; sorry to have wasted your time.

Installing a new USB doodad

Like most computer add-ons, many USB gadgets come with special software to place on the iMac itself. You'll find this software, if it's necessary, on a CD that came with the USB gadget. Just insert the CD and look for an icon called Installer; double-click the icon and follow whatever instructions appear.

After you've installed the software, connect your gadget to the USB jack on the iMac. If the circuitry gods are smiling, your USB device should now work as advertised.

Attaching more USB gear

Even after you've hooked up your keyboard and mouse, you still have three free USB jacks. But for certain gadget fans, even three may not be enough. Maybe you've plugged in your printer, scanner, and digital camera — great — but now where are you supposed to plug your Palm organizer?

Easy: buy an adapter box that gives you more USB jacks. Those so-called *USB hubs* multiply your USB jack so that you wind up with four, eight, or even more jacks. Connect enough of these hubs to one another, in fact, and you can have up to 127 USB gadgets connected to your iMac all at once.

The only thing that could conceivably go wrong with USB has to do with *power*. Many USB gadgets draw power from the iMac itself, sparing you the ugliness and hassle of power cords and plugs for all your external equipment. It turns out, however, that the back-panel jacks provide more power than the keyboard jacks do.

You can take away two lessons from this. First, if you ever plug in some USB gizmo to the end of your keyboard and discover that it doesn't work, try plugging the gizmo into one of the back-panel USB jacks instead. Second, when you buy a USB hub, shop for a *powered* one (one that requires its own electrical plug), so that you won't run into the same trouble as you did with the keyboard-end jack.

External Monitor

If you use your iMac to give slide shows or classroom lectures, you may sometimes wish you could project images onto a big screen.

That's exactly the purpose of this *video-output* jack. Unfortunately, the other piece you need for this stunt — something called the VGA Display Adapter cable — doesn't come with the iMac; you have to buy it for $20 from an Apple store, or from *www.apple.com/store.*

One end of this little adapter connects to the back of your iMac; the other end connects to the standard *VGA connector* of the sorts of projectors found in schools, businesses, and presentation halls. If you've ever been to a user-group meeting and seen a Mac demonstration projected onto a huge screen, now you know how it's done.

The Power Button

The On button for your iMac is also on the back panel, at the far right as you look at it.

Yes, I realize that it's not technically a jack or connector. But it's the tenth *thing* back there, and that's good enough for me.

Index

• *Numbers & Symbols* •

 (Apple) logo (menu), 14–15, 30, 262
* (asterisk), 138
{ } (braces), 138
⌘ (command) key, 38–39
= (equal sign), 210
4-pin-to-6-pin FireWire cables, 236, 349–350
- (hyphen), 211
- (minus sign), 211
1-click accounts, 229
100BaseT cables, 281
/ (slash), 334
' (straight apostrophes), 113
" (straight quotes), 113
10BaseT cables, 281

• *A* •

About This Mac command, 17, 30–31
accent marks, creating, 194
Access keyword, America Online (AOL), 137
access privileges, error messages, 276, 309–310
accessing
   America Online (AOL), 135
   desktop automatically, 14
   Internet, access options, 12, 133
   Internet, using AirPort, 284
   World Wide Web, previous pages viewed, 157
   World Wide Web, via America Online (AOL), 155–156
   World Wide Web, via the desktop, 161
   World Wide Web, via Internet Service Providers, 156
accounts
   Create Your Account screen, 11–12
   deleting user accounts, 278
   EarthLink, signing up, 141
   e-mail, setting up, 173–174
   Internet, signing up for, 141
   multiple-user systems, setting up, 273–275, 287
   1-click accounts, 229
Acrobat files, 121
activating screen savers, 72. *See also* opening; starting
Activation tab, 72
active programs, determining, 63–64, 99–100
adapters, musical-keyboards, 352
adding. *See also* creating; installing
   credits, iMovie, 243–244
   icons, 57
   inkjet printers, 116–117
   laser printers, 118–119
   music soundtracks, iMovie, 246–247
   printers, for faxing, 327
   signatures, e-mail, 179–180
   text, TextEdit program, 84
   titles, iMovie, 243–244
   toolbar buttons, 256
   toolbar icons, personal, 345
address books
   Address Book program, 80
   e-mail, 175, 184
   faxes, 328–329
addresses
   typing format, Internet Explorer (Microsoft), 163
   typing new, World Wide Web, 157–158
   typing shortcuts, Internet Explorer (Microsoft), 164
adjusting
   brightness, iPhoto, 222–223
   column widths, 46
   contrast, iPhoto, 222–223
   monitors, computers, 7
administrators
   defining permissions, 274–275
   file sharing capabilities, 291
   purpose, 271–272, 273
ads, blinking, 168

.aif files, 246
aim keyword, America Online (AOL), 140
AirPort Setup Assistant, 284
AirPort (wireless) connections, 281–285
albums, iPhoto, 223–225
aliases, 338–339
AltaVista search engine, 158
amazon.com, 163
America Online (AOL). *See also* Internet
    Service Providers; World Wide Web
  access phone numbers, 135
  chat rooms, 138, 139–140
  e-mail, 138–139
  Favorite Places, 137–138
  features listing, 133
  first session, setup steps, 135–136
  fonts, acquiring new, 123–124
  free software, downloading, 140–141
  hanging up, 146
  icon, 134
  installing, 134
  Instant Message, 139–140
  Internet versus, 134
  keywords, 137, 139–140
  newsgroups, 143
  Personal Finance page, 136
  Research & Learn button, 136
  screen names, defining, 135
  screen names, looking up, 139
  table of contents, 136
  Travel button, 136
  Web browsers, 145
animated ads, 168
answering e-mail, 139
antennas, radio transmitter, 281–282
AOL. *See* America Online
apostrophes, straight ('), 113
Apple logo (menu), 14–15, 30, 262
Apple DVD Player Help, 257
Apple DVD Player program, 256–257
Apple IDs, 229
Apple iPod MP3 player, 231, 349
Apple Knowledge Base, 316
Apple System Profiler program, 81
Apple Web site, 250, 316
AppleCare, 316
AppleWorks
  databases, creating, 192–193, 195
  databases, data entry, 195–196

databases, purpose, 192
databases, records, creating, 196–197
databases, records, finding, 197
databases, records, sorting, 197
drawing, 192, 201–204
fonts, defining favorite, 201
icon, 191
mailing labels, 216
modules, summary, 192
painting, 192, 215–216
slide shows, designing, 212–214
slide shows, presenting, 215
spreadsheets, creating, 206–210
spreadsheets, formulas, creating, 210–211
spreadsheets, grand totals, creating,
  210–211
spreadsheets, purpose, 192, 206
starting, 191–192
word processing, 198–200, 201
Zoom buttons, 203
applications. *See* programs
Applications folder, 56
.ARC files, 148
arranging. *See* sorting
arrow tip, 14
arrows, downward-pointing, menus, 39
asterisk (*), 138
attachments, e-mail
  opening, 184
  sending, 177–178
audio CDs. *See also* iTunes
  burning, 233–234
  copying to hard drives, 232–233
  playlists, creating, 233
  title display, 231–232
audio fade control, iMovie, 246
Authentication dialog box, 335
available memory, displaying, 30–31, 34

• *B* •

Back button
  Apple DVD Player, 256
  general purpose, 22
  iTunes, 230
background colors, changing (Drawing
  module, AppleWorks), 202
backspace (Delete) key, 78

backups
  importance of, 104
  methods, backup drives, 108–109
  methods, burning CDs, 105–107
  methods, iDisk, 107–108, 151–153
  methods, onto other Macs, 108
  what to back up, 104–105
bad news voice, Sing program, 323
Banking keyword, America Online
    (AOL), 137
base stations, AirPort
  cost, 282
  setting up, 284–285
  usage, 283
Beginners keyword, America Online
    (AOL), 137
Beginning button (QuickTime Player), 325
Billing keyword, America Online (AOL), 137
blind carbon copy (Bcc), 179
blinking ads, stopping, 168
blinking cursors, 84
blue screen problems, 297
blue underlined phrases, Web pages, 158
boldface text, printout spacing, 128
bolding text, 91, 93
bookmarking, 167–168. *See also* Favorite
    Places, America Online; Favorites
    option, Internet Explorer
books, iPhoto, designing, 227–229
bottom of page text, 113
braces ({}), 138
breaks, page, 79
brightness, iPhoto, adjusting, 222–223
browsers, Web, 145, 156
bulleted lists, 213
bulletin boards for troubleshooting, Web
    sites, 316
burning
  audio CDs, 233–234
  CDs for backups, 105–107
  DVDs, time to complete, 255
  DVDs, verifying capability, 250
busy phone lines, Internet usage, 146
buttons
  Back button, general purpose, 22
  Back button (Apple DVD Player), 256
  Back button (iTunes), 230
  Beginning button (QuickTime Player), 325

Camera angle button (Apple DVD
    Player), 256
Camera button (iMovie), 239
Close button, 17, 20
Continue button, 11
divider buttons, 72
Effects button (iMovie), 239
Eject CD button (iTunes), 230
End button (QuickTime Player), 325
Equalizer button (iTunes), 230
Forward button (Apple DVD Player), 256
Forward button (iTunes), 230
frame advance button (Apple DVD
    Player), 256
Full-screen playback button (iMovie), 239
Import/Stop button (iPhoto), 220
Loop button (iTunes), 230
Minimize button, 20, 58
movie buttons, creating, 253–254
mute button, iMovie, 246
New Album button (iPhoto), 220
New Playlist button (iTunes), 230
On (Power) button, 8, 347, 355
Play/Stop button (Apple DVD Player), 256
Play/Stop button (iTunes), 230
Play/Stop button (QuickTime Player), 325
PPP Options button, 142
previous location button (Apple DVD
    Player), 256
Research & Learn button, America Online
    (AOL), 136
Rotate button (iPhoto), 220
Search Tips button (Google search
    engine), 160
Shuffle button (iTunes), 230
Slow button (Apple DVD Player), 256
Subtitles button (Apple DVD Player), 256
Toolbar button, 20
toolbar buttons, adding, 256
Trash button (iMovie), 239
Travel button, America Online (AOL), 136
View buttons (AppleWorks), 203
Visual Effects button (iTunes), 230
Volume button (Apple DVD Player), 256
YOU HAVE MAIL button (America
    Online), 139
Zoom buttons, 20, 49–50, 203
buy.com, 55

buying
   DVDs, 250
   fonts, 123–124
   software, 55
   USB cables, 117
bypassing locked files, 302

• C •

cable modems, 132, 156
cabled (Ethernet) connections, 280–281
cables
   Cat 5 cables, 281
   crossover cables, 280
   Ethernet cables, 118, 280
   4-pin-to-6-pin FireWire cables, 236, 349–350
   Kensington Security cables, 347
   100BaseT cables, 281
   10BaseT cables, 281
   USB cables, purchasing, 117
calculations (formulas), spreadsheets,
      210–211
Calculator program, 61, 64, 65
camcorders, digital, 235–237, 238
Camera angle button (Apple DVD
      Player), 256
Camera button (iMovie), 239
cameras, digital. See also iPhoto
   described, 217–218, 351–352
   iPhoto compatible, 219
canceling print jobs, 123
Canon
   cameras, 219, 351
   printers, 115, 119–120
carbon copy (Cc), 175
Casio cameras, 351
cassettes, Mini DV, 236
Cat 5 cables, 281
CD drawers, not opening, 304
CD icon, 18
CD-ROM Movie, Medium setting
      (QuickTime), 249
CD-Rs
   for backups, 105
   for music, 234
CD-RWs
   for backups, 105, 106
   for music, 234
cellos voice, Sing program, 323

cells, spreadsheets, 206
centered paragraphs, 93
channels, 162
character formatting, 90–91
characters, special, creating, 194
chat rooms, America Online (AOL), 138,
      139–140
Chess program, 80, 189
chimes, not sounding on startup, 295–296
Classic
   dialog box, 266
   icon, 263
   returning to Mac OS 9 method, 262
   shutting down (exiting), 265–266
   as simulator, 262, 263
   starting automatically, 264
   starting manually, 263
   usage, 265
Clear key, 78
clearing. See deleting; removing
clicking (mouse), 10
clicking tension (mouse), 303
clicktv.com, 163
Clipboard, 64–66, 113
clip-on microphones, 238
clips, iMovie
   assembling into movies, 242–243
   capturing, 240
   playing, 241
   renaming, 241
   superimposing titles, 244
   trimming (cropping), 241–242
clock, setting, 13
Clock program, 81
clock tab, iMovie, 246
Close button, 17, 20
closing. See also quitting
   Classic, 265–266
   documents, 98–99
   e-mail, 139
   files, 99
   windows, all, 337
color effects, iMovie, 244–245
colors, changing (Drawing module,
      AppleWorks), 202
columns
   column view, windows, 41, 45–46
   long names, reading, 46
   rearranging, 44

sorting (list view), 44
widths, adjusting, 46
command bars. *See* toolbars
command ⌘ key, 38–39
command line, displaying at startup, 310
commands
grayed out, 15
highlighted, 15
noun-verb structure, 19–20
syntax, 19–20
commands, listed by name. *See also*
keyboard shortcuts
About This Mac command, 17, 30–31
Cut command, 113
Empty Trash command, 49
Force Quit command, 294
Layout command, 121
Log Off command, 277
Make Alias command, 338–339
New Finder Window command, 22
New Folder command, 37
Output Options command, 121–122
Quality & Media command, 122
Reset Password command, 276
Save As command, 184
Save command, 94
Save Custom Setting command, 122
Show Clippings command, 203
Shut Down command, 15
Speech commands, 324
Summary command, 122
Undo Paste command, 67
comparison-shopping Web sites, 163
compatibility, inkjet printers, 116
compressed files, 147–148
CompUSA, 280
computer memory
amount available, displaying, 30–31, 34
concept explained, 28–29
cost, 33
erasing contents, 94
hard drives versus, 33
installing, 295
random access memory (RAM), 30–31
resolving slowness, 295
computers, naming, 287
connecting two Macs, 280
Connectix, VirtualPC for Mac OS X, 333
Continue button, 11

contrast, iPhoto, adjusting, 222–223
Control key, 79
converting movies for other computers,
248–250
cookies, 169
Copies & Pages menu commands
Layout command, 121
Output Options command, 121–122
Quality & Media command, 122
Save Custom Setting command, 122
Summary command, 122
copying
CDs, 232–233
files, 49, 107
folders to other folders (dragging), 40
movies to videotape, 248
songs to hard drives, 232–233
copying and pasting, 64–67, 204
costs, Apple help line, 315–316
Courier font, 125
cover sheets, faxes, 329–330
Create Your Account screen, 11–12
creating. *See also* adding; burning
accent marks, 194
albums, iPhoto, 223–225
aliases, 338–339
databases, AppleWorks, 192–193, 195
folders, 37, 39
form letters, 198–200
formulas in spreadsheets, AppleWorks,
210–211
grand totals in spreadsheets,
AppleWorks, 210–211
letterhead, 201–204
mailbox folders, 183
movie buttons, 253–254
playlists, iTunes, 233
QuickTime movies, 248–250
records in databases, AppleWorks,
196–197
screenshots, 333
special characters, 194
spreadsheets, AppleWorks, 206–210
creator codes, 306
credits, iMovie, adding, 243–244
cropping pictures, iPhoto, 221–222
cross-fading, 242, 243
crossover cables, 280
Cubase VST sequencing program, 352

curly double quotes, 113
curly single quotes, 113
cursors, 84
Cut command, 113
cutting. *See* copying and pasting
.cwk files, 197

• D •

databases
  creating, 192–193, 195
  data entry, 195–196
  purpose, 192
  records, creating, 196–197
  records, finding, 197
  records, sorting, 197
Date and Time options, System
    Preferences, 75–76
date (system), setting, 75–76
Dave program (Thursby), 333
dealtime.com, 163
decompressing files, 148
Del key, 79
Delete (backspace) key, 78, 79, 195
Delete folder, 278
deleting
  accounts, user, 278
  aliases, 339
  files and folders, 47–48, 49
  fonts, 125
  icons, 57
  mail, 185
  print jobs, 123
  text, TextEdit program, 85–87
  toolbar icons, 344
  trashing, general steps, 47–48, 49
deselecting text, TextEdit program, 87
designing slide shows, 212–214
desktop. *See also* Finder
  accessing automatically, 14
  figure of, 16
Desktop feature, iPhoto, 226
Desktop options, System Preferences, 69–71
diacritical marks, 194
dialog boxes
  Authentication dialog box, 335
  Classic dialog box, 266
  DVD player dialog box, 255
  Export dialog box (File menu), 249

Identity dialog box, 275
Modem Center dialog box, 329, 331
New User dialog box, 273
Open dialog box, 102
Print dialog boxes, 119–120, 329
Software Update dialog box, 76
Starting Points dialog box, 191–192
  tab key usage, dialog boxes, 120–121
dictionaries Web site, 164
digital camcorders, 235–237, 238
digital cameras. *See also* iPhoto
  described, 217–218, 351–352
  iPhoto compatible, 219
digital hub concept, 54
digital jukeboxes, 229
digital movies. *See also* iMovie
  camcorders, digital, 235–237, 238
  production tips, 237–238
  requirements, hardware, 235–236
digital subscriber lines (DSL), 132, 156
Digital8 camcorders, 237
digitized images, 351
Dilbert cartoon Web site, 163
dim screen displays, 304
directories. *See* folders
disappearing work, 32
disconnecting, America Online (AOL), 146
disk drives
  for backups, 108–109
  concept explained, 28
  costs, 33
  erasing completely, 312–313
  megabytes (MB), explained, 29–30
  memory versus, 33
  problems, 310–311
  space available, displaying, 33–34
disk image files, 148–149
disk repair programs, 310–311
Disk Utility, 310–311
displaying. *See also* viewing
  command line, at startup, 310
  commands, shortcuts, 50
  documents open in programs, 343
  garbage on screen, 296–297
  location paths, windows, 341–342
  memory available, 30–31, 34
  screen picture, not displaying on
    startup, 295
  space available, disk drives, 33–34

Displays options, System Preferences, 73
divider buttons, 72
.dmg files, 148–149
DNS Entry not found error message, 310
.doc files, 150
Dock
  folder burrowing, 342–343
  icons, adding and removing, 57
  icons, enlarging, 59–60
  icons described, 56–57
  minimizing windows, 58
  opening icons, 57
  positioning, 59
  purpose, 56
  triangles, 63
  usage tips, 59–60
Dock icons, described, 56–57
document icons, 100
documents. *See also* files; programs
  closing, 98–99
  filing in other folders, 96–98
  graphics documents, opening, 309
  launching, at startup, 339–340
  locating, 96
  open in programs, displaying, 343
  position in a document, determining, 112
  programs versus, 100–101
  reassigning to programs, 306–308
  retrieving, 102–103
  Save File Sheet, 95–98
  saving, 94–98, 103
dots per inch (dpi), 116
double clicking. *See also* opening
  described, 21
  problems, 303
double quotes, curly, 113
downloading free software, 140–141
downloading problems, Internet
  disk image files, 148–149
  encoded files, 147–148
  wrong formats, 149–150
downward-pointing arrow, menus, 39
dpi (dots per inch), 116
dragging and dropping, 88–89
dragging icons, 18, 40
drawing, 192, 201–204
Drive 10 disk repair program
    (Micromat), 311

Drop Box, 277, 290–291
DSL (digital subscriber lines), 132, 156
DVD club Web sites, 255
DVD player dialog box, 255
DVD Player program (Apple), 256
DVDovernight.com, 255
DVDs
  burning on iMacs, time to complete, 255
  burning on iMacs, verifying capability, 250
  menu screens, designing, 251–253
  menu screens, previewing, 254–255
  movie buttons, creating, 253–254
  movie capacity, 253
  playing on iMacs, 255–257
  purchasing, 250

● **E** ●

EarthLink
  accounts, signing up, 141
  setup options, 142–143
EarthLink Total Access sign-up
    program, 141
EasyBeat sequencing program, 352
Edit menu commands
  Cut command, 113
  Undo Paste command, 67
editing down videos, 238
efax.com, 163
Effects button (iMovie), 239
Eject CD button (iTunes), 230
Eject key, 78
ejecting CDs, 107, 230
E-mail, Small setting (QuickTime), 249
e-mail (Internet Service Providers)
  account setup, 173–174
  address books, 175, 184
  America Online (AOL) e-mail, 138–139
  answering e-mail, 139
  attachments, opening, 184
  attachments, sending, 177–178
  blind carbon copy (Bcc), 179
  carbon copy (Cc), 175
  checking for mail, 180–182
  closing e-mail, 139
  deleting mail, 185
  draft e-mails, 179

e-mail (Internet Service Providers) *(continued)*
 etiquette, message content, 181
 filing mail, 183–184
 formatted e-mail, 176
 forwarding mail, 183
 junk e-mail, 185–186
 listening to mail, 182, 322
 Mail program, 173
 offline messages, composing, 179
 pictures, sending (iPhoto), 225–226
 plain text format, 176
 printing mail, 139, 184
 processing mail, 182–185
 recipients, 175, 179
 replying to e-mail, 139, 182–183
 Rich Text format, 176
 saving mail, 139
 search e-mail addresses icon
  (Sherlock), 162
 sending e-mail, 139, 174–178
 signatures, adding, 179–180
 spam, 185–186
 usage tips, 179
 Windows users, sending attachments
  to, 178
Empty Trash command, 49
encoded files, 147–148
Encyclopedia, World Book program,
 190–191
Encyclopedia keyword, America Online
 (AOL), 137
End button (QuickTime Player), 325
End key, 78
ending. *See* closing
Energy Saver options, System
 Preferences, 74
enlarging icons, 59–60
Enter key, 79
Entourage (Microsoft), 55, 144
Epson printers, 115
equal sign (=), 210
Equalizer button (iTunes), 230
equipment, connecting to iMacs, 280–281
erasing
 CD-RWs, 106
 hard drives, 312–313
 memory contents, 94
Error 404 message, 310

error messages. *See also* problems,
  hardware; problems, software;
  problems, startup
 aliases, 339
 DNS Entry not found message, 310
 Error 404 message, 310
 sounds made, changing, 75
 There is no application available
  message, 308–309
 You do not have sufficient access
  privileges message, 309–310
Esc (Escape) key, 78
Ethernet (cabled) connections, 280–281
Ethernet cables
 crossover cables, 280
 for laser printers, 118
Ethernet hubs, 280–281
Excel (Microsoft), 54–55, 206. *See also*
  spreadsheets
.exe files, 150
executable files, 150
exiting. *See* closing; quitting
Expert setting (QuickTime), 250
Export dialog box, 249
extensions, file-names (suffixes)
 described, 304–305
 hidden extensions, 305
 listing, 150
 viewing, 101
external disk drives, 28, 349

• *F* •

fast motion control, iMovie, 246
Favorite Places, America Online (AOL),
 137–138. *See also* bookmarking
Favorites option, Internet Explorer
 (Microsoft), 171. *See also* bookmarking
faxes
 address books, 328–329
 installing FAXstf program, 326–327
 receiving faxes, 328–329
 sending steps, 327–330
FAXstf Installer icon, 326
FAXstf program, installing, 326–327
fees, Apple help line, 315–316
fields, defined, 193
file folder tabs, 72

File menu commands
  Make Alias command, 338–339
  New Finder Window command, 22
  New Folder command, 37
  Save As command, 184
  Save command, 94
  Show Clippings command, 203
file sharing. *See also* files
  capabilities, administrators, 291
  computer setup, 285–287
  connecting, 287–290
  disconnecting, 291
  usage, 290–291
FileMaker Pro database program, 55
files. *See also* documents; file sharing;
    programs
  Acrobat files, 121
  .aif files, 246
  aliases, 338–339
  .ARC files, 148
  closing, 99
  compressed files, 147–148
  copying, 49, 107
  creator codes, 306
  .cwk files, 197
  decompressing files, 148
  disk image files, 148–149
  .dmg files, 148–149
  .doc files, 150
  encoded files, 147–148
  .exe files, 150
  executable files, 150
  file-name suffixes (extensions),
      described, 304–305
  file-name suffixes (extensions), listing, 150
  file-name suffixes (extensions),
      viewing, 101
  GIF files, 309
  .gif files, 150
  .gz files, 147
  hidden extensions, 305
  hidden files, 302
  .html files, 150
  JPEG files, 309
  .jpg files, 150
  locked files, 302
  mach file, 302
  mach_kernel file, 302

mach.sym file, 302
MP3 files, 229
parent-and-child relationships,
    100–101, 304
PDF files, 121–122
.pdf files, 150
permissions, 303
PICT files, 309
.plist files, 300
preference files, 299–300
searching for, using file contents, 110–111
searching for, using file names, 109–110
.sit files, 147
strangely-named files, 302
stuffed files, 147, 148
.tar files, 147
TIFF files, 307–308
type codes, 306
unstuffing files, 148
untarring files, 148
updating files, general processing, 32
.uu files, 148
Word (Microsoft) files, 150
.z files, 148
.zip files, 147, 148
filesearch keyword, America Online
    (AOL), 140
Finale sheet music program, 353
Finder menu commands, 49
Finder screen. *See also* desktop
  purpose, 18
  text only display mode, 344
  toolbar, hiding, 343
  toolbar, making smaller, 344
finding, AppleWorks databases, 197. *See
    also* searching
FireWire cables, 236, 349–350
F-keys (function keys), 78
floppy-disk drives, 107, 352
folder burrowing, 342–343
folder icon, 18, 35
folders
  Applications folder, 56
  copying to other folders (dragging), 40
  creating, 37, 39
  Delete folder, 278
  documents, filing in other folders, 96–98
  folders display, not icons, 310

folders *(continued)*
  Fonts folders, 124
  Home folder, backing up, 104–105
  Home folder, described, 36
  locating, 21
  mailbox folders, creating, 183
  opening, 21
  Public folder, 277
  purpose, 35
  shared folders, 276–277
  Sites folder, 277
  System folder, with 9, 261
  System folder, with X, 21, 261
Font Panel, 125–126
fonts
  acquiring new, America Online (AOL),
    123–124
  changing, 92, 209
  Courier font, 125
  defining favorite, AppleWorks, 201
  document limits, 112
  examples, in font menus, 127
  Font Panel, 125–126
  Fractional Character Widths feature, 128
  installing, 124
  Monaco font, 125
  monospaced fonts, 125
  point size, 92
  PostScript fonts, 123
  proportional fonts, 125
  purchasing, 123–124
  removing, 125
  sans serif, 127–128
  serif, 127–128
  sizes, changing, 92
  storage locations, 124
  symbol fonts, 127
  text-smoothing, 126–127
  TrueType fonts, 123
  word spacing, printouts, 128
Fonts folders, 124
Force Quit command, 294
force quitting programs, 294
force restarting iMacs, 294
forgotten passwords, 298
form letters, creating, 198–200

formatted e-mail, 176
formatting
  paragraphs, 93–94
  text, 91–92
formulas, spreadsheets, 210–211
Forward button
  Apple DVD Player, 256
  iTunes, 230
Forward Delete key, 79
forwarding mail, 183. *See also* replying to
    e-mail
4-pin-to-6-pin FireWire cables, 236, 349–350
Fractional Character Widths feature, 128
frame advance button (Apple DVD
    Player), 256
free fax number Web site, 163
free help sources, 316–317
free software, downloading, 140–141
freezing up, resolving, 297, 310
frozen programs, 293–294
Fuji cameras, 219
Full Quality, Large setting (QuickTime), 249
full-screen mode (Apple DVD Player), 256
Full-screen playback button (iMovie), 239
fully justified paragraphs, 93
function (F) keys, 78

game playing, 353
garbage on screen, 296–297
GB (gigabytes), defined, 29
General options, System Preferences, 71
GIF files, 309
.gif files, 150
gigabytes (gigs), defined, 29
glass surfaces, effecting mouse usage, 303
glossy prints, converting to, 226
good news voice, Sing program, 323
Google search engine, 158–160
grand totals, spreadsheets, 210–211
graphics documents, opening, 309
Graphics Equalizer button (iTunes), 230
grayed out commands, 15
guests, file sharing capabilities, 290–291
.gz files, 147

• H •

Halime newsgroup-reading program, 144
Handspring, 331
hanging up, America Online (AOL), 146
hard drives (disks)
  for backups, 108–109
  concept explained, 28
  costs, 33
  erasing completely, 312–313
  megabytes (MB), explained, 29–30
  memory versus, 33
  problems, 310–311
  space available, displaying, 33–34
hardware problems
  CD drawers, not opening, 304
  dim screen displays, 304
  disk (hard drive) problems, 310–311
  mouse problems, 303
  Universal Serial Bus (USB) power
    problems, 354
Harmon/Kardon iSub, 353
Help
  AirPort, installing, 284
  Apple DVD Player, 257
  in iMacs, 23–24
Help key, 79
Help keyword, America Online (AOL), 137
help line phone numbers, Apple, 284,
  315–316
help sources, free, 316–317
Hewlett-Packard (HP)
  cameras, 219
  printers, 115
hidden extensions, 305
hidden files, 302
hiding
  programs, 79–80
  toolbar, 343
highlighted commands, 15
Hints, Password, setting, 12, 274
History option, Internet Explorer
  (Microsoft), 171
Home folder
  backing up, 104–105
  described, 36
Home icon, 36

Home key, 78
home pages, defining, 166
HomePage feature, iPhoto, 226
Homework keyword, America Online
  (AOL), 137
Horizontal Scroll Bar, 20
Hot Corners tab, 72, 73
hot keys. *See* keyboard shortcuts
hot spots, 73
HP (Hewlett-Packard)
  cameras, 219
  printers, 115
.html files, 150
hubs. *See also* routers
  digital hub concept, 54
  Ethernet hubs, 280–281
  USB hubs, 354
hyperlinks (links), 156, 158
hyphen (-), 211

• I •

I-beam cursor, 85, 275–276
iCab Web browser, 156
icon view, windows, 41–43
icons. *See also* icons, listed by name
  adding, 57
  arranging in windows, 51
  arranging on desktop, 52
  dragging, 18, 40
  enlarging, 59–60
  moving, 18
  names, finding out, 16
  purpose, 18
  removing, 57
  renaming, 48
  selecting individual, 19–20
  selecting multiple, adjacent, 40
  selecting multiple, non-adjacent, 42
  toolbar icons, adding personal, 345
  toolbar icons, rearranging, 345
  toolbar icons, removing, 344
icons, listed by name. *See also* icons
  America Online icon, 134
  AppleWorks icon, 191
  CD icon, 18
  Classic icon, 263

icons, listed by name *(continued)*
  Dock icons, described, 56–57
  document icons, 100
  FAXstf Installer icon, 326
  folder icon, 18, 35
  Home icon, 36
  Macintosh HD (hard drive) icon, 18, 19
  Newsgroup List icon (Entourage), 144
  picture icon, 18
  program icons, 18, 100
  search Apple's Web site icon
     (Sherlock), 162
  search auction sites icon (Sherlock), 162
  search dictionaries icon (Sherlock), 162
  search e-mail addresses icon
     (Sherlock), 162
  search encyclopedia icon (Sherlock), 162
  search entire Web icon (Sherlock), 162
  search for financial reports icon
     (Sherlock), 162
  search for news icon (Sherlock), 162
  search hard drive icon (Sherlock), 162
  search movie databases icon
     (Sherlock), 162
  search phone numbers icon
     (Sherlock), 162
  search shopping sites icon (Sherlock), 162
  search showbiz magazines icon
     (Sherlock), 162
  Sherlock icon, 109
  Title Bar icon, 20
  Trash can icon, 47
Identity dialog box, 275
iDisk, 107–108, 151–153
iDVD 2 program, 251
iMac general information Web sites, 317
iMac-compatible, downloadable, 144
images
  digitized, 351
  disk image files, 148–149
iMovie. *See also* digital movies; DVDs,
     burning
  clips, assembling into movies, 242–243
  clips, capturing, 240
  clips, playing, 241
  clips, renaming, 241
  clips, trimming (cropping), 241–242
  color effects, 244–245

converting movies for other computers,
     248–250
copying movies to videotape, 248
credits, adding, 243–244
cross-fading, 242, 243
DVDs, exporting to, 251
footage capacity, iMacs, 240–241
launching, 238–239
music soundtracks, adding, 246–247
QuickTime movies, creating, 248–250
reviewing recorded movies, 247
screen display, 239
the Shelf, 239, 240
sound effects, 247
sounds, editing, 247
speed versus quality, 240
timeline, 240
titles, adding, 243–244
Import/Stop button (iPhoto), 220
incorrect programs opening, 304–308
inkjet printers, 115–117
inserting text, TextEdit program, 85. *See
     also* adding
insertion points, 84
Installer menu commands, Reset
     Password, 276
installing. *See also* adding
  AirPort cards, 282–283
  America Online (AOL), 134
  camcorders, 238, 348
  FAXstf program, 326–327
  fonts, 124
  inkjet printers, 116–117
  iPhoto, 218
  laser printers, 118–119
  Mac OS X, reinstalling, 312–313
  memory, computer, 295
  programs, reinstalling, 301
  USB devices, 354
Instant Message, America Online (AOL),
     139–140
Internet. *See also* Internet Service
     Providers; World Wide Web
  access options, 12, 133
  accessing using AirPort, 284
  America Online (AOL) versus, 134
  as backup tool, 151–153
  best aspects of, 154

downloading problems, disk image files, 148–149

downloading problems, encoded files, 147–148

downloading problems, wrong formats, 149–150

newsgroups, 143–145

online services, defined, 133–134

radio, 166, 234

worst aspects of, 154

Internet Connect program, 146

Internet Explorer (Microsoft)

additional browser windows, opening, 168

addresses, typing format, 163

addresses, typing shortcuts, 164

blinking ads, stopping, 168

bookmarking, 167–168

cookies, 169

Favorites option, 171

general information, typing shortcuts, 165

History option, 171

home pages, defining, 166

Page Holder option, 172

plug-ins, 165–166

radio broadcasts, listening to, 166

Scrapbook option, 172

Search option, 172

usage described, 157–158

viewing area, increasing, 170

Web surfing speed, increasing, 166–167

Internet Service Providers (ISPs). *See also* America Online; EarthLink; e-mail (Internet Service Providers); Internet

defined, 133

hanging up, 146

Internet accounts, signing up for, 141

interview, startup, 11

invisible storage windows, 65

iPhoto

albums, creating, 223–225

books, designing, 227–229

brightness, adjusting, 222–223

cameras, erasing, 219, 220

cameras, iPhoto-compatible, 219

contrast, adjusting, 222–223

cropping pictures, 221–222

Desktop feature, 226

HomePage feature, 226

installing, 218

locating, 218

magnifying pictures, 220–221

Mail feature, 225–226

Order Book feature, 227–229

Order Prints feature, 226

purpose, 218

redeye, correcting, 223

regular glossy prints, converting to, 226

resolution, 225

rotating pictures, 221

Screen Saver feature, 226–227

Slide Show feature, 225

starting, 219

trimming pictures, 221–222

version 1.1, upgrading to, 218

Web pages, converting pictures to, 226

iPod MP3 player (Apple), 231, 349

ISPs (Internet Service Providers). *See also* America Online; EarthLink; e-mail (Internet Service Providers); Internet

defined, 133

hanging up, 146

Internet accounts, signing up for, 141

iSub (subwoofers), 353

italicizing text, 91, 93

iTunes

audio CDs, burning, 233–234

audio CDs, copying to hard drives, 232–233

audio CDs, playlists, creating, 233

audio CDs, title display, 231–232

iPod MP3 player (Apple), 231, 349

iTunes Setup Assistant, 229

locating, 229

purpose, 229

radio, Internet, 234

screen display, 230

Setup Assistant, 229

songs, playing, 230–231

• J •

jacks

Ethernet jacks, 347, 350

external monitor jacks, 347, 355

FireWire jacks, 347, 348–350

headphone jacks, 347, 348

jacks *(continued)*
 lock jacks, 347
 phone line jacks, 347, 350
 power cord jacks, 347, 350
 speaker jacks, 347, 348
 Universal Serial Bus (USB) jacks, compatible devices, 350–354
 Universal Serial Bus (USB) jacks, example, 347
 Universal Serial Bus (USB) jacks, installing USB devices, 354
 video-output jacks, 355
joysticks, 353
JPEG files, 309
.jpg files, 150
jukeboxes, digital, 229
junk e-mail, 185–186

● *K* ●

Kensington Security cables, 347
Kensington Security Web site, 347
kernel panics, 296–297
Key Caps program, 81
keyboard (iMacs), described, 77–79
Keyboard options, System Preferences, 74
keyboard shortcuts. *See also* commands, listed by name
 Add to Favorite Places (America Online), 138
 commands, displaying, 50
 deleting items, 47
 explained, 38–41
 folders, creating, 39
 folders, locating, 21
 No shortcut, 77
 saving, 94
 typing shortcuts, Internet Explorer (Microsoft), 164
keys, listed by name. *See also* buttons
 backspace (Delete) key, 78
 Clear key, 78
 command ⌘ key, 38–39
 Control key, 79
 Del key, 79
 Delete (backspace) key, 78, 79
 Eject key, 78
 End key, 78

Enter key, 79
Esc (Escape) key, 78
F-keys (function keys), 78
Forward Delete key, 79
Help key, 79
Home key, 78
modifier keys, 38
NumLock key, 78
Option key, 79
Pg Down key, 78
Pg Up key, 78
Return key, 79, 90–91
Shift key, 38
speaker volume keys, 78
symbols keys, 81, 194
Tab key usage, dialog boxes, 120–121
keywords, America Online (AOL), 137, 139–140
Knowledge Bases, Apple, 316
Kodak cameras, 219, 351

● *L* ●

labels, mailing, 216
landscape mode, 221
laser printers, 117–119
launching. *See also* opening
 AppleWorks, 191–192
 Classic, automatically, 264
 Classic, manually, 263
 documents, at startup, 339–340
 iMovie, 238–239
 iPhoto, 219
 programs, at startup, 296, 339–340
 programs, manually, 57
Layout command, 121
layouts, mailing labels, 216
left-justified paragraphs, 93
letterhead, creating, 201–204
letters, creating, 198–200
lining up text, 111
links, World Wide Web, 156, 158
list view, windows, 41, 44–45
listening to mail, 182, 322
live numbers, spreadsheets, 208
loading updaters, 76–77. *See also* starting
local access numbers, America Online (AOL), 135

locating. *See also* searching
　documents, 96
　folders, 21
　fonts, storage locations, 124
　iPhoto, 218
　iTunes, 229
　location paths, windows, 341–342
　previous location button (Apple DVD
　　Player), 256
　TextEdit program, 83
locked files, 302
Log Off command, 277
logging off, multiple-user systems, 277
logging on
　multiple-user systems, 275–276, 297–298
　problems, 297–298
logo, Mac OS, 9
logo (menu), Apple ⌘, 14–15, 30, 262
long-term storage, 29
Loop button (iTunes), 230
losing work, 32
lost passwords, 298
Louvre museum Web site, 163

• *M* •

Mac Help, 23–24
Mac OS 9
　characteristics, 268
　file sharing setup, 287
　restarting iMac in, 266
　returning to methods, 262–263
　simulating, 262, 263
　startup screen, 264
　switching to, 267–268
　System folder, 261
Mac OS 10.2, upgrading to, 317–318
Mac OS logo, 9
Mac OS X
　advantages, 261
　file sharing setup, 285–286
　reinstalling, 312–313
　switching to methods, 268–269
　System folder, 261
　versions, determining, 17
MacAddict, 317, 326
MacCentral Web site, 317
macdownload.com, 55

MacFixIt Web site, 316
Macgame keyword, America Online
　　(AOL), 137
mach file, 302
mach_kernel file, 302
MacHome Journal, 317
mach.sym file, 302
Macintosh HD (hard drive) icon, 18, 19
Macintosh Startup Slide Show, 9
macmall.com, 55, 123
macro viruses, 299
MacSurfer Web site, 317
macwarehouse.com, 55, 123
Macworld, 317, 326
Macworld Mac Secrets, 123
magazines, iMac, 317
magnifying pictures, iPhoto, 220–221
Mail feature, iPhoto, 225–226
mail merges, 198–200, 205
Mail program, 173
mailbox folders, creating, 183
mailing labels, 216
mail-order software store Web sites, 55
Make Alias command, 338–339
master slide designs (AppleWorks), 214
megabytes (MB), explained, 29–30
megapixels, 352
members keyword, America Online
　　(AOL), 139
memory, computer
　amount available, displaying, 30–31, 34
　concept explained, 28–29
　cost, 33
　erasing contents, 94
　hard drives versus, 33
　installing, 295
　random access memory (RAM), 30–31
　resolving slowness, 295
memory card readers, 219
menu bar, described, 14, 16
menu screens, DVDs
　designing, 251–253
　previewing, 254–255
menus
　Apple ⌘ menu, 14–15, 30, 262
　downward-pointing arrow, 39
　pop-up menus, defined, 69
　right-pointing triangle, 39

merges, mail, 198–200, 205
Micromat Drive 10 disk repair program, 311
Micromat Web site, 311
microphones, clip-on, 238
Microsoft Entourage, 55, 144
Microsoft Excel, 54–55, 206. *See also* spreadsheets
Microsoft Internet Explorer
  additional browser windows, opening, 168
  addresses, typing format, 163
  addresses, typing shortcuts, 164
  blinking ads, stopping, 168
  bookmarking, 167–168
  cookies, 169
  Favorites option, 171
  general information, typing shortcuts, 165
  History option, 171
  home pages, defining, 166
  Page Holder option, 172
  plug-ins, 165–166
  radio broadcasts, listening to, 166
  Scrapbook option, 172
  Search option, 172
  usage described, 157–158
  viewing area, increasing, 170
  Web surfing speed, increasing, 166–167
Microsoft Office X for Macintosh, 54
Microsoft PowerPoint, 55
Microsoft Windows programs, running on iMacs, 333
Microsoft Word, 54, 150. *See also* word processing
MIDI (Musical Instrument Digital Interface), 352
Mini DV cassettes, 236
MiniDV camcorders, 237
Minimize button, 20, 58
minimizing windows, 58
Minolta cameras, 219
minus sign (-), 211
mirrored surfaces, effecting mouse usage, 303
Modem Center program, 329, 331
modems, 132–133
modifier keys, 38
Monaco font, 125
monitor window, iMovie, 239

monitors, computers
  adjusting, 7
  resolution controls, 73
monospaced fonts, 125
MOS keyword, America Online (AOL), 316
motion control, iMovie, 246
mouse problems, 303
mouse usage, 10, 21
movie buttons, creating, 253–254
movie capacity, DVDs, 253
movie information Web site, 164
Movie Player, 325
movies, digital. *See also* iMovie
  camcorders, digital, 235–237, 238
  production tips, 237–238
  requirements, hardware, 235–236
moving. *See also* dragging and dropping
  icons, 18
  windows, 20, 23
MP3. *See also* iTunes
  files, 229
  players, 231, 349
multiple-user systems. *See also* passwords
  accounts, deleting, 278
  accounts, setting up, 273–275, 287
  concept explained, 271–272
  logging off, 277
  logging on, 275–276, 297–298
  shared folders, 276–277
multitasking, 63–64, 337–338
music soundtracks, adding, 246–247
Musical Instrument Digital Interface (MIDI), 352
musical-keyboard adapters, 352
mute button, iMovie, 246
mysimon.com, 163

names, on Welcome screen, 13–14
naming computers, 287
navigating, Save File Sheet, 95–98
Net. *See* Internet
netflix.com, 255
Netscape Navigator Web browser, 156
networking iMacs
  advantages, 279
  AirPort (wireless) connections, 281–285
  cabling requirements, 280

connecting two Macs, 280
Ethernet (cabled) connections, 280–281
sharing files, computer setup, 285–287
sharing files, connecting, 287–290
sharing files, disconnecting, 291
sharing files, usage, 290–291
Windows computers, iMac networking
   steps, 333–335
New Album button (iPhoto), 220
New Finder Window command, 22
New Folder command, 37
New Playlist button (iTunes), 230
New User dialog box, 273
Newsgroup List icon (Entourage), 144
newsgroups, 143–145
newsgroups for troubleshooting Web
   sites, 316
newsgroups keyword, America Online
   (AOL), 143
Nightingale sheet music program, 353
Nikon cameras, 219
noun-verb structure, commands, 19–20
NumLock key, 78

• *O* •

obsolescence, software, 54
Office X for Macintosh (Microsoft), 54
offline e-mail messages, 179
Olympus cameras, 219, 351
On (Power) button, 8, 347, 355
1-click accounts, 229
100BaseT cables, 281
online services, defined, 133–134
Open dialog box, 102
opening. *See also* starting
   attachments, e-mail, 184
   browser windows, Internet Explorer
      (Microsoft), 168
   CD drawers, not opening, 304
   folders, 21
   graphics documents, 309
   icons, 57
   problems, programs, 301
   programs, individual, 57
   programs, multiple, 63–64, 337–338
   System Preferences, 67
   windows, multiple, 22–23
   wrong programs opening, 304–308

Opera Web browser, 156
operating systems
   Classic, as simulator, 264
   Classic, returning to Mac OS 9 method, 262
   Classic, shutting down (exiting), 265–266
   Classic, starting automatically, 264
   Classic, starting manually, 263
   Classic, usage, 265
   defined, 17
   Mac OS 9, characteristics, 268
   Mac OS 9, file sharing setup, 287
   Mac OS 9, restarting iMacs in, 266
   Mac OS 9, returning to methods, 262–263
   Mac OS 9, switching to, 267–268
   Mac OS 9, System folder, 261
   Mac OS 10.2, upgrading to, 317–318
   Mac OS X, advantages, 261
   Mac OS X, file sharing setup, 285–286
   Mac OS X, reinstalling, 312–313
   Mac OS X, switching to methods, 268–269
   Mac OS X, System folder, 261
   Mac OS X, versions, determining, 17
   two operating systems, reasons for in
      iMac, 261–262
optical mouse, 303
Option key, 79
orange bar, iMovie, 246
Order Book feature, iPhoto, 227–229
Order Prints feature, iPhoto, 226
ordering. *See* sorting
OS 9, Mac
   characteristics, 268
   file sharing setup, 287
   restarting iMacs in, 266
   returning to methods, 262–263
   simulating, 262, 263
   switching to, 267–268
   System folder, 261
OS 10.2, Mac, upgrading to, 317–318
OS X, Mac
   advantages, 261
   file sharing setup, 285–286
   reinstalling, 312–313
   switching to methods, 268–269
   System folder, 261
   versions, determining, 17
Otto Matic program, 190
Output Options command, 121–122

• P •

page breaks, 79
Page Holder option, Internet Explorer (Microsoft), 172
pages, Web
  basic screens, described, 157–158
  converting pictures to, 226
painting, 192, 215–216
Palm Desktop, 332
Palm Web site, 332
PalmPilots (Palm), 331–332, 352
paragraphs, formatting, 93–94
parent-and-child relationships, files, 100–101, 304
Password Hint, setting, 12, 274
passwords. *See also* multiple-user systems
  forgotten, resolving, 298
  resetting, 276
  setting, 12, 274
pasting and copying, 64–67, 204
patches, updating, 76–77
pausing print jobs, 123
PDF files, 121–122
.pdf files, 150
peripherals, connecting to Macs, 280–281
permanent storage, 29
permissions
  defining, administrators, 274–275
  files, 303
Personal Finance page, America Online (AOL), 136
personal toolbar icons, adding, 345
Pg Down key, 78
Pg Up key, 78
phone lines, Internet usage, 132, 146
PICT files, 309
picture icon, 18
pictures, e-mail, sending, 225–226
pictures, World Wide Web, saving, 158
picture-size slider (iPhoto), 220
pipe organ voice, Sing program, 323
pixels, 73
plain text format, e-mail, 176
playhead (iMovie), 239, 241
playing games, 353

playlists, creating, 233
Play/Stop button
  Apple DVD Player, 256
  iTunes, 230
  QuickTime Player, 325
.plist files, 300
plugging in iMacs, 7
plug-ins, Internet Explorer (Microsoft), 165–166
point size, 92
pointers, 10
pointing, 15
pop-up menus, defined, 69
positioning, Dock, 59
PostScript fonts, 123
powering off iMacs, 15
powering on iMacs
  internal processing, 29
  steps, 8–9
PowerPoint (Microsoft), 55. *See also* slide shows, AppleWorks
PPP Options button, 142
preference files, 299–300
presentation templates, 212
presenting slide shows, 215
Preview program, 81
previous location button (Apple DVD Player), 256
Print Center program, 122–123
Print dialog boxes, 119–120, 329
print jobs, managing, 123
printers. *See also* printing
  adding for faxing, 327
  dots per inch (dpi), 116
  inkjet printers, 115–117
  laser printers, 117–119
  Universal Serial Bus (USB) compatibility, 351
printing. *See also* printers
  canceling print jobs, 123
  deleting print jobs, 123
  mail, 139, 184
  options (Copies & Pages pop-up menu), 121–122
  pausing print jobs, 123
  Print Center program, 122–123

print queues, 123
screenshots, creating, 333
steps, 119–120
waiting printouts, controlling, 123
privacy issues. *See* multiple-user systems
problems, hardware. *See also* error
    messages
  CD drawers, not opening, 304
  dim screen displays, 304
  disk (hard drive) problems, 310–311
  mouse problems, 303
  Universal Serial Bus (USB) power
    problems, 354
problems, software (programs). *See also*
    error messages
  opening problems, 301
  renaming problems, 301
  single program problems, 299–301
  strangely-named files, 302
  System Preferences dimmed, 301
  trash, can not empty, 302
  wrong programs opening, 304–308
problems, startup. *See also* error messages
  blue screen problems, 297
  chimes, not sounding on startup, 295–296
  command line displays, 310
  folders display, not icons, 310
  freezing up, resolving, 297, 310
  frozen programs, 293–294
  garbage on screen, 296–297
  logging in problems, 297–298
  passwords, forgotten, 298
  programs launching automatically, 296
  screen picture, not displaying on
    startup, 295
  slowness, 295
  viruses, 299
production tips, digital movies, 237–238
program icons, 18, 100
programs. *See also* AppleWorks; iMovie;
    iPhoto; iTunes; problems, software
    (programs)
  active programs, determining, 63–64,
    99–100
  Address Book program, 80
  Apple DVD Player program, 256–257

Apple System Profiler program, 81
Calculator program, 61, 64, 65
Chess program, 80, 189
Clock program, 81
creator codes, 306
Cubase VST sequencing program, 352
Dave program (Thursby), 333
disk repair programs, 310–311
Disk Utility, 310–311
documents versus, 100–101
DVD Player program (Apple), 256
EarthLink Total Access sign-up
    program, 141
EasyBeat sequencing program, 352
Entourage (Microsoft), 55, 144
FAXstf program, installing, 326–327
Finale sheet music program, 353
free software, downloading, 140–141
frozen programs, 293–294
Halime newsgroup-reading program, 144
hiding, 79–80
iDisk program, 151–153
iDVD 2 program, 251
iMac-compatible, downloadable, 144
Internet Connect program, 146
iTunes program, 81
Key Caps program, 81
launching, at startup, 296, 339–340
launching, manually, 57
Mail program, 173
Modem Center program, 329, 331
Movie Player, 325
newsgroup-reading programs, 144
Nightingale sheet music program, 353
obsolescence, 54
open documents, displaying, 343
open programs, determining, 63
opening one program, 57
opening two programs, 63–64, 337–338
Otto Matic program, 190
Palm Desktop, 332
Preview program, 81
Print Center program, 122–123
purchasing, 55
Quicken program, 81, 189
QuicKeys X program, 78

programs *(continued)*
  quitting, 67
  reinstalling, 301
  restarting, 299
  sequencing programs, 352
  shareware, 55
  sheet music programs, 353
  Sibelius sheet music program, 353
  Sing program, 322–323
  speech recognition program, 323–325
  standard with iMac, 54
  starting, 57
  Stickies program, 62–63
  Stufflt Expander program, 148
  Talk program, 321–322
  TextEdit program, 81, 83
  VirtualPC for Mac OS X (Connectix), 333
  Windows (Microsoft) programs, running on iMacs, 333
  World Book Encyclopedia program, 190–191
  wrong programs opening, 304–308
proportional fonts, 125
Public folder, 277
punctuation, chat rooms, 138
purchasing
  DVDs, 250
  fonts, 123–124
  software, 55
  USB cables, 117
purple bar, iMovie, 246

• Q •

Quality & Media command, 122
queues, print, 123
Quicken program, 81, 189
QuicKeys X program, 78
QuickTime
  creating movies, 248–250
  playing movies, 325–326
quitting. *See also* closing
  force quitting programs, 294
  programs, 67
  System Preferences, 77
quotes, curly, 113
quotes, straight ("), 113

• R •

radio, Internet, 166, 234
radio transmitter antennas, 281–282
random access memory (RAM), 30–31
readers, memory cards, 219
Real plug-in Web site, 166
rearranging
  columns, 44
  toolbar icons, 345
reassigning documents, 306–308
receiving faxes, 328–329
recipients, e-mail, 175
records, databases, 196–197
redeye, correcting, 223
registering iMacs, 12
Registration Information screen, 11
reinstalling
  Mac OS X, 312–313
  programs, 301
relevance (Sherlock), 111
removable disks, 28
removing. *See also* deleting
  fonts, 125
  icons, 57
  toolbar icons, 344
renaming
  icons, 48
  iMovie clips, 241
  renaming problems, 301
rendering, 243
replacing windows, 22
replying to e-mail, 139, 182–183. *See also* forwarding mail
Research & Learn button, America Online (AOL), 136
Reset Password command, 276
resetting passwords, 276
Resize Box, 20
resizing windows, 20, 49
resolution, iPhoto, 225
resolution controls, computer monitors, 73
restarting
  force restarting iMacs, 294
  iMacs in Mac OS 9, 266
  programs, 299

retrieving
  documents, 102–103
  previously opened windows, 22
Return key, 79, 90–91, 195
reversing. *See* Undo Paste command
revising. *See* Edit menu commands
Rich Text format, e-mail, 176
right-justified paragraphs, 93
right-pointing triangles, menus, 39
ripping CDs, 232–233
Rotate button (iPhoto), 220
rotating cursors, 293
rotating pictures, iPhoto, 221
routers, 281. *See also* hubs
rules, word processing, 83–84
running footer feature, 113
running header feature, 113

• S •

salary calculator Web site, 164
sans serif, 127–128
satellite photographs Web site, 163
Save As command, 184
Save as File option (printing), 121–122
Save command, 94
Save Custom Setting command, 122
Save File Sheet, 95–98
saving
  documents, 94–98, 103
  internal processing, described, 32
  mail, 139
  pictures, World Wide Web, 158
scanners, 351
Scrapbook option, Internet Explorer
    (Microsoft), 172
screen names, America Online (AOL). *See
    also* screens, listed by name
  defining, 135
  looking up, 139
screen picture, not displaying on
    startup, 295
Screen Saver feature, iPhoto, 226–227
Screen Saver options, System Preferences,
    71–73

screens, listed by name. *See also* screen
    names, America Online; screens
    (computer monitors); windows
  blue screens, 297
  Create Your Account screen, 11–12
  Mac OS 9 startup screen, 264
  Registration Information screen, 11
  valid users screen, 272
  Welcome screen, 13–14
screens (computer monitors). *See also*
    screens, listed by name; windows
  adjusting height, 7
  resolution controls, 73
screenshots, creating, 333
scroll bars, 20, 340–341
scrolling pages, World Wide Web, 158
search Apple's Web site icon (Sherlock), 162
search auction sites icon (Sherlock), 162
Search blanks, World Wide Web, 157
search dictionaries icon (Sherlock), 162
search e-mail addresses icon
    (Sherlock), 162
search encyclopedia icon (Sherlock), 162
search engines, 158–160
search entire Web icon (Sherlock), 162
search for financial reports icon
    (Sherlock), 162
search for news icon (Sherlock), 162
search hard drive icon (Sherlock), 162
search movie databases icon
    (Sherlock), 162
Search option, Internet Explorer
    (Microsoft), 172
search phone numbers icon (Sherlock), 162
search shopping sites icon (Sherlock), 162
search showbiz magazines icon
    (Sherlock), 162
Search Tips button (Google search
    engine), 160
searching. *See also* locating
  for files, using file contents, 110–111
  for files, using file names, 109–110
  World Wide Web, searching tools, 158
  World Wide Web, using Google, 159–160
  World Wide Web, using Sherlock, 160–163
secret recipients, e-mail, 179

security issues. *See* multiple-user systems
selecting icons
  selecting individual, 19–20
  selecting multiple, adjacent, 40
  selecting multiple, non-adjacent, 42
selecting text
  entire document, 112
  several pages, 113–114
  single words, 111
  TextEdit program, 86–87
self-powered speakers, 348
sending
  e-mail, 139, 174–178
  faxes, 327–330
sequencing programs, 352
serif, 127–128
servers, time, 75
setting passwords, 12, 274
Setup Assistant, 11–13
shared folders, 276–277
shareware, 55
shareware.com, 124
sharing files
  computer setup, 285–287
  connecting, 287–290
  disconnecting, 291
  usage, 290–291
sheet music programs, 353
sheets, defined, 94–95
Sherlock
  iMac searching, 109–111
  World Wide Web searching, 160–163
Sherlock icon, 109
shielded speakers, 348
Shift key, 38
Shockwave Player plug-in, 166
shopper.com, 163
short names, 274
shortcut keys. *See also* commands, listed
  by name
  Add to Favorite Places (America
    Online), 138
  commands, displaying, 50
  deleting items, 47
  explained, 38–41
  folders, creating, 39
  folders, locating, 21
  No shortcut, 77

saving, 94
  typing shortcuts, Internet Explorer
    (Microsoft), 164
Show Clippings command, 203
Shuffle button (iTunes), 230
Shut Down command, 15
shutting down. *See* closing
Sibelius sheet music program, 353
signatures, e-mail, adding, 179–180
simulating Mac OS 9, 262, 263
Sing program, 322–323
single documents, reassigning to
  programs, 307
single quotes, curly, 113
.sit files, 147
SiteLink Web site, 317
Sites folder, 277
slash (/), 334
sleep mode, 15–16
slide designs, master (AppleWorks), 214
Slide Show, Startup, Macintosh, 9
Slide Show feature, iPhoto, 225
slide shows, AppleWorks. *See also*
  PowerPoint
  designing, 212–214
  presenting, 215
Slow button (Apple DVD Player), 256
slow motion control, iMovie, 246
slowness, resolving, 295
smiling Macintosh, 9
software. *See also* AppleWorks; Dock;
  documents; files; software problems
  active programs, determining, 63–64,
    99–100
  Address Book program, 80
  Apple DVD Player program, 256–257
  Apple System Profiler program, 81
  Calculator program, 61, 64, 65
  Chess program, 80, 189
  Clock program, 81
  creator codes, 306
  Cubase VST sequencing program, 352
  Dave program (Thursby), 333
  disk repair programs, 310–311
  Disk Utility, 310–311
  documents versus, 100–101
  DVD Player program (Apple), 256

EarthLink Total Access sign-up
    program, 141
EasyBeat sequencing program, 352
Entourage (Microsoft), 55, 144
FAXstf program, installing, 326–327
Finale sheet music program, 353
free software, downloading, 140–141
frozen programs, 293–294
Halime newsgroup-reading program, 144
hiding, 79–80
iDisk program, 151–153
iDVD 2 program, 251
iMac-compatible, downloadable, 144
iTunes program, 81
Key Caps program, 81
launching, at startup, 296, 339–340
launching, manually, 57
Mail program, 173
Modem Center program, 329, 331
Movie Player, 325
newsgroup-reading programs, 144
Nightingale sheet music program, 353
obsolescence, 54
open documents, displaying, 343
open programs, determining, 63
opening one program, 57
opening two programs, 63–64, 337–338
Otto Matic program, 190
Palm Desktop, 332
Preview program, 81
Print Center program, 122–123
purchasing, 55
Quicken program, 81, 189
QuicKeys X program, 78
QuickTime, playing movies, 325–326
quitting, 67
reinstalling, 301
restarting, 299
sequencing programs, 352
shareware, 55
sheet music programs, 353
Sibelius sheet music program, 353
Sing program, 322–323
speech recognition program, 323–325
standard in iMacs, 54
starting, 57
Stickies program, 62–63
StuffIt Expander program, 148
Talk program, 321–322

TextEdit program, 81, 83
VirtualPC for Mac OS X (Connectix), 333
Windows (Microsoft) programs, running
    on iMacs, 333
World Book Encyclopedia program,
    190–191
wrong programs opening, 304–308
software problems. *See also* software
    opening problems, 301
    renaming problems, 301
    single program problems, 299–301
    strangely-named files, 302
    System Preferences dimmed, 301
    trash, can not empty, 302
    wrong programs opening, 304–308
Software Restore CDs, 312–313
Software Update dialog box, 76
Software Update options, System
    Preferences, 76–77
songs
    CDs, copying to hard drives, 232–233
    iTunes, playing, 230–231
Sony cameras, 219, 351
sorting
    columns (list view), 44
    databases, AppleWorks, 197
    records, 197
sound effects, iMovie, 247
Sound options, System Preferences, 75
soundtracks, adding, 246–247
space available, hard drives, 33–34
spam, 185–186
speaker volume keys, 78
speakers
    iMac requirements, 348
    subwoofers (iSub), 353
special characters, creating, 194
Speech commands, 324
speech controls (Talk program), 322
speech recognition program, 323–325
spinning cursor, 293
splitters, 132
spreadsheets
    cells, 206
    creating, 206–210
    formulas, 210–211
    grand totals, 210–211
    purpose, 192, 206

Star Trek keyword, America Online (AOL), 137
starting. *See also* opening
    AppleWorks, 191–192
    Classic, automatically, 264
    Classic, manually, 263
    documents, at startup, 339–340
    iMovie, 238–239
    iPhoto, 219
    programs, at startup, 296, 339–340
    programs, manually, 57
Starting Points dialog box, 191–192
Startup Disk control panel, 268–269
startup interview, 11
startup problems
    blue screen problems, 297
    chimes, not sounding on startup, 295–296
    command line displays, 310
    folders display, not icons, 310
    freezing up, resolving, 297, 310
    frozen programs, 293–294
    garbage on screen, 296–297
    logging in problems, 297–298
    passwords, forgotten, 298
    programs launching automatically, 296
    screen picture, not displaying on startup, 295
    slowness, 295
    viruses, 299
Startup Slide Show, Macintosh, 9
Stickies program, 62–63
Stocks keyword, America Online (AOL), 137
storage, computer, 29
storage windows, invisible, 65
straight apostrophes ('), 113
straight quotes ("), 113
strangely-named files, 302
Streaming Web Movie, Small setting (QuickTime), 249
structure, commands, 19–20
stuffed files, 147, 148
StuffIt Expander program, 147, 148
Subtitles button (Apple DVD Player), 256
subwoofers (iSub), 353
suffixes, file-names
    described, 304–305
    listing, 150
    viewing, 101
Summary command, 122

SuperDrive option, 250
superimposing titles, iMovie, 244
surfaces, effecting mouse usage, 303
switching off iMacs, 15
switching on iMacs
    how to, 8–9
    internal processing, 29
switching to Mac OS X, 268–269
symbol characters, creating, 194
symbol fonts, 127
symbols keys, 81, 194
syntax, iMac commands, 19–20
synthesizers, 352
system clock, setting, 13
system date, setting, 75–76
System folder, 261
System Preferences
    Date and Time options, 75–76
    Desktop options, 69–71
    dimmed, 301
    Displays options, 73
    Energy Saver options, 74
    General options, 71
    Keyboard options, 74
    opening, 67
    purpose, 68
    quitting, 77
    Screen Saver options, 71–73
    Software Update options, 76–77
    Sound options, 75
system time, setting, 13, 75–76

• T •

Tab key usage, dialog boxes, 120–121
tab stops, using, 111
table of contents, America Online (AOL), 136
tabs, dialog boxes, 72
Talk program, 321–322
.tar files, 147
telephone lines, Internet usage, 132, 146
telephone numbers
    accessing America Online (AOL), 135
    help line numbers, Apple, 284, 315–316
templates, presentation, 212
temporary storage, 29
10BaseT cables, 281
tension, clicking (mouse), 303

text, moving, 90–91. *See also* dragging and
dropping
text, selecting. *See also* TextEdit program
  entire document, 112
  several pages, 113–114
  single words, 111
  TextEdit program, 86–87
text clippings, 89
Text tool (AppleWorks), 201
TextEdit program, 81, 83. *See also* text,
selecting
  adding text, 84–85
  deleting text, 85–87
  deselecting text, 87
  inserting text, 85
  locating, 83
  purpose, 81
  selecting text, 86–87
text-smoothing, 126–127
the Shelf, 239, 240
There is no application available
  error message, 308–309
Thursby, Dave program, 333
tied up phone lines, Internet usage, 146
TIFF files, 307–308
time servers, 75
time (system), setting, 13, 75–76
time zones, setting, 76
timeline, iMovie, 239
Title Bar, 20
titles, iMovie, adding, 243–244
Toolbar button, 20
toolbar buttons, adding, 256
toolbar icons
  adding personal, 345
  rearranging, 345
  removing, 344
toolbars
  general description, 20
  hiding, 343
  making smaller, 344
transitions, 243
Trash button (iMovie), 239
Trash can icon, 47
trashing items. *See also* deleting
  aliases, 339
  general steps, 47–48, 49
  problems, trash can not empty, 302
Travel button, America Online (AOL), 136

triangles
  in the Dock, 63
  right-pointing, menus, 39
trimming
  clips, iMovie, 241–242
  pictures, iPhoto, 221–222
tripod usage, camcorders, 238
troubleshooting, hardware problems
  CD drawers, not opening, 304
  dim screen displays, 304
  disk (hard drive) problems, 310–311
  mouse problems, 303
  Universal Serial Bus (USB) power
    problems, 354
troubleshooting, software (program)
problems
  opening problems, 301
  renaming problems, 301
  single program problems, 299–301
  strangely-named files, 302
  System Preferences dimmed, 301
  trash, can not empty, 302
  wrong programs opening, 304–308
troubleshooting, startup problems
  blue screen problems, 297
  chimes, not sounding on startup, 295–296
  command line displays, 310
  folders display, not icons, 310
  freezing up, resolving, 297, 310
  frozen programs, 293–294
  garbage on screen, 296–297
  logging in problems, 297–298
  passwords, forgotten, 298
  programs launching automatically, 296
  screen picture, not displaying on
    startup, 295
  slowness, 295
  viruses, 299
troubleshooting-related Web sites, 316
TrueType fonts, 123
turning off iMacs, 15
turning on iMacs
  how to, 8–9
  internal processing, 29
TV listings Web site, 163
type codes, 306
type sizes, changing, 92
typefaces. *See* fonts

• U •

underlined phrases, Web pages, 156
underlining text, 91
Undo Paste command, 67
Universal Serial Bus (USB)
  cables, purchasing, 117
  compatible devices, 350–354
  cradles, 352
  hubs, 354
  installing USB devices, 354
  jacks, 347
  power problems, 354
Unix, 147, 302
unstuffing files, 148
untarring files, 148
updaters, loading, 76–77
updating files, general processing, 32
URLs, 157
user groups, 317
.uu files, 148

• V •

valid users screen, 272
verbs, commands, 19–20
version 1.1, iPhoto, upgrading to, 218
version 10.2, Mac OS, upgrading to, 317–318
versiontracker.com, 55, 144
Vertical Scroll Bar, 20
VGA connectors, 355
View buttons (AppleWorks), 203
viewing. See also displaying
  area, Internet Explorer (Microsoft),
    increasing, 170
  extensions, file names (suffixes), 101
views, windows
  column view, 41, 45–46
  icon view, 41–43
  list view, 41, 44–45
  View buttons (AppleWorks), 203
VirtualPC for Mac OS X (Connectix), 333
viruses, 299
Visual Effects button (iTunes), 230
voices, choosing (Talk program), 322
Volume button (Apple DVD Player), 256
volume control, iMovie, 246

• W •

waiting printouts, controlling, 123
wallpaper, choosing, 69–71
Web. See World Wide Web
Web browsers, 145, 156
Web Movie, Small setting (QuickTime), 249
Web pages
  basic screens, described, 157–158
  converting pictures to, 226
Web sites. See also World Wide Web
  Apple Web site, 250, 316
  bulletin boards for troubleshooting Web
    sites, 316
  cameras, iPhoto-compatible Web site, 219
  comparison-shopping Web sites, 163
  dictionaries Web site, 164
  Dilbert cartoon Web site, 163
  DVD club Web sites, 255
  free fax number Web site, 163
  iMac general information Web sites, 317
  Kensington Security Web site, 347
  Louvre museum Web site, 163
  MacCentral Web site, 317
  MacFixIt Web site, 316
  MacSurfer Web site, 317
  mail-order software store Web sites, 55
  Micromat Web site, 311
  movie information Web site, 164
  newsgroups for troubleshooting Web
    sites, 316
  Palm Web site, 332
  Real plug-in Web site, 166
  salary calculator Web site, 164
  satellite photographs Web site, 163
  Shockwave Player plug-in, 166
  SiteLink Web site, 317
  troubleshooting-related Web sites, 316
  TV listings Web site, 163
Welcome screen, 13–14
widths
  columns, adjusting, 46
  Fractional Character Widths feature, 128
windows. See also screens, listed by name
  closing all, 337
  column view, 41, 45–46
  icon view, 41–43

iDVD window, 253
list view, 41, 44–45
location path, displaying, 341–342
minimizing, 58
monitor window, iMovie, 239
moving, 20, 23
multiple windows, opening, 22–23
replacing, 22
resizing, 20, 49
retrieving previously open, 22
Windows computers, iMac networking
    steps, 333–335
Windows (Microsoft) programs,
    running on iMacs, 333
wireless connections (AirPort), 281–285
Word (Microsoft), 54, 150
word processing
  advantages, 90
  AppleWorks, 198–200, 201
  bottom of page text, 113
  formatting paragraphs, 93–94
  formatting text, 91–92
  lining up text, 111
  Return key usage, 90–91
  rules, 83–84
  running footer feature, 113
  running header feature, 113
  selecting text, entire document, 112
  selecting text, several pages, 113–114
  selecting text, single words, 111
  top of page text, 113
  usage tips, 111–114
word spacing, printouts, 128
word wrap, 84
World Book Encyclopedia program, 190–191
World Wide Web. *See also* Internet;
    Web sites
  accessing, via America Online (AOL),
    155–156
  accessing, via the desktop, 161

accessing, via Internet Service
    Providers, 156
addresses, typing new, 157–158
links, explained, 156, 158
pictures, saving, 158
previous pages viewed, accessing, 157
scrolling pages, 158
Search blanks, 157
searching, using Google, 159–160
searching, using Sherlock, 160–163
searching tools, 158
Web browsers, 156
wrong programs opening, 304–308
WWW. *See* World Wide Web

• ¥ •

Yahoo search engine, 158
yellow sticky notes, electronic version,
    62–63
You do not have sufficient access
    privileges error message, 309–310
YOU HAVE MAIL button (America
    Online), 139
yourdictionary.com, 164

• Z •

.z files, 148
Zip drives, 28, 352
.zip files, 147, 148
Zoom buttons, 20, 49–50, 203
zooming techniques, camcorders, 237–238

Notes